Dog Decor

Canines
Living Large

Dog Decor

Canines Living Large

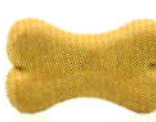

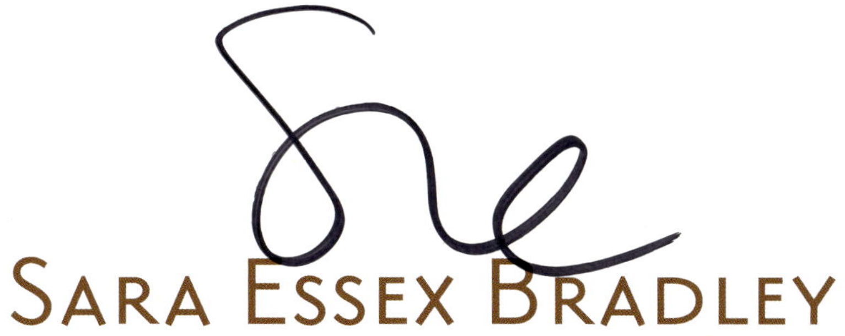

Sara Essex Bradley

Foreword by Valorie Hart

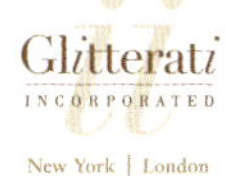

New York | London

Dedication

This book is dedicated to my awesome husband, Mike Bradley.
It is also dedicated to my cat, Steve, who got this whole ball rolling by jumping into a set at my home studio and posing for a photo.

First published in 2017 by

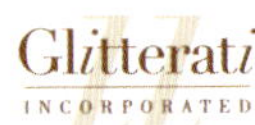

New York Office:
630 Ninth Ave, Ste 603
New York, NY 10036
Telephone: 212 362 9119

London Office:
1 Rona Road
London NW3 2HY
Tel/Fax +44 (0) 267 8339
www.GlitteratiIncorporated.com
media@GlitteratiIncorporated.com for inquiries

First edition, 2017

Library of Congress Cataloging-in-Publication data is available from the publisher.

Editor: Phil Columns
Design: Liz Trovato

Hardcover edition
ISBN: 978-1-943876-40-2
Printed and bound in China
10 9 8 7 6 5 4 3 2 1

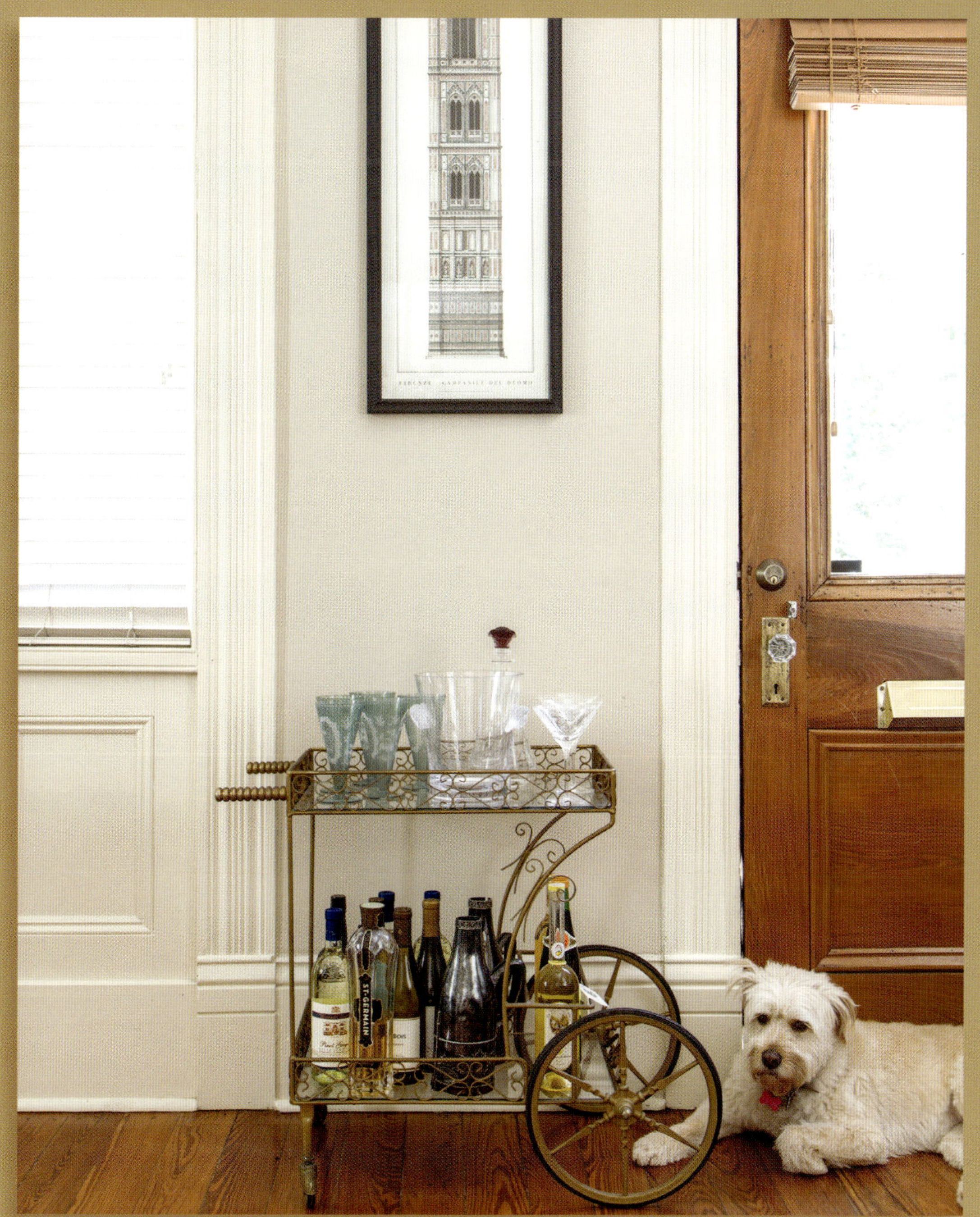

Lottie Leona

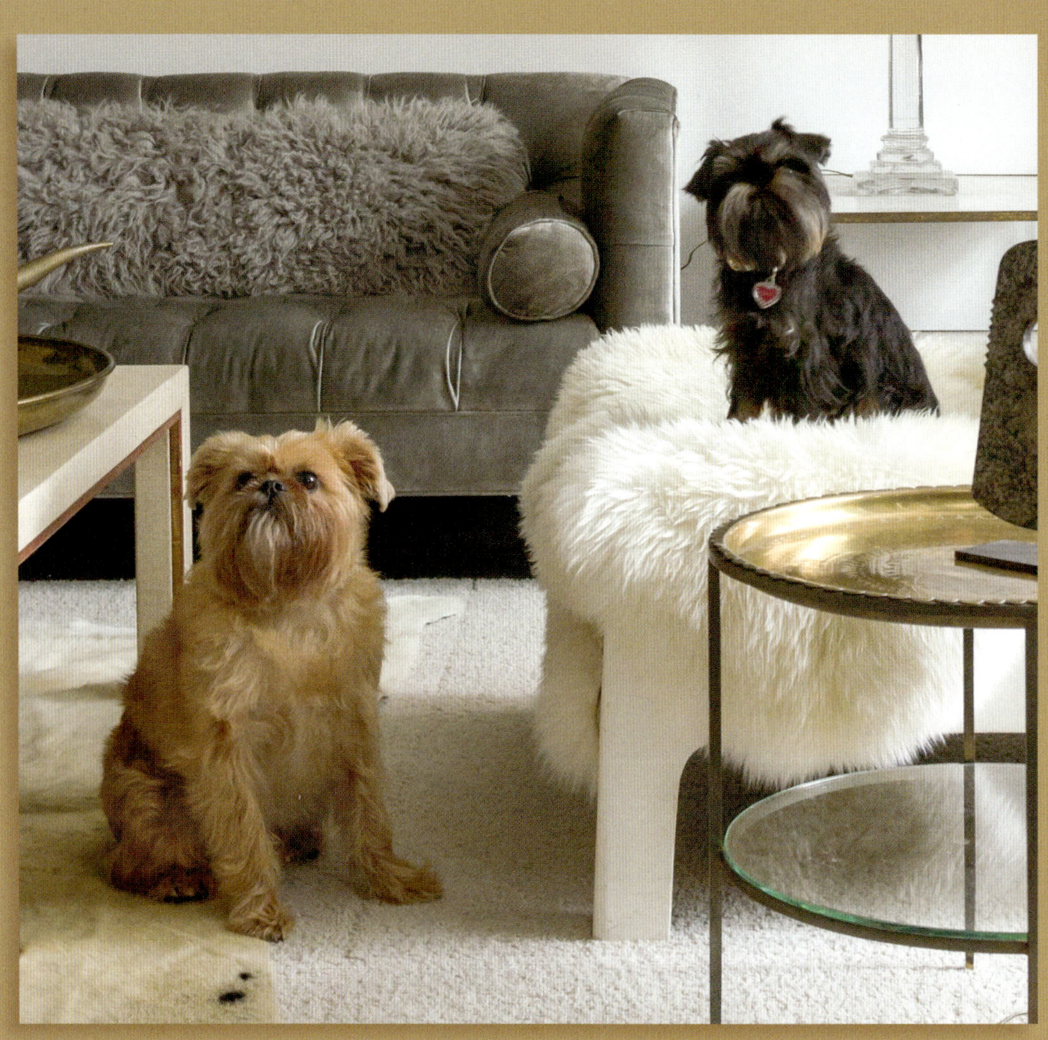

Otto and Inky

Contents

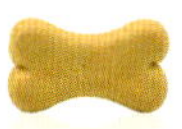

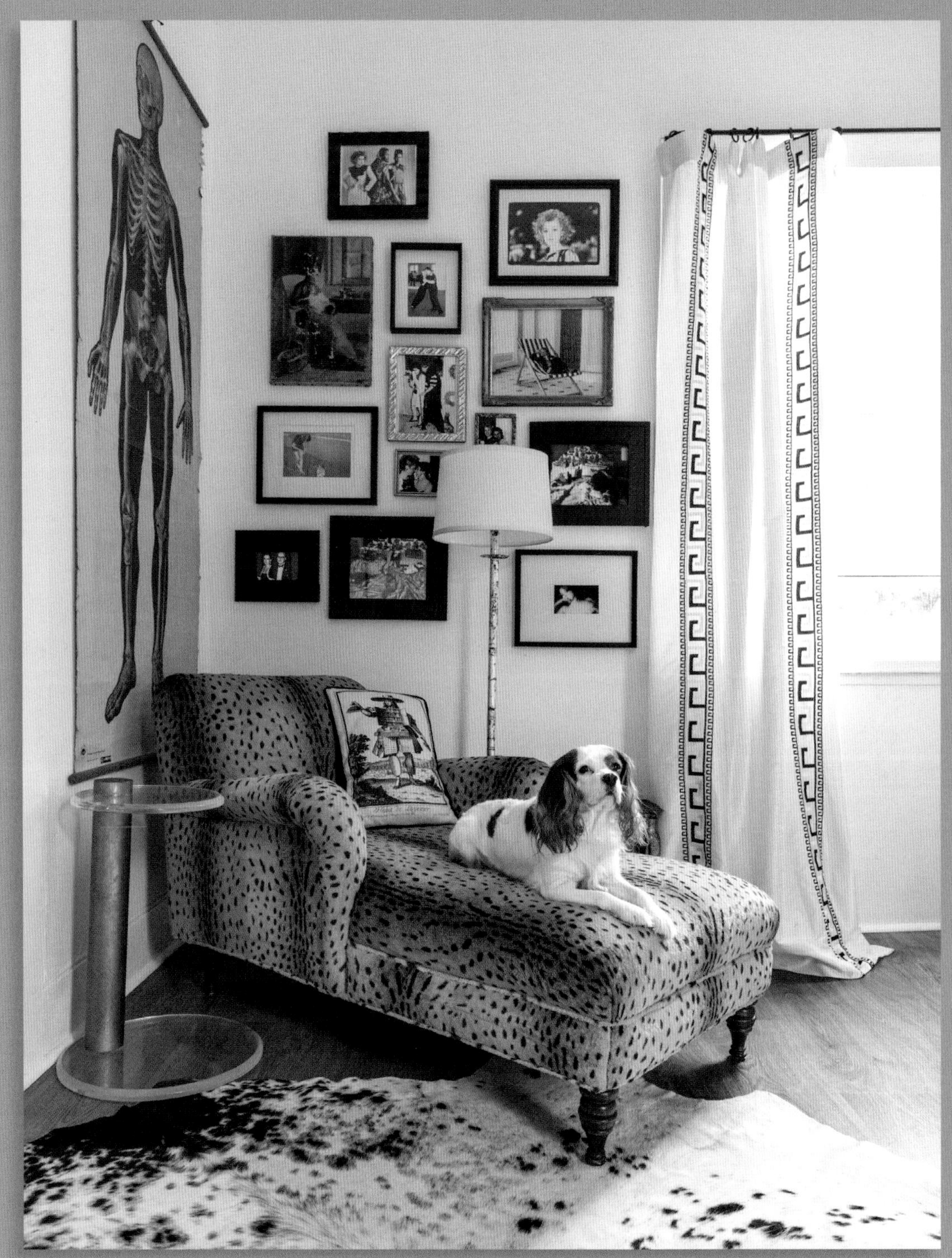

Cholo

Foreword

"Dogs are definitely the things that make your house a home. You can spend millions on a house, have everything just perfect and have the best of everything, but without these messy hairy animals it's not QUITE right. . . . I wouldn't trade my brand-new scratched-up oak floors and Swifter and vet bills in for the world!"

—Tracy Gielbert, Gallery Orange

The oldest fossils of a domesticated dog are from a 14,000-year-old dog grave. DNA evidence suggests dogs diverged from wolves much earlier than that, with estimates ranging from 15,000 to more than 100,000 years ago. Regardless, historians agree that humans domesticated dogs before any other animal, making dog man's oldest friend, if not his best.

From cave-dwellers to the ancient cultures of Egypt, Italy, and Greece, and later cultures of China, England, Scotland, and France, to modern-day universal cultures, the dog has been welcomed into the homes of humans. You are sure to remember your first childhood dog, brought into your house by your parents. In a way, the dog and you were young pups growing up together. When it came time to leave home for college or marriage or just life on your own as an adult, the hardest goodbye to say was to the family dog.

Our picture of domestic bliss includes cozy hearths, comfortable furniture, and a faithful dog lying at its master's feet, or snuggled up in a human lap, or surrounded by children playing playing fetch with the beloved pet.

Sara Essex Bradley and I have worked on many photo shoots of beautiful homes for various publications and books. We always are happy when there is a family pet in the house. Homeowners will often ask if we want the pet sent away for the day so as not to be underfoot while we work, and we always emphatically decline. To us having a dog in the shot makes the room more human, more alive. It's better than any home décor any interior designer can place in a room.

Getting the perfect shot of a dog is always an interesting proposition. Some are natural-born supermodels and camera-lovers who strike a perfect pose and hold it. Others are super active or shy and may sit or lie down for a split second. Sara has her little dog-whisperer tricks to get a dog to look into the lens. Sometimes these backfire when the dog cannot resist her magical siren call. They happily lunge to give her a lick, or offer a head or a belly for a rub. Homeowners by design or accident seem to choose dogs that fit nicely with their décor. You often wonder if they chose the dog to match the rug or chair, or the other way around. No matter how precious the fabrics are, how fine the furnishings, how polished the floors, the dogs rule the roost and occupy a home right alongside their people.

In these pages you will see dogs in living rooms perched on chairs and lounging on sofas; in bedrooms on beds and chaise lounges; outdoors poolside or on porches or in pretty gardens; in kitchens—the nerve center of a home; underfoot in dining rooms. No place is off-limits to this most important family member. Each dog has its own unique habitat and backstory, and that is why we love them so much, because they become almost "human" to owners.

If you take your thumb and cover the image of the dog in the photo, you will see a beautiful photograph of a beautiful room. Remove your thumb to reveal the dog in the shot, and you will see a space made complete, the very vision we hold of a happy home. Whether a pure-breed, a mixed-breed, a shelter dog, or a dog rescued—these ancient companions have found their way to us, into our hearts and into our houses.

—Valorie Hart

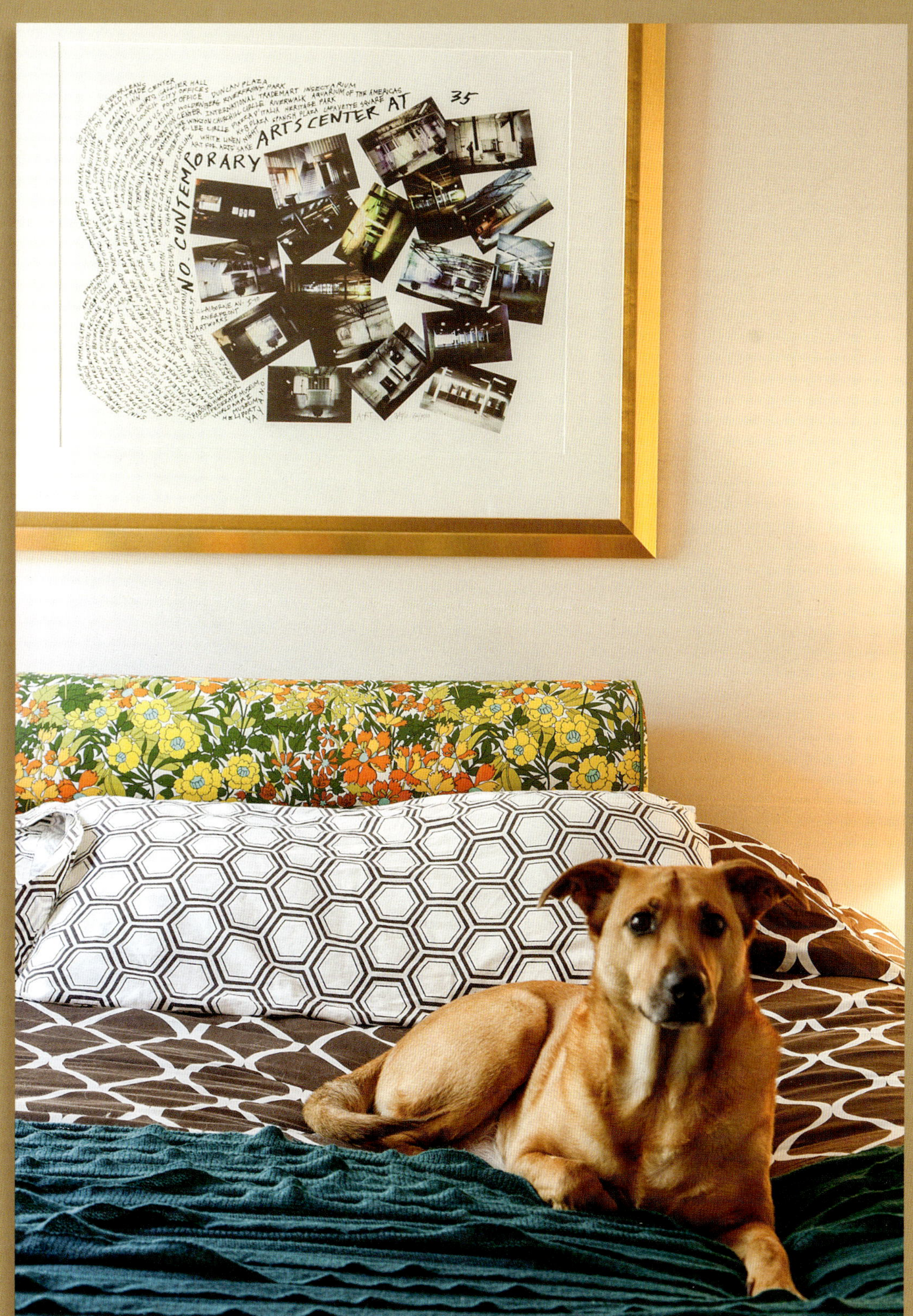

Dude

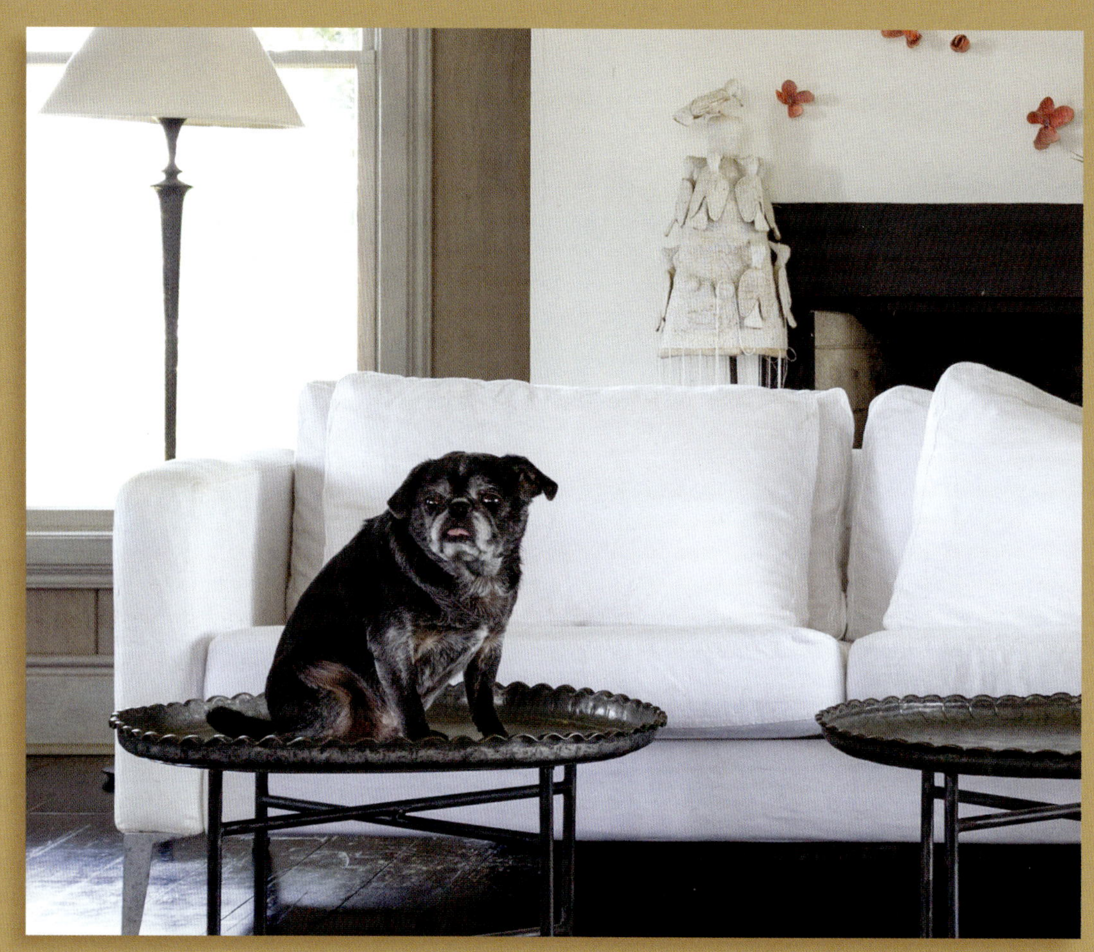

Boudreaux

Introduction

Full disclosure: I am not a writer, and I do not own dogs. I'm a photographer, currently residing with two spoiled cats. I was inspired to create this book because of dogs I've met and photographed over the years while shooting interiors for magazines and designers.

As a photographer, I like to keep my production simple. I don't like to bring a lot of gear and put on a show. It's usually just me and my holy trinity: camera bag, tripod, and reflector. I'm a natural-light photographer. I have and use lighting when necessary, but I find the best look is achieved by manipulating window light. There's contrast, depth, and imperfection. It looks real and more beautiful to me. Working this way creates a laid-back, natural flow, and that's where the dogs come in.

Usually when I arrive, there is barking at the door ("Oh, good! A new friend!" I think). I am greeted with slobber and jumps. The dog goes nuts trying to sniff my gear, possibly getting intel on all the other dogs that have sniffed before. The owners apologize, pull the dog off, and say they'll put the dog up for the day. I ask that they don't. I assure them I'm a dog lover and that he'll calm down in a bit. Eventually, the dog mellows and becomes curious about what's going on. He follows me around, and I enjoy the company—and usually can coax the dog to pose in one of the shots. This actually goes better when the owner is not around. The dog is so surprised by a stranger saying "Sit! Stay!" that he plops his butt down and cocks his head.

I love all of these dogs, and the rooms are beautiful and varied. Looking through the shots as a collection, I'm surprised by how often it seems like the space was designed to match the dog. The stories the owners shared with me made me laugh, and cry more than a few times. Many of the dogs in these pages have since passed on, and those dogs are described in the third person, out of respect, and I hope their portraits will bring happy memories. For all the other dogs, still with us and communicating through barks and other methods, I have taken the liberty of interpreting looks, behavior, and sounds, to present their profiles and living environments "in their own voices." Most of these were shot in New Orleans, and I'm delighted to showcase so many talented local designers and artists. I hope these portraits will not only make you smile because these dogs are so darned cute, but will inspire you with their décor and their stories.

—Sara Essex Bradley

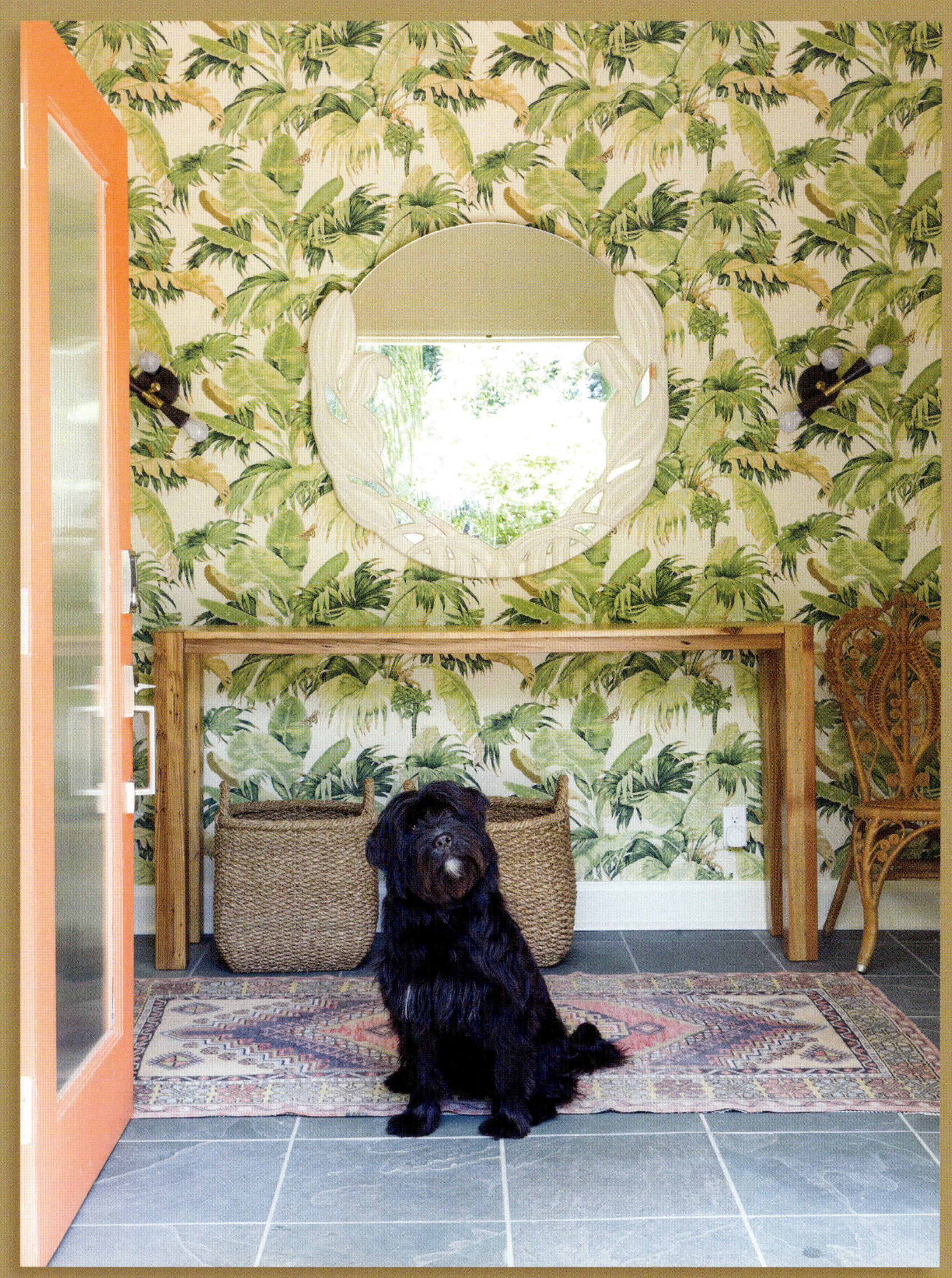

Jet

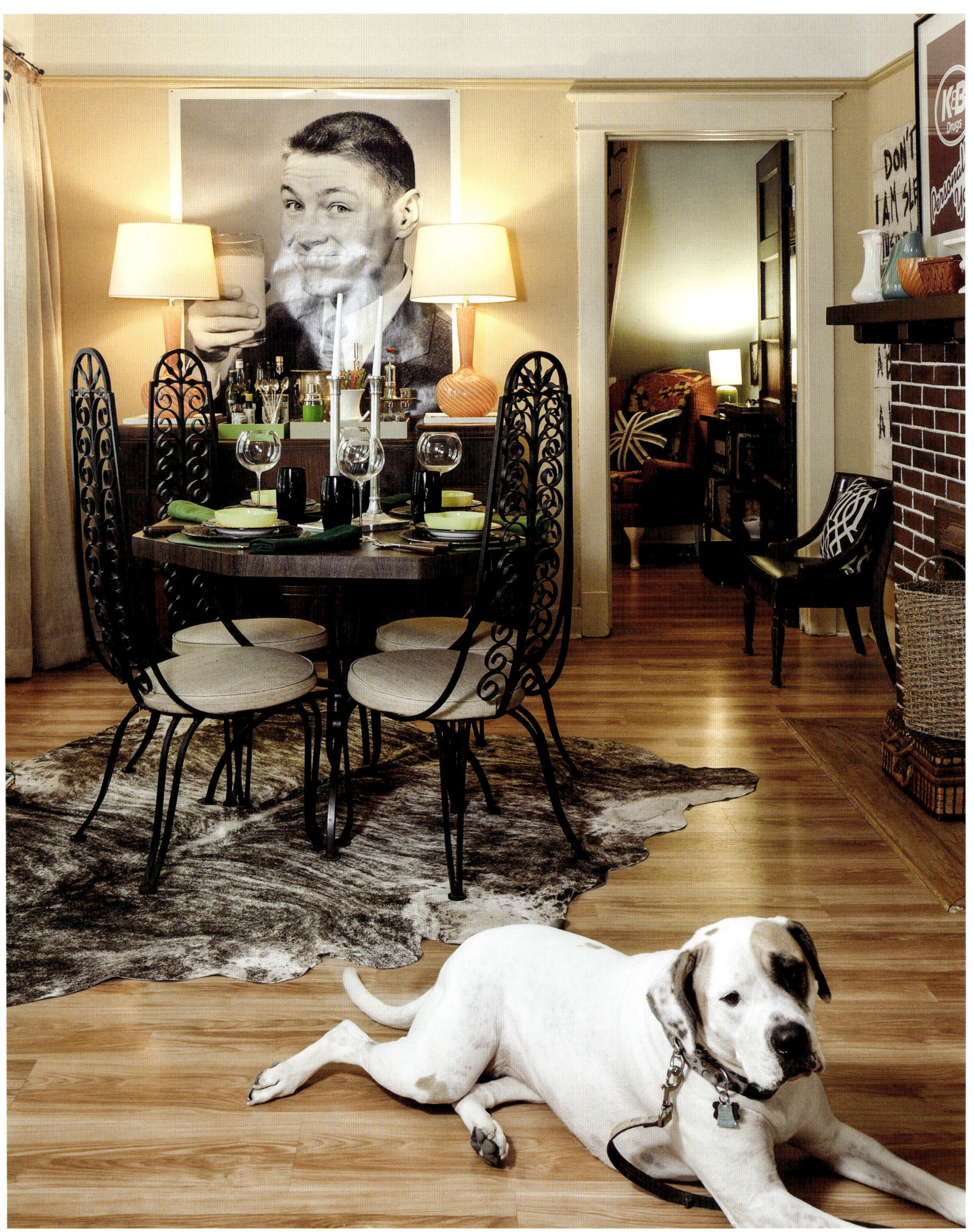
DON'T
Drugs

Cleopatra

"At ninety pounds, I might be the biggest lapdog you'll meet. Born near Dallas, I was adopted by Mitchell Settoon and Thomas Ecker from a friendly, reputable breeder. I was not named for the Egyptian queen but rather for Cleopatra Shwartz, from *The Kentucky Fried Movie*. Most of my friends call me Cleo, and I am enthusiastically greeted by neighbors, most times before Mitchell and Tom. I'm a very sweet girl, and I love to cuddle.

The Mid-City neighborhood in New Orleans where we live flooded badly after Katrina, and a complete renovation of the first floor had to take place. Mitchell is a talented artist, designer, and fabricator, and he steered most of the decorating decisions. I am lounging in the dining room, in front of a dining set from the sixties, with throne chairs. The large-scale photo is a former display from Restoration Hardware. Peeking in on the right is an old sign from the now closed K&B drugstore, an iconic New Orleans institution. Just past that you can see a bit of a hand-painted sign, plucked from Katrina debris, that was spray painted with a warning to would-be looters. Mitchell manages to combine a myriad of styles and layers, and describes the overall effect as 'Bohemian Hellhole.'"

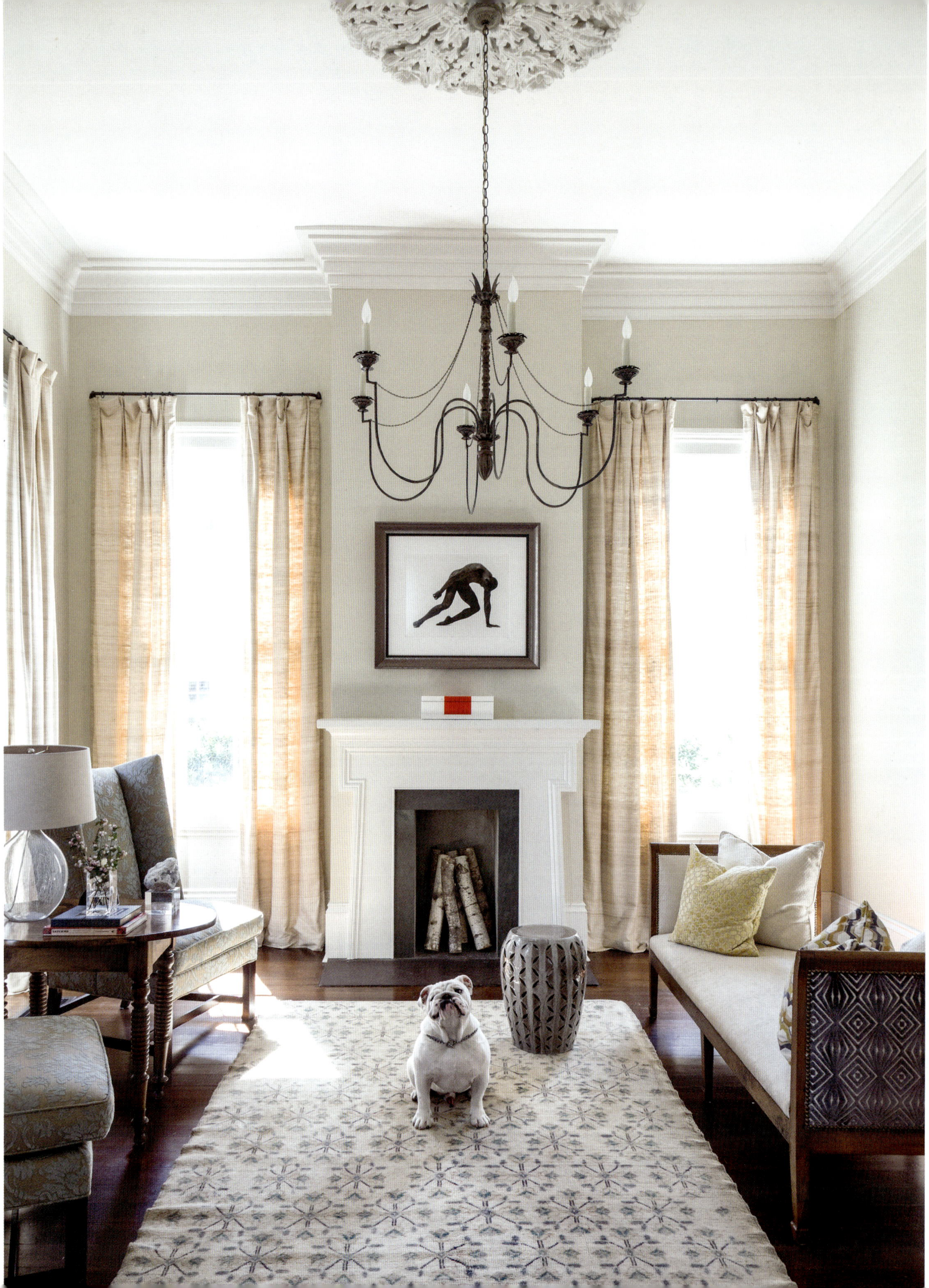

BAXTER

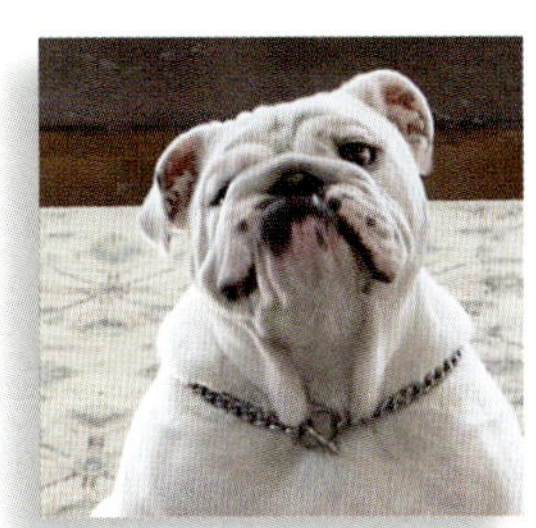

"You know that weekend guest who just won't leave? Well, that's me. I'm Baxter the Bulldog, and I was originally adopted by a busy attorney, but after a few months it was obvious her workload was taking a toll on my happiness. She knew her friend, Dr. Troy Scroggins, was a big Bulldog lover, so she called and asked if he was up for a new one. Troy had recently lost a beloved Bulldog in a terrible accident at home and was not sure he was up for another dog, but I was welcome to come stay for the weekend to try it out. I had other plans. I showed up with all of my worldly possessions, trotted through the front door, and plopped down on the previous dog's bed and said, 'when's dinner? I'm famished!'

I have been ruling the house ever since. I am a confident, sweet dog who never met a stranger. Here I pose in the front parlor of our beautifully renovated center-hall Creole mansion in the Garden District of New Orleans. Troy decorated the home himself. The photo is by Herb Ritts, the chandelier is by Julie Neill, and the daybed is from Source. The lamps are from Eclectic Home, and I think it all looks just dandy."

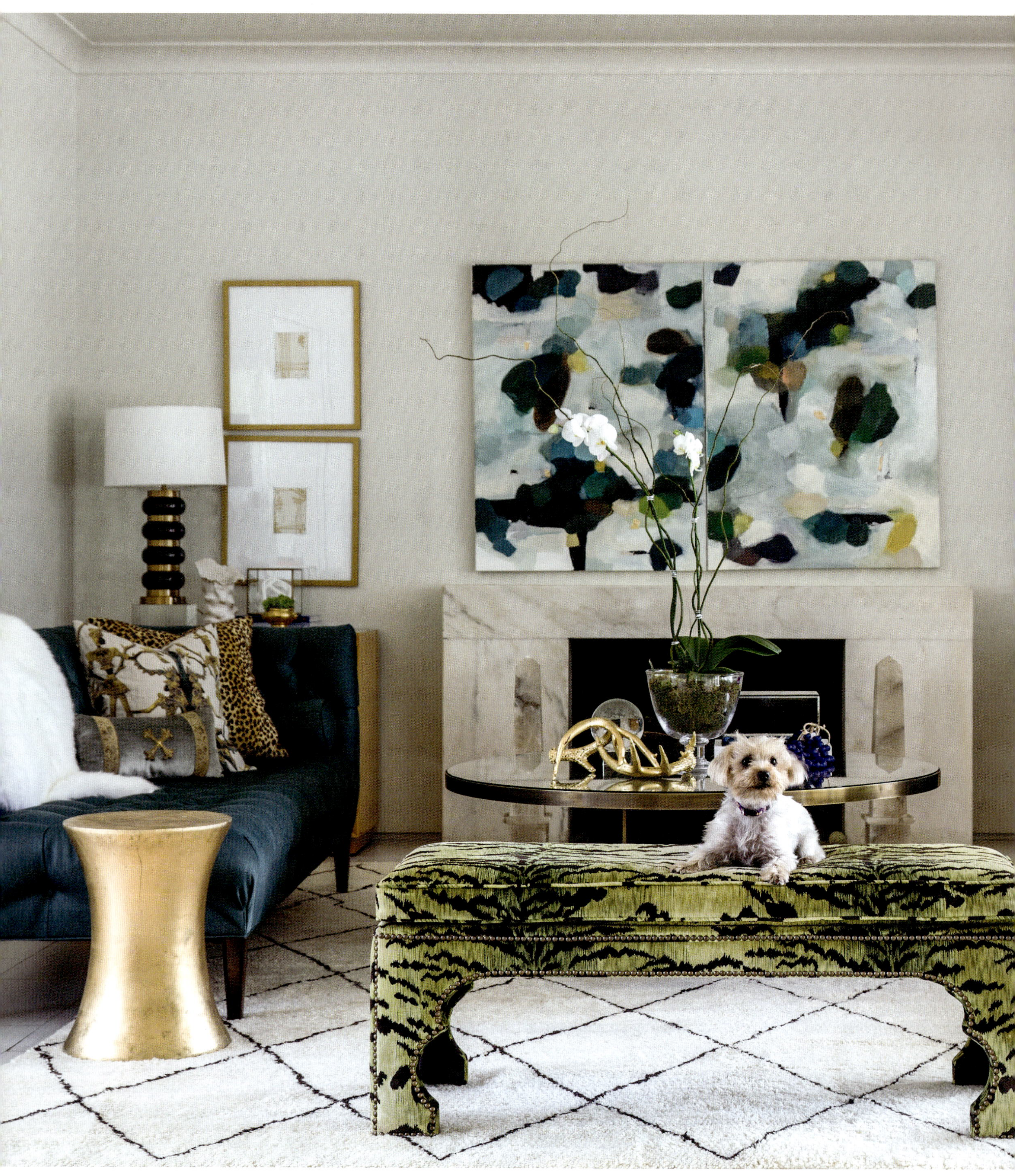

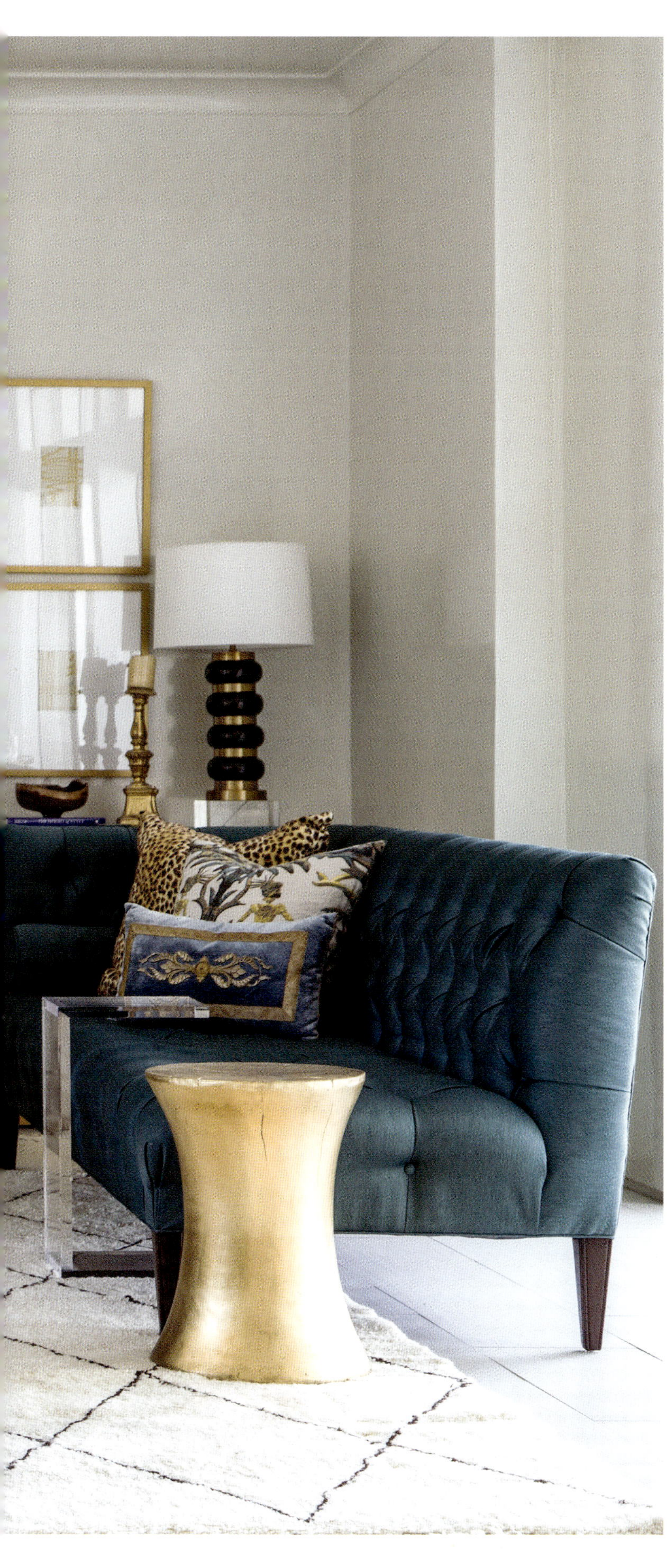

JADE

"I joined the Rabalais family with a specific career in mind: shop dog. The shop and I even have the same name. I possess all of the necessary cuteness and friendliness, but I just can't seem to settle down and work. I have more energy than one shop can harness, and I prefer to stay home doing puppy things. I did manage to quit wiggling for 1/20th of a second so this portrait could be snapped. It was harder than you might think.

Kenny and Jennifer Rabalais are a complete package in the world of design; Jennifer is an interior designer and owns the home furnishings store Jade on Metairie Road in New Orleans, and Kenny owns The Plant Gallery, a full-service garden center. Kenny and Jennifer have helped so many New Orleanians with their own homes, inside and out, that it was a particular joy for them to design their own space. The ultra modern house is outfitted in bright and elegant contemporary furnishings from Jennifer's store, and the grounds are sumptuous and stylish."

Rudy and Riley

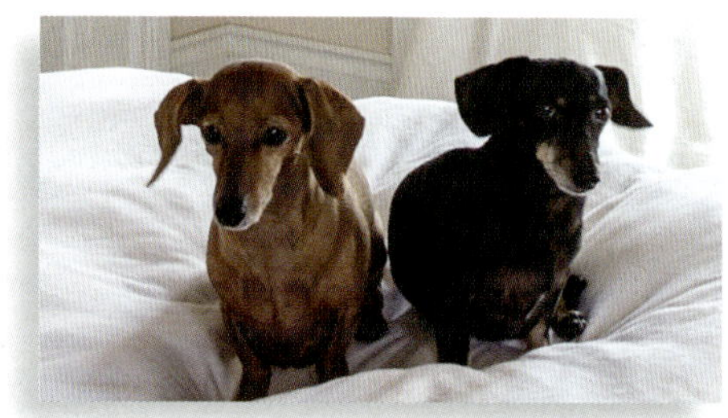

"When Michael DeGeorge and Deborah Hinson saw the beautiful Italianate neoclassical double-gallery home in the Lower Garden District of New Orleans, it only took them ten minutes to make an offer and sign a contract. The gorgeous house, designed by famous architect Henry Howard, needed a fairly extensive renovation, and the couple were involved with every step. Michael took on the duties of decorating the interiors, and scoured local shops and auctions for a mix of antiques and classic pieces.

I came to live in this beautiful home from the small town of Vidalia, Louisiana, but I was such a pup when I moved here, I really am a city dog. My older sister Riley and I enjoy lying about on the silk furnishings, watching the tourists ogle our beautiful home. I will occasionally bark at them to let them know a vicious guard dog is on premises. Riley and I are sweet and loving dogs, and we enjoy our family and living the good life."

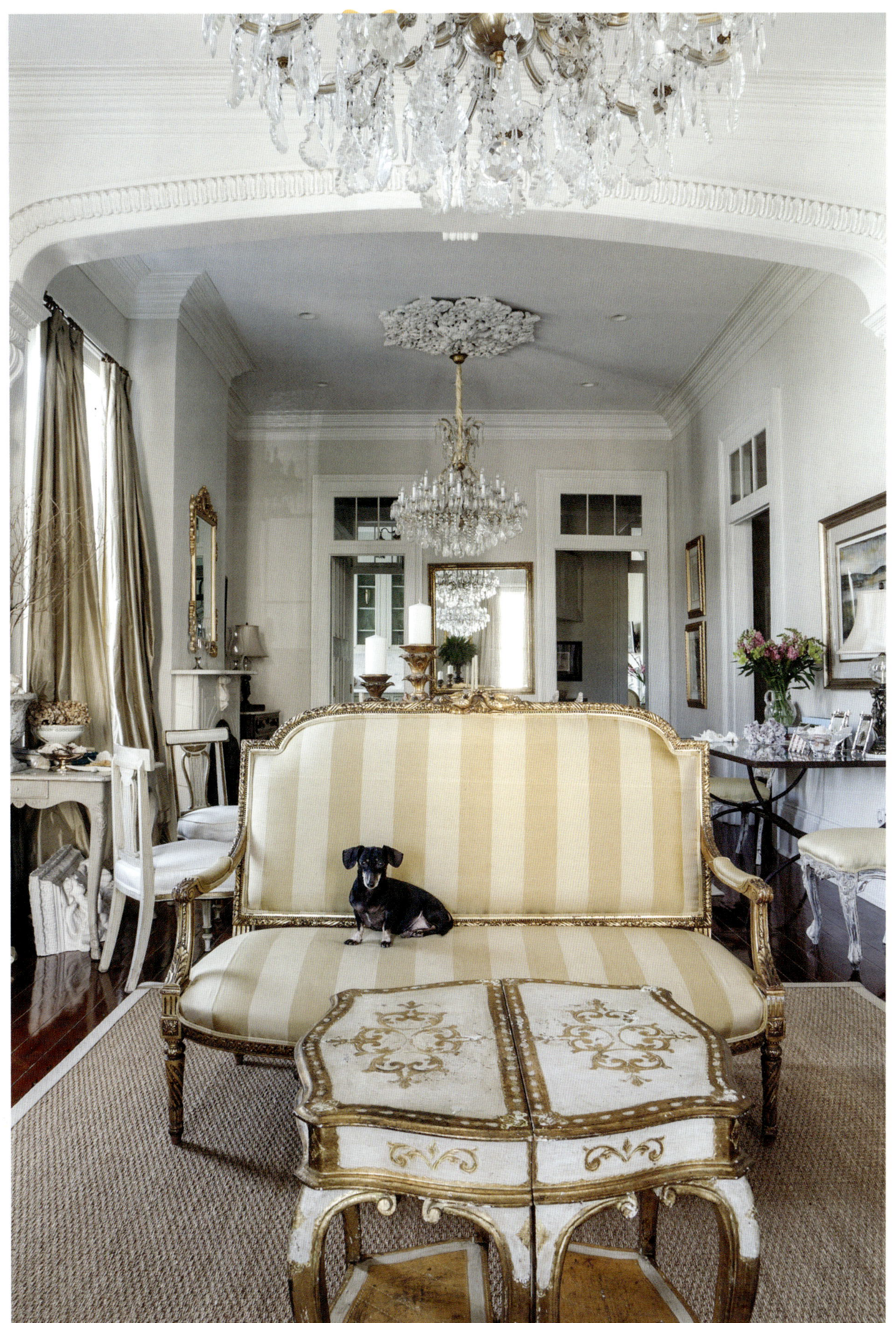

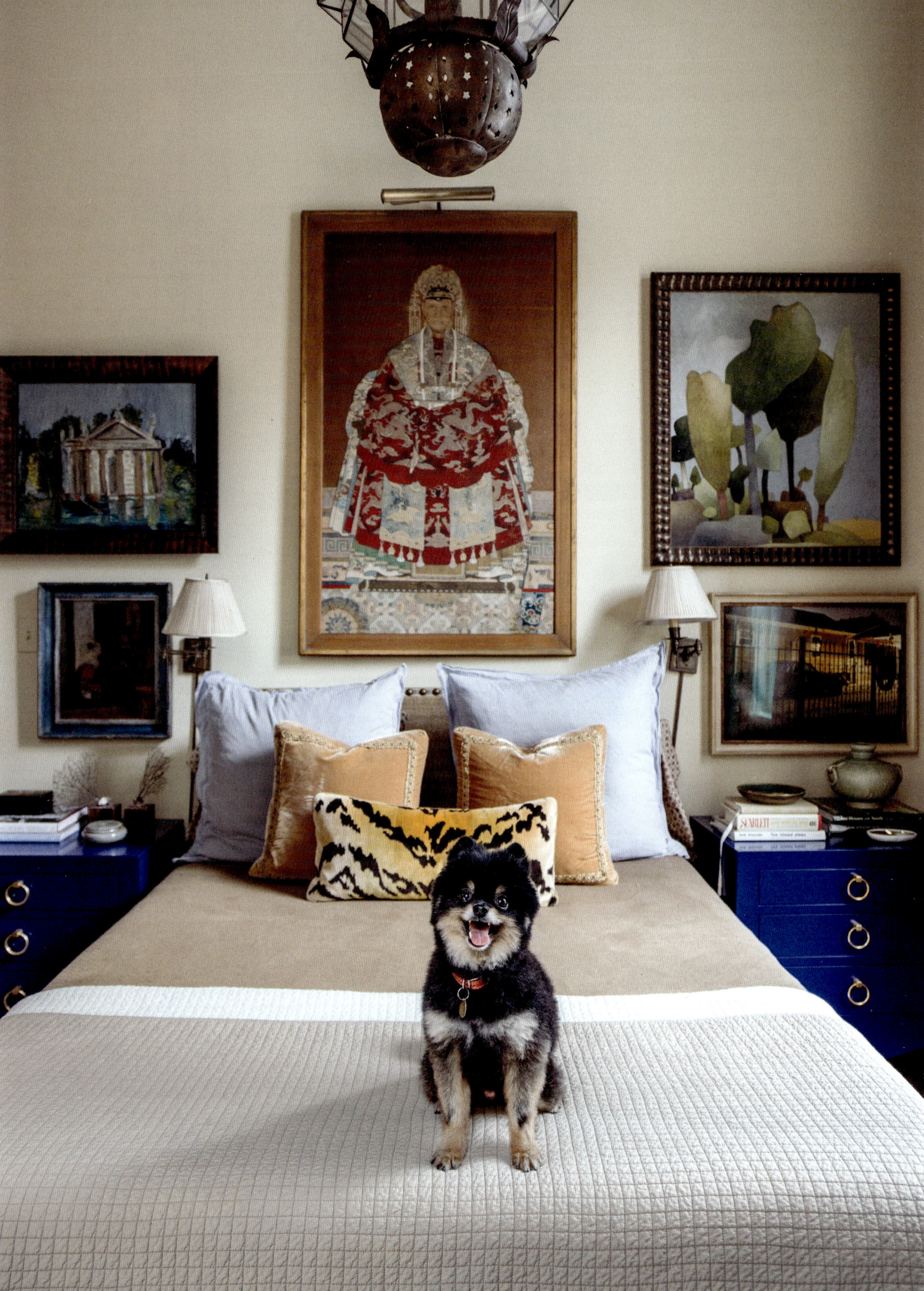

Baron

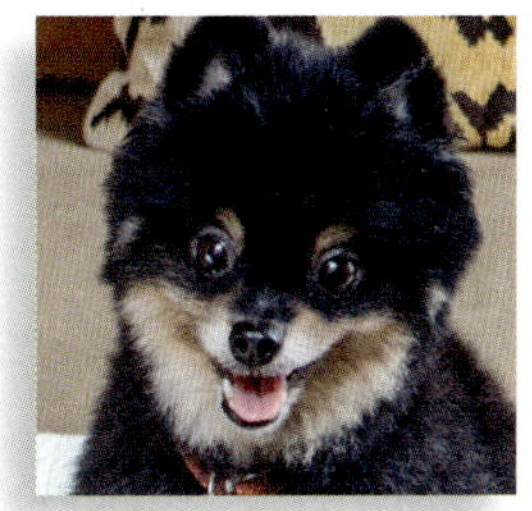

"Hi! I'm Baron, and I have the classic gutter-to-glam story: I had been looking for a home through Zeus' Place for over six weeks when Chad Graci found me. I weighed under three pounds and was riddled with heart worms. Look at me now! It is impossible to feel sad when I'm around. I have boundless energy and an irrepressible attitude toward life, and I keep the busy designer grounded and smiling. I am especially excited in the morning for my walk where I will greet my many neighborhood admirers and grant them my belly for rubbing. I am quite popular, you see.

I am a bit of an aesthete myself, and am particularly fond of animal prints, as evidenced in the pillow behind me. Chad designed his bedroom with his customary blend of high-style antiques, and vintage finds. The Moroccan pendant light was found on the street in New York years ago. The main painting is a Chinese ancestral portrait."

Roxy

"It's a common problem. You want to go to a resort, but you don't want to leave beloved Fido behind. Well, look no further. Carmel Valley Ranch resort in California is your destination. Your arrival will be greeted by me, Roxy, the hotel concierge.

I enjoy hanging out in the lobby surveying check-ins, and will generously offer my head for a scratch and slobber for your shoes. My team and I have developed a menu of amenities for doggie guests, including special custom dog beds and a room service menu. Finally your dog will get the treatment he knows he deserves!

The lobby was designed in a rustic, but elegant lodge style with large leather club chairs and a roaring fire. The painting is by Joyce Treiman and was gifted to the hotelier John Pritzker. I especially love hunkering near the hearth on chilly days, and I'll happily snooze at your feet while you read the morning paper."

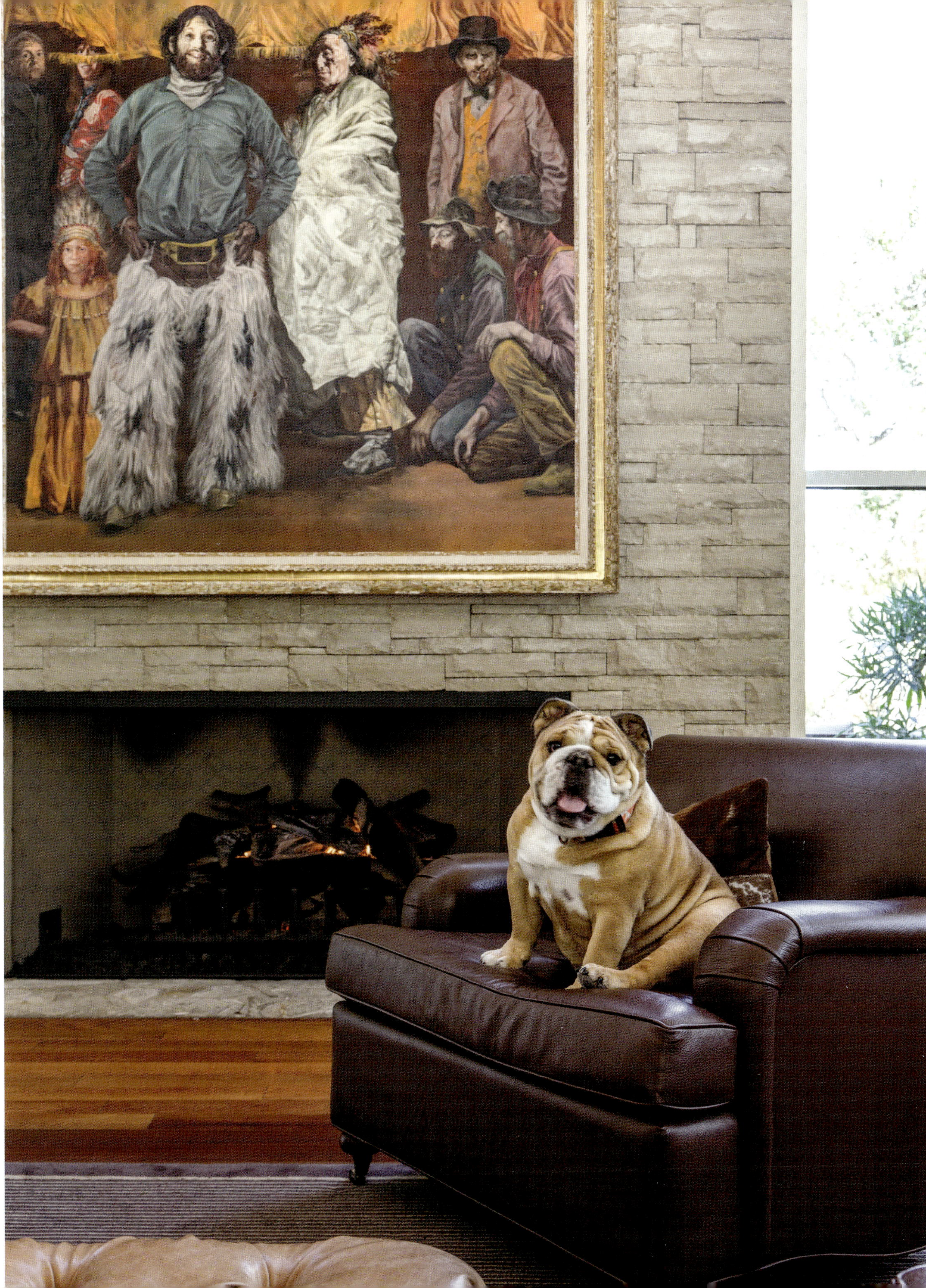

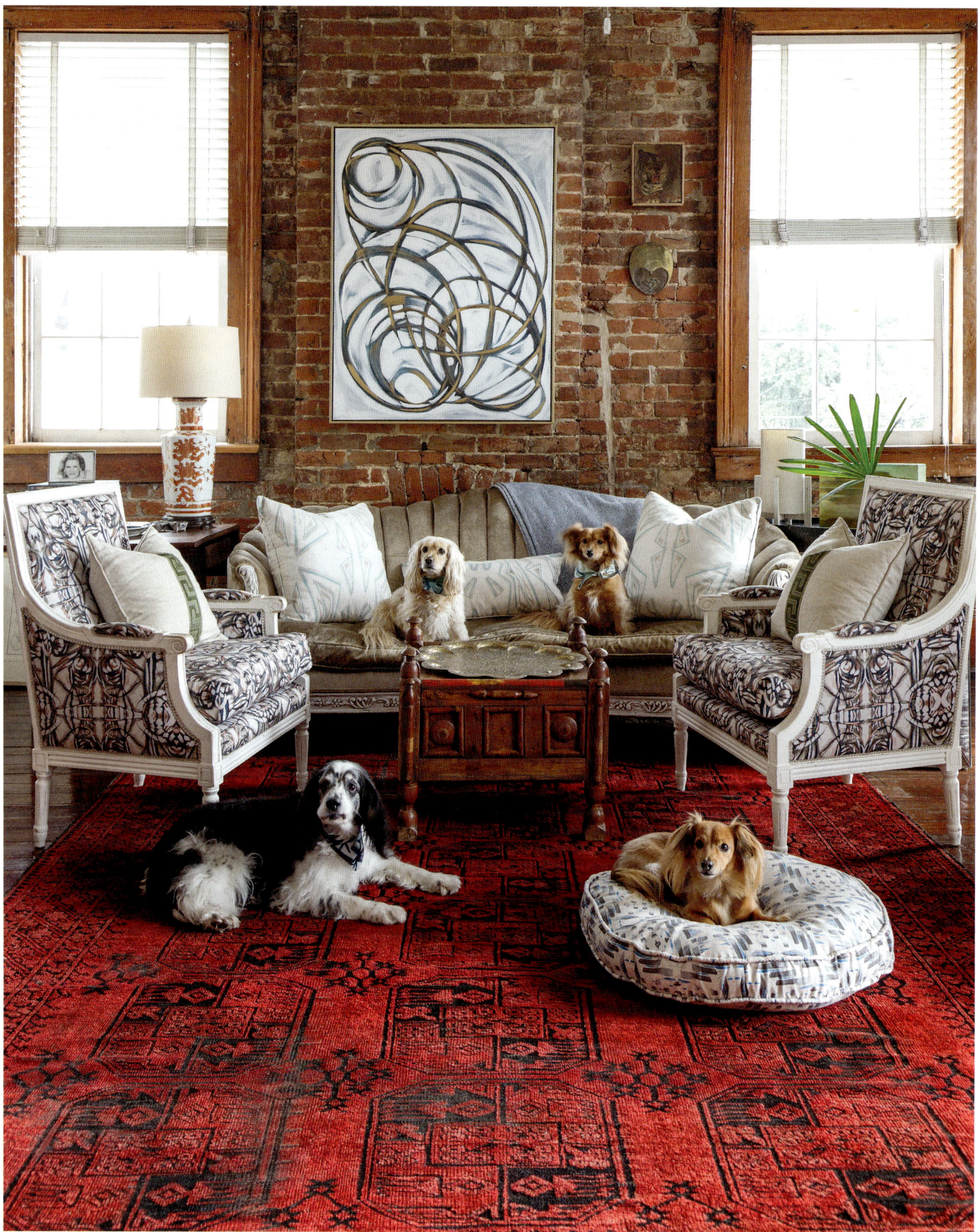

Phil, Ladybug, Ginger, and Zippy

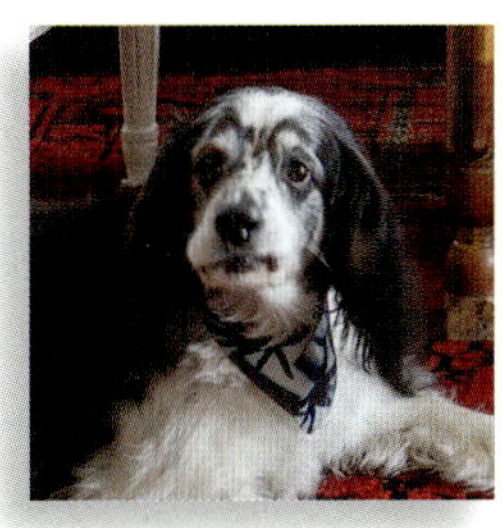
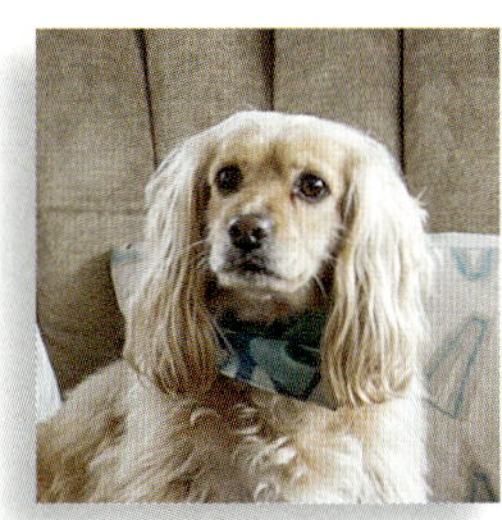
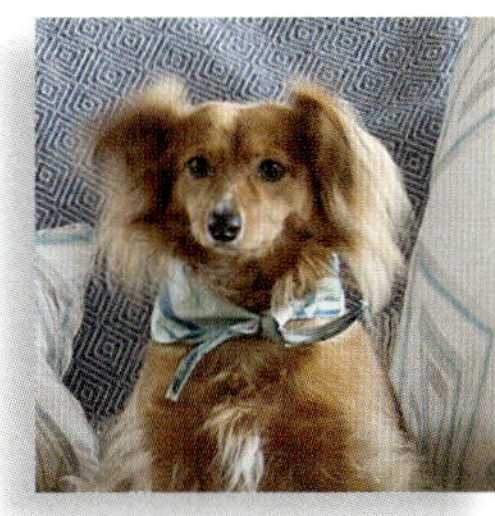
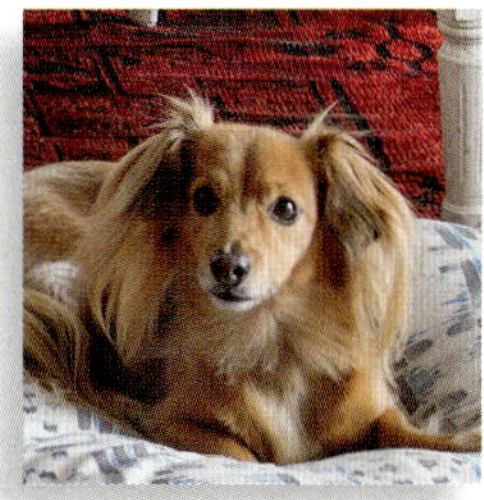

"I'm Phil (the black-and-white one) and I'm here to applaud New Orleans-based artist Amanda Talley. As if she doesn't have enough on her plate, executing commissions for her large abstract paintings, converting her designs to fabric, and running a busy gallery, she also found the time to rescue and mother the four of us! All but yours truly were adopted from the Sabine Humane Society/Animal Shelter in Sabine, Louisiana, where Amanda's mother is an independent rescuer. Featured in this wonderful family photograph are (clockwise from bottom left) myself, Ladybug, Ginger, and Zippy. We have the run of her lovingly restored nineteenth-century townhouse, from the apartment upstairs to the gallery below. Amanda's beautiful work is seen in the painting above the couch and in the fabric design of the armchairs and the dog bed . . . and, of course, in this lovely array of dog family, as well."

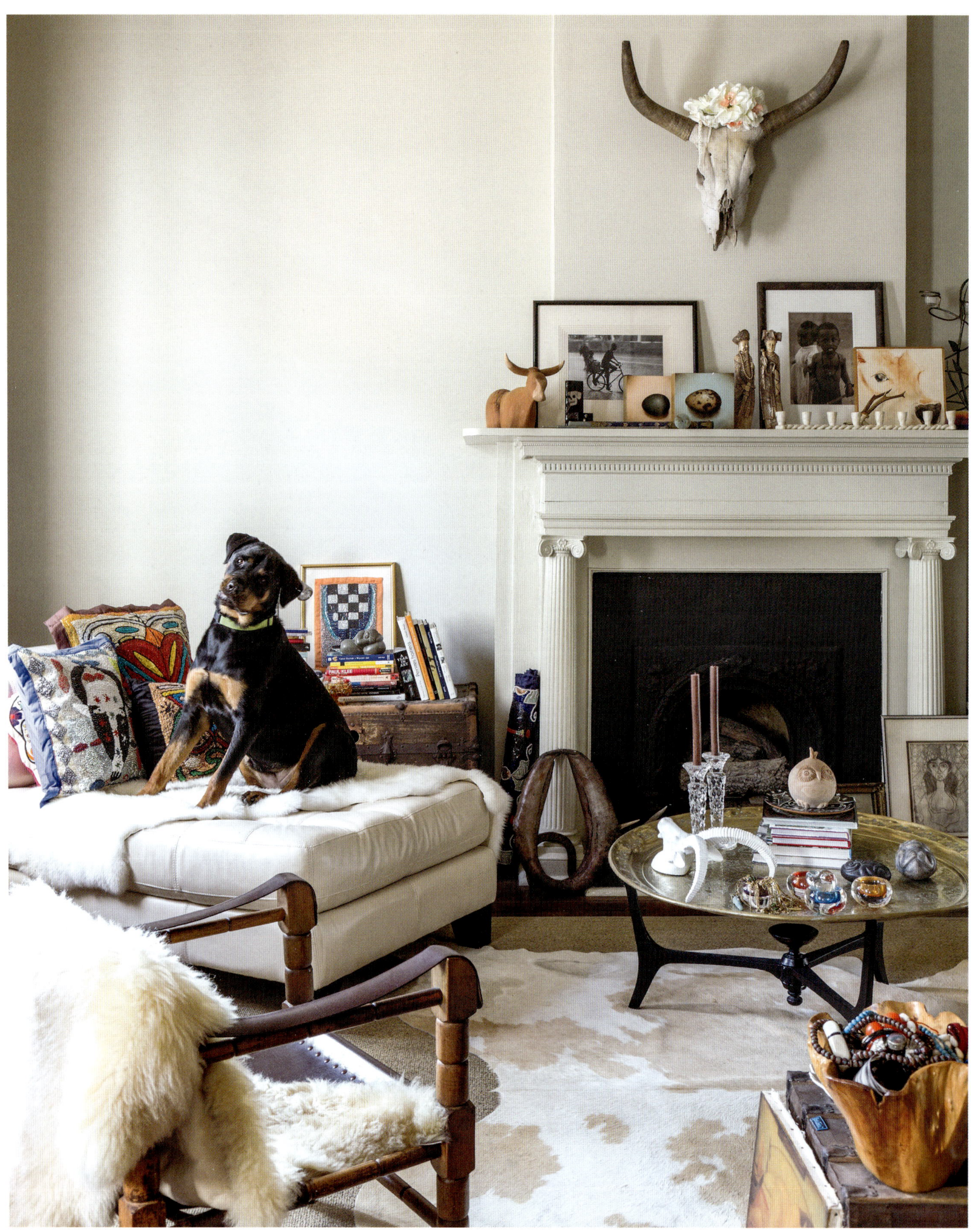
PAUL KLEE

Big Freda

"I got my name from the blending of the names of hip-hop artist Big Freedia and the Mexican painter Frida Kahlo—hence Big Freda. Unlike my rowdy namesakes, I am a 'total Zen dog.' While my lawyer-owner Nathalie is at work, I chill out to Bob Marley while resting on the chaise lounge by the window overlooking my French Quarter street. The vintage Moroccan table is a hand-me-down from Nathalie's aunt, who practiced medicine in Morocco in the sixties and seventies. The chairs are from Sterling Provision. The pillows are made from Haitian voodoo flags. I am such a mellow dog that I don't even chew my own toys, much less Nathalie's beautiful things."

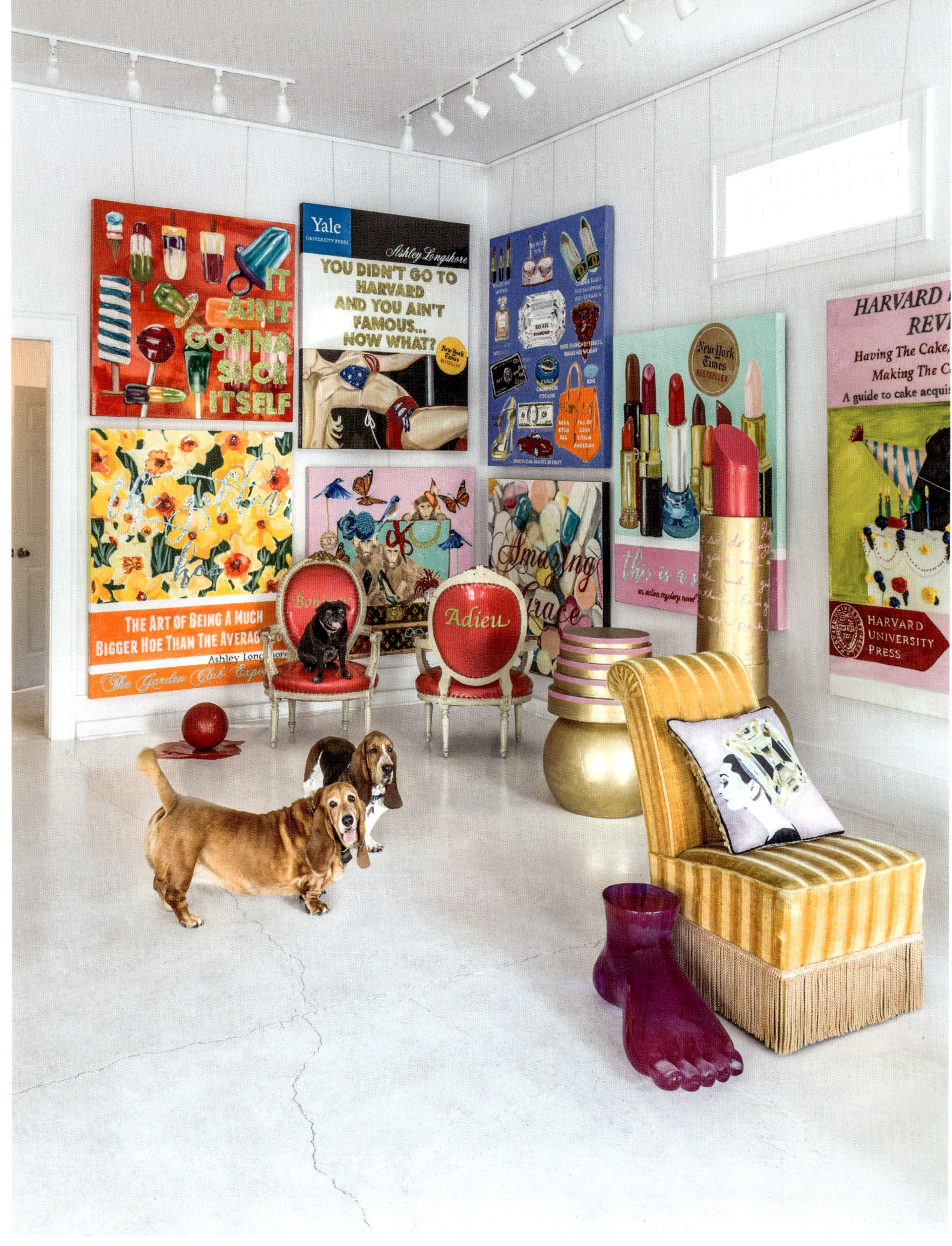
IT AINT GONNA SUCK ITSELF
Yale
UNIVERSITY PRESS
Ashley Longshore
YOU DIDN'T GO TO HARVARD AND YOU AIN'T FAMOUS... NOW WHAT?
New York Times
BESTSELLER
THE ART OF BEING A MUCH
Adieu
HARVARD
UNIVERSITY
PRESS

Miles, Buttercup, and Honeybee

"Funky and fearless pop artist Ashley Longshore found the perfect mellow foils to her ebullient personality in Basset Hounds Buttercup (me!, left) and Honeybee (right). We are not only low-slung; we enjoy chilling out on the painted concrete floor of Ashley's gorgeously psychedelic studio. In contrast with the many demands of Ashley's business, our requirements are simple: love, food, sleep. Absolutely in that order.

Joining us in this photo is Miles, the mellow pug, parented by Gallery director Kate Grace Bauer Rouchell, who fields inquiries from collectors worldwide, as well as from corporations that commission Ashley for branding imagery. Excitable and adoring, Miles is something of a camera-hog—he is also a natural-born model and will sit and smile for the camera indefinitely. KGB is his number one human, even though he originally belonged to Kate's now-husband, before they met.

We're happy to have Miles visit us, but happy too that he goes home with Kate when she departs!"

Rukus

"Fate intervened in my destiny on multiple occasions. First, I was returned to the shelter by my first adopted family after eight months, for reasons the Caplan family cannot fathom. Then, I was placed in a transport program to be sent to Wisconsin. Awaiting the transfer, the shelter was overcrowded, and I needed to be fostered in the meantime.

The Caplans agreed to take me in, but it became quickly clear that I would remain a New Orleans boy. I was named Rukus for my boundless energy and sometimes mischievous nature, but I am a docile and sweet guy. I greet newcomers with a lick and a smile. I am smart and mostly obedient, but not much of a guard dog. I'm a lover, not a fighter. Andrea Caplan utilized the expertise of designer Nomita Gupta, who created an environment that is stylish and modern, just like me! The carpet squares, my favorite part of the décor, are from Nomita's shop, Spruce, on Magazine Street."

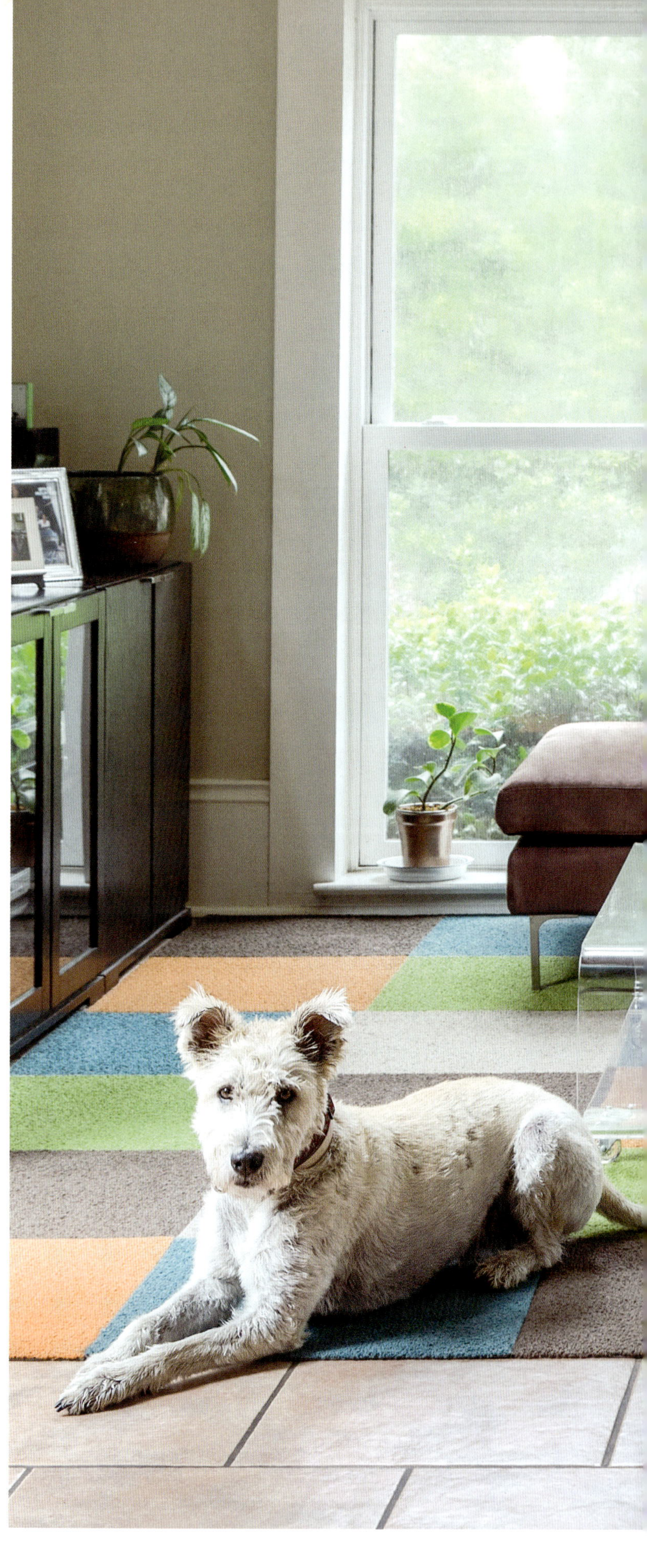

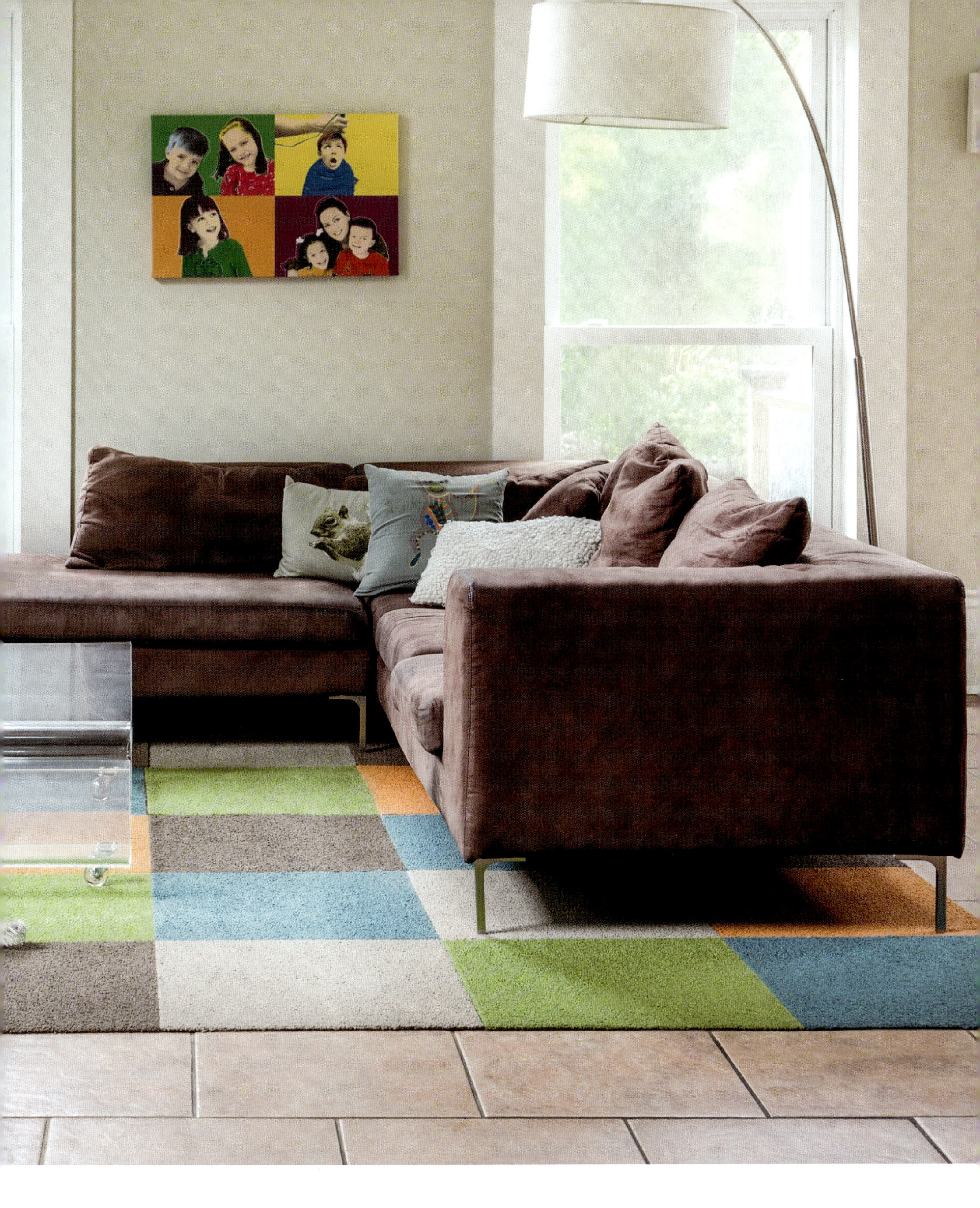

JAKE Despite his indifference to tossed balls, Jake nonetheless picked up Lina and James Jacobs, owners of the Magpie Cafe in Baton Rouge. One day Lina and James came home from work to discover the neglected dog under their carport. They had an instant rapport, and after no one claimed him, he became a member of their family, overcoming terrible heart worms to live a happy and full life. Labrador Jake was never a retriever, but he displayed many other characteristics of his breed: loyalty, a mellow disposition, and a fondness for swimming. Lina steered the home design herself, with guidance from designer Valorie Hart. Valorie helped Lina brightly combine family pieces with new finds. On the back porch, where Jake loved to hang out, James devised a serene and stylish oasis by hanging an antique bed, creating privacy with a slatted screen.

Jake has gone to doggy heaven, and he is sorely missed.

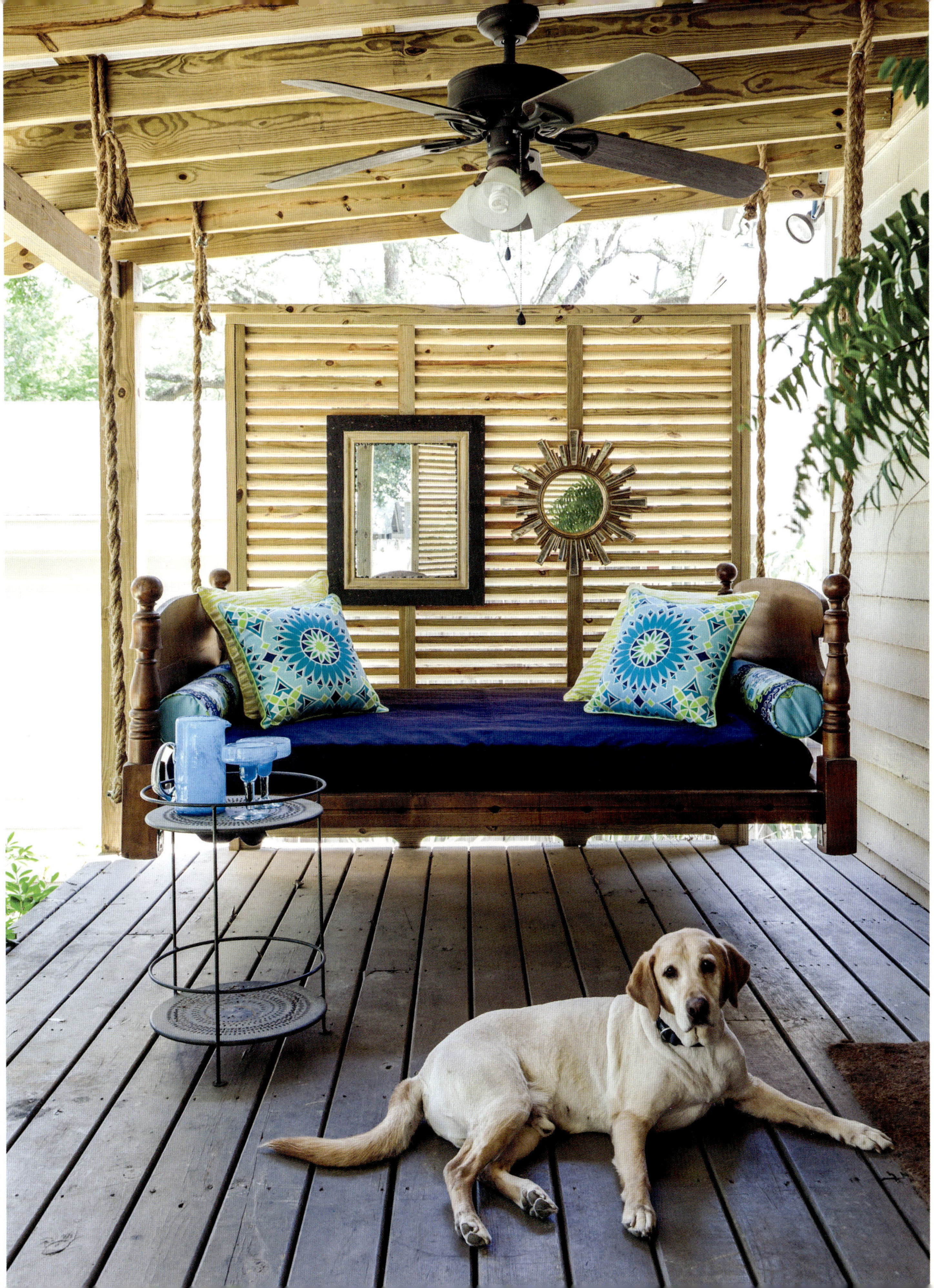

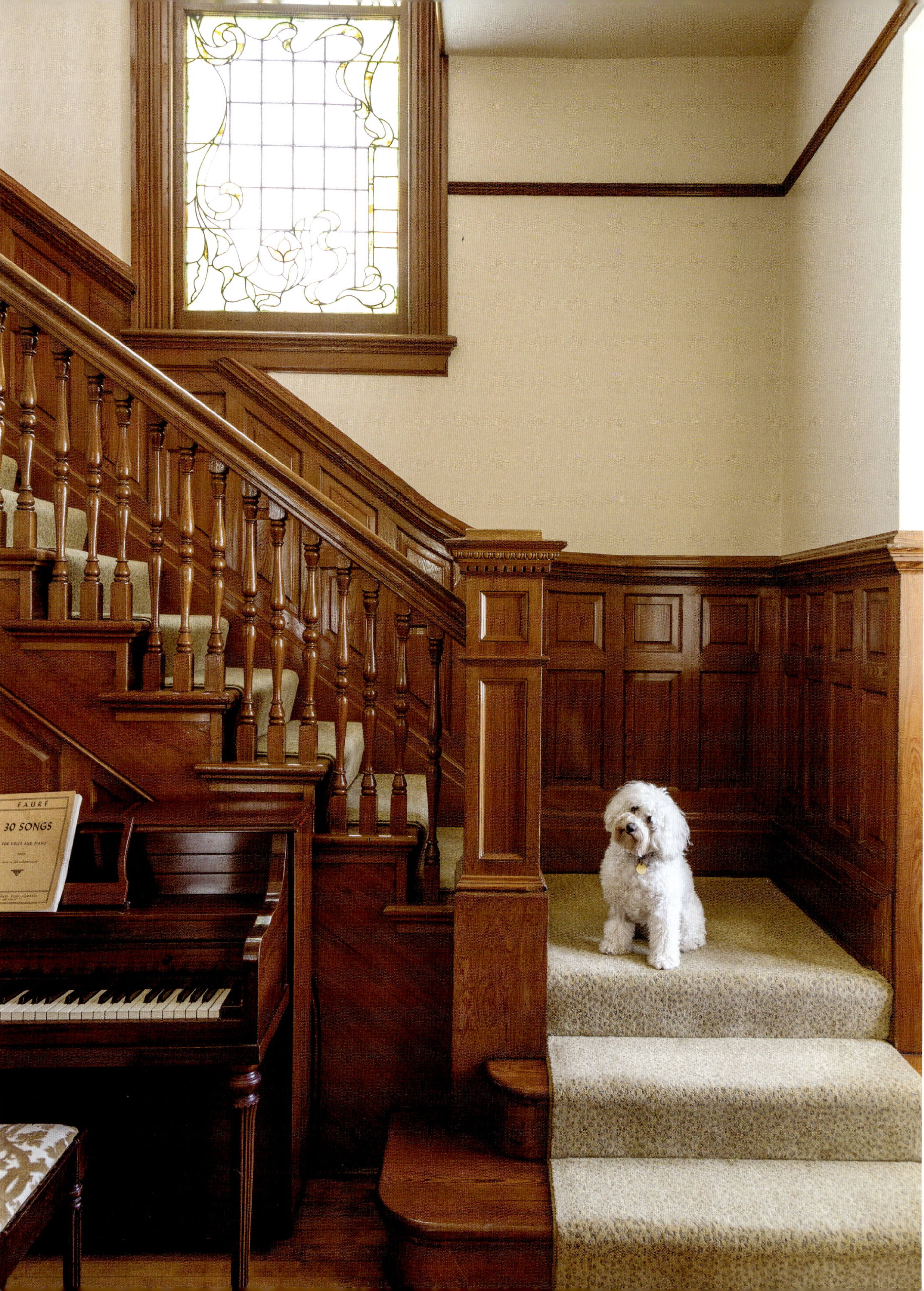
FAURÉ
30 SONGS
FOR VOICE AND PIANO

Molly

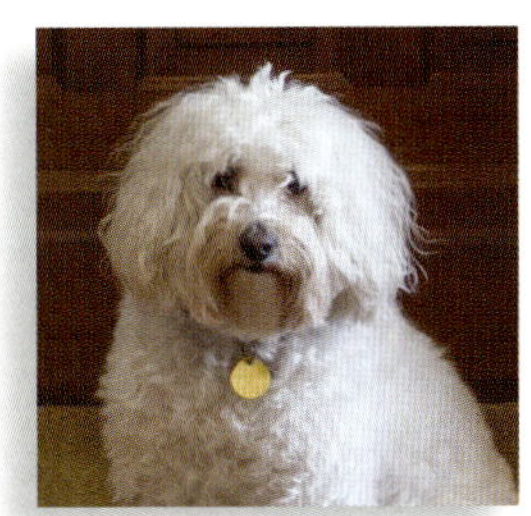

"I reside in a beautiful New Orleans home built in 1904 in the Edwardian style by a German immigrant. The stained glass throughout is attributed to Kokomo (Indiana) Opalescent Glass Works Company, which also supplied glass to Louis Comfort Tiffany. The staircase and wainscoting are original to the house. Designer Chad Graci is handling the second round of renovations, under way now. I'm a Schnoodle (Schnauzer/Poodle) and I like to know everything that's going on in the house. I'm too busy to cuddle but I keep tabs on all members of the family. When the house's occupants are scattered, I am sure to hold vigil on the steps, keeping track of who's up and who's down."

Birdie

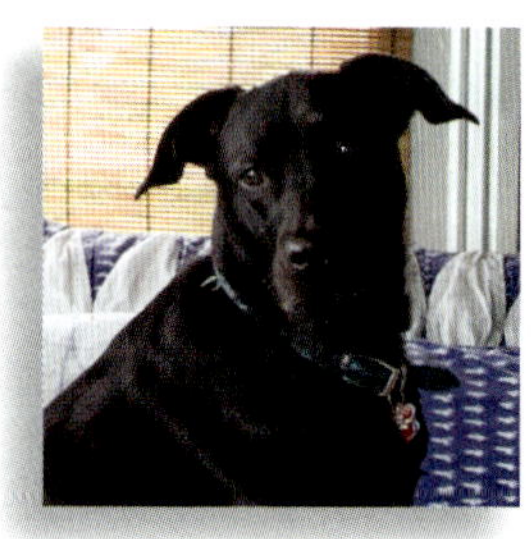

"One day in the spring of 2009, artist Miranda Lake found herself facing multiple challenges: her aging, beloved dog Stretch was in his final days, she had a large one-person exhibit on the horizon with much work yet to complete, and it was raining more than it had since Hurricane Katrina. The storm was so fresh that New Orleans residents still got very nervous whenever it rained, much less when it flooded the streets, as was the case that day. As Miranda monitored the rising water from her front window, she discovered that a scrawny black puppy had squeezed through her fence rails. While she thought the last thing she needed at the time was a soaked puppy, deep down she knew that this pup wasn't going anywhere.

And that pup was me, Birdie! Miranda was so taken with my 'colors' and the colors of Mr. Whipple, my roommate (not shown here), that she was compelled to repaint the entire interior of her house in a bolder, deeply saturated, jewel-toned color palette.

The bedroom where you see me is in what was originally a side porch addition. The room is long and skinny, with lots of screened-in windows and a functioning fireplace and sitting area opposite the bed. Miranda the overall vibe, likening it to sleeping in a cabin or on a boat. She handled all the décor herself in her unique creative style, finding most items in junk stores or on eBay. She's amazing when it comes to rescue: whether furniture or dogs!"

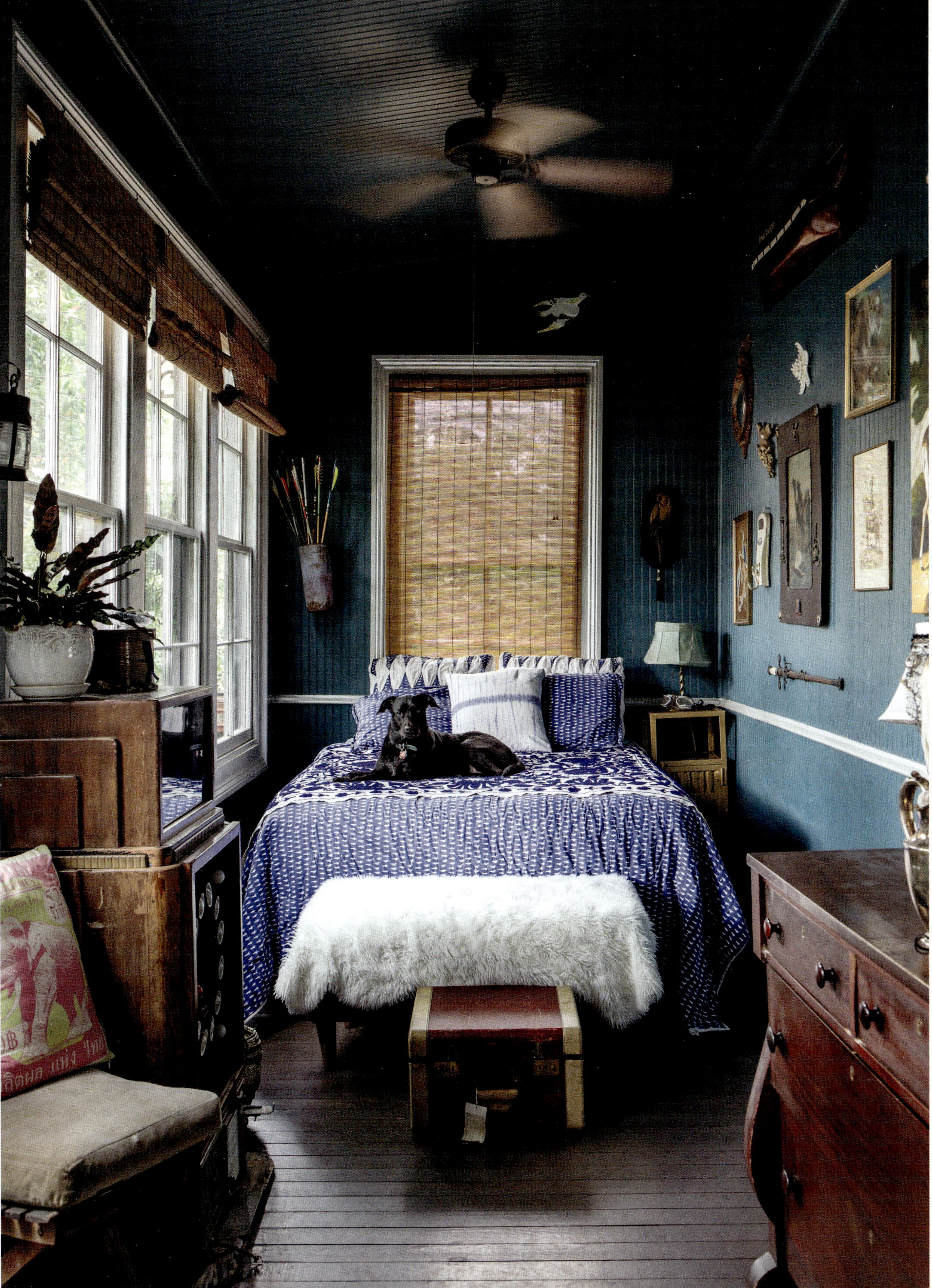

Henry

"As a guard dog, I'm useless. Years ago Julia Reed's Garden District home was burglarized, while I was on-duty. But I'm docile and friendly, so how could I not greet a visitor and not be agreeable as I was placed in my kennel? It's just good Southern manners to welcome guests.

A prolific writer, Julia had just completed her latest book at the time, *The House on First Street*, detailing the agonies and ecstasies of renovating her beloved home. The book, stored on her computer, was ready to be sent to her publisher; the television, some jewelry, and other personal items were all lost to the thief, but the loss of the computer was most daunting. Except for the first chapter, the book was not backed-up and Julia had to rewrite the whole thing.

I have been forgiven, after all I am a stoic and loyal companion.

You see me here in the kitchen, the least renovated part of the house. In this space Julia replaced some fixtures, added a wooden floor, repainted, and installed a bookshelf where the breakfast bar stools once would have been placed. I think it's kind of cozy in here and we decided that our mutual affection for one another could get us through anything—even a robbery."

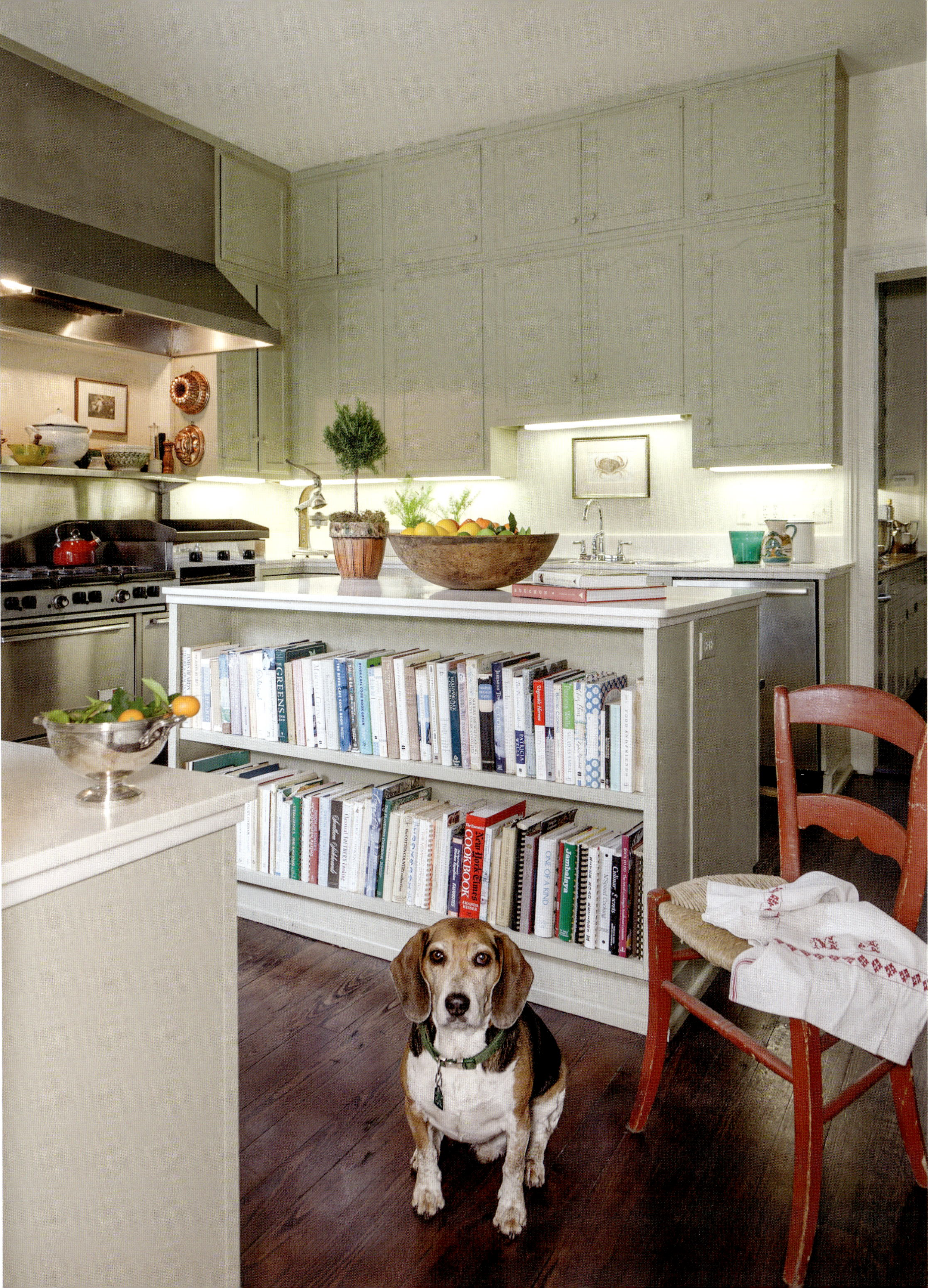
PATRICIA WELLS
The Essential
New York Times
COOKBOOK
AMANDA HESSER
FAVORITES
ONE OF A KIND
Jambalaya
RIVER ROAD RECIPES II
Culinary Secrets

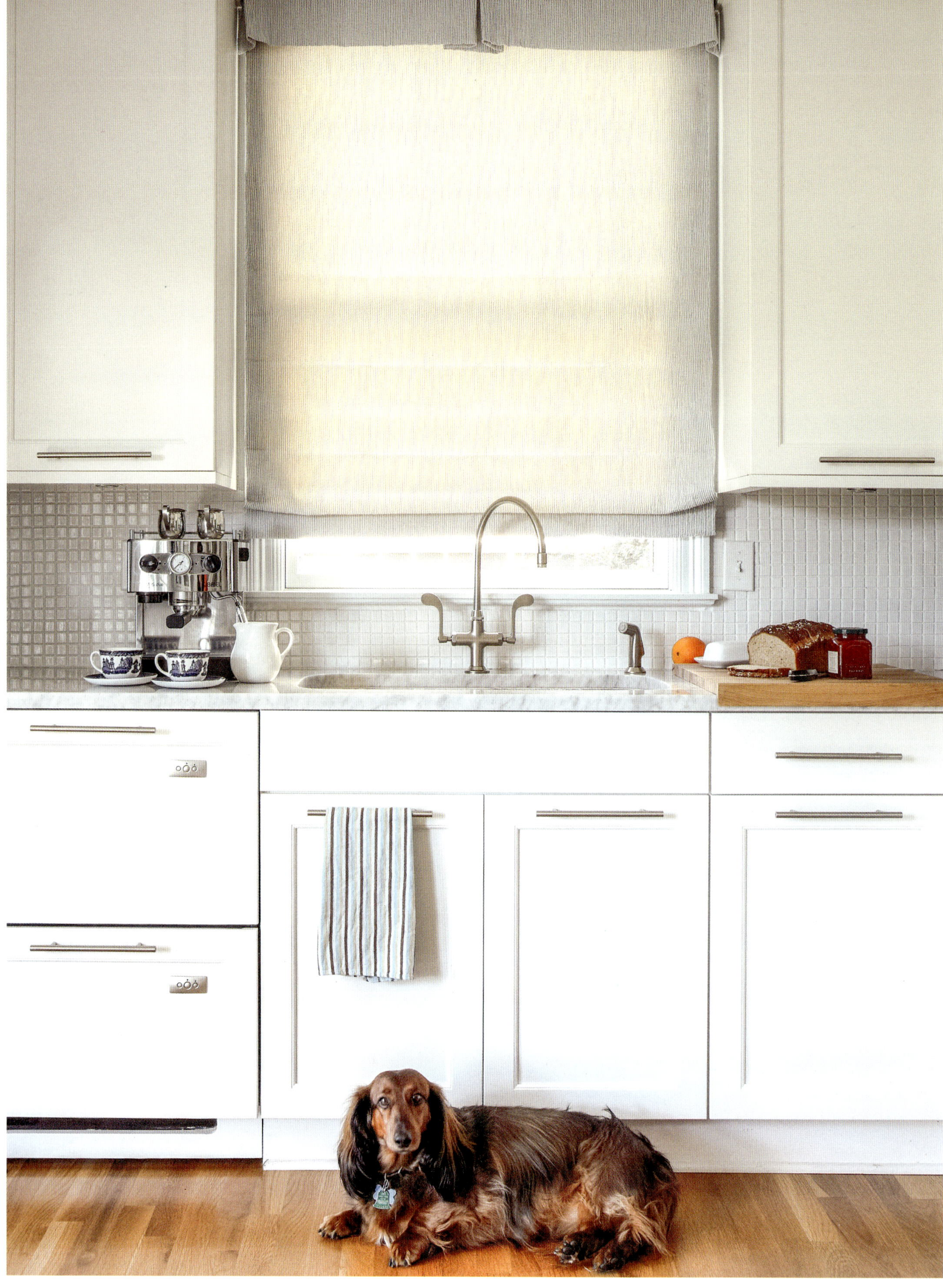

Emma

"Following Hurricane Katrina, interior designer Curtiss Herring had to completely gut and rebuild his 160-square-foot kitchen, which sat at ground level and took on water. Through it all, I stayed by his side. I am a long-haired Dachshund and, despite my advanced years, still look and act like a puppy, following Curtiss around and saying hi to visitors.

Curtiss says I am the sweetest dog he has ever known, and while I am perfectly happy to loll about in the kitchen, I do not do dishes. Curtiss selected cabinets by WoodMode/Classic Cupboards and the roman shade is by Peyroux's Custom Curtains. The mosaic backsplash is from Stafford Tile and the Carrara marble countertops are by Carr Stone.

Aren't I lucky to live in such a bright environment?"

Boudreaux

Guy and Poe Carpenter bought their opulent double-gallery Italianate mansion in 2007 and carefully restored it under the guidance of Guy, principal of Supreme Restoration LLC. Their vision for the décor was to create a space both elegant and comfortable for their family.

Guy applied his signature lacquered paint technique to walls of the dining room. The chandelier was found at New Orleans Auction Gallery, and the framed silk tapestry was found in a market in Chile by Poe's parents for $20. The dining set is a refurbished family heirloom.

Boudreaux, a 145-pound Newfoundland, was laid back and gentle. He lumbered quietly around the house, calmly saying hello to guests and soliciting a head pat. He was beloved by the family until his passing. In memoriam, Poe's daughter Chloe Carpenter wrote this poem:

To the eye he is a fright.
To the touch, he is as soft as black velvet
A gentle giant who loves and protects me,
who follows me like a dark shadow.
He speaks through his sad, brown,
droopy eyes,
and I speak back.
He sits as if he were a king, proud
and strong.
He instinctively swims gracefully
to my rescue like a lifeguard on duty.
I love my Newfie.
Not many understand.

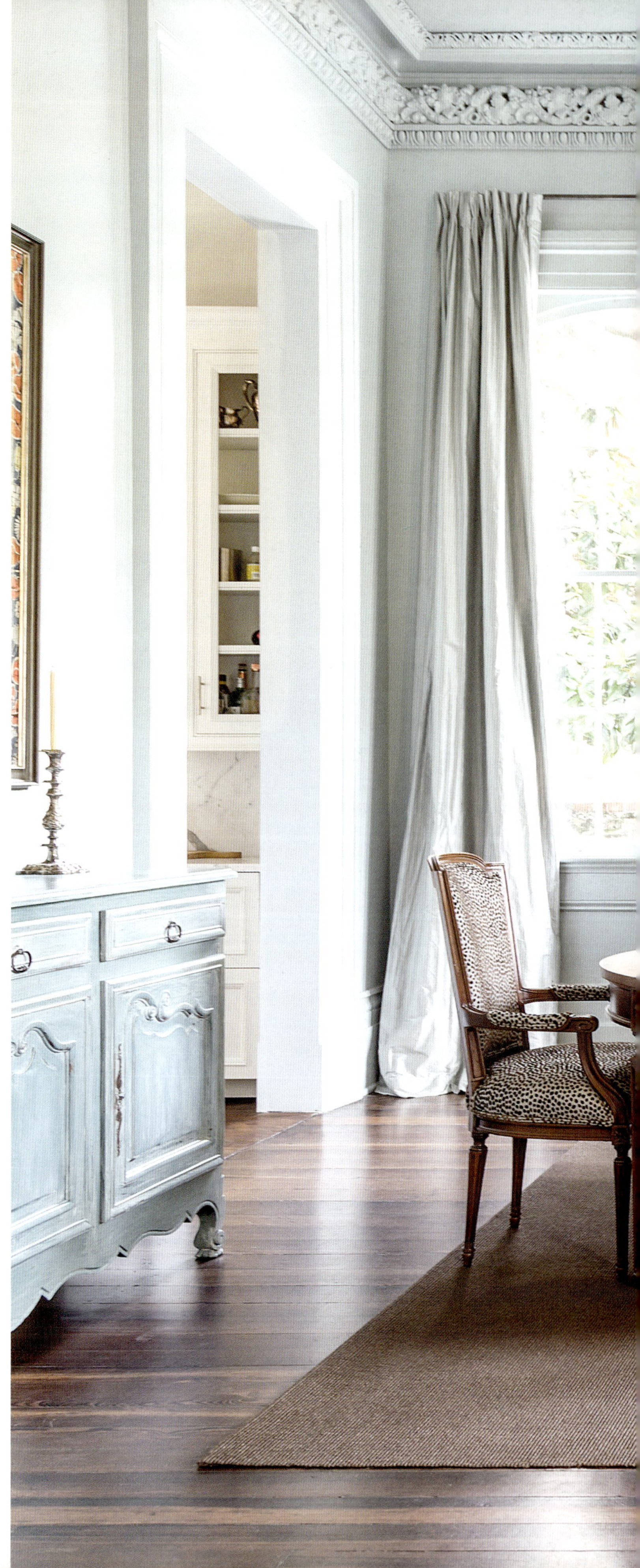

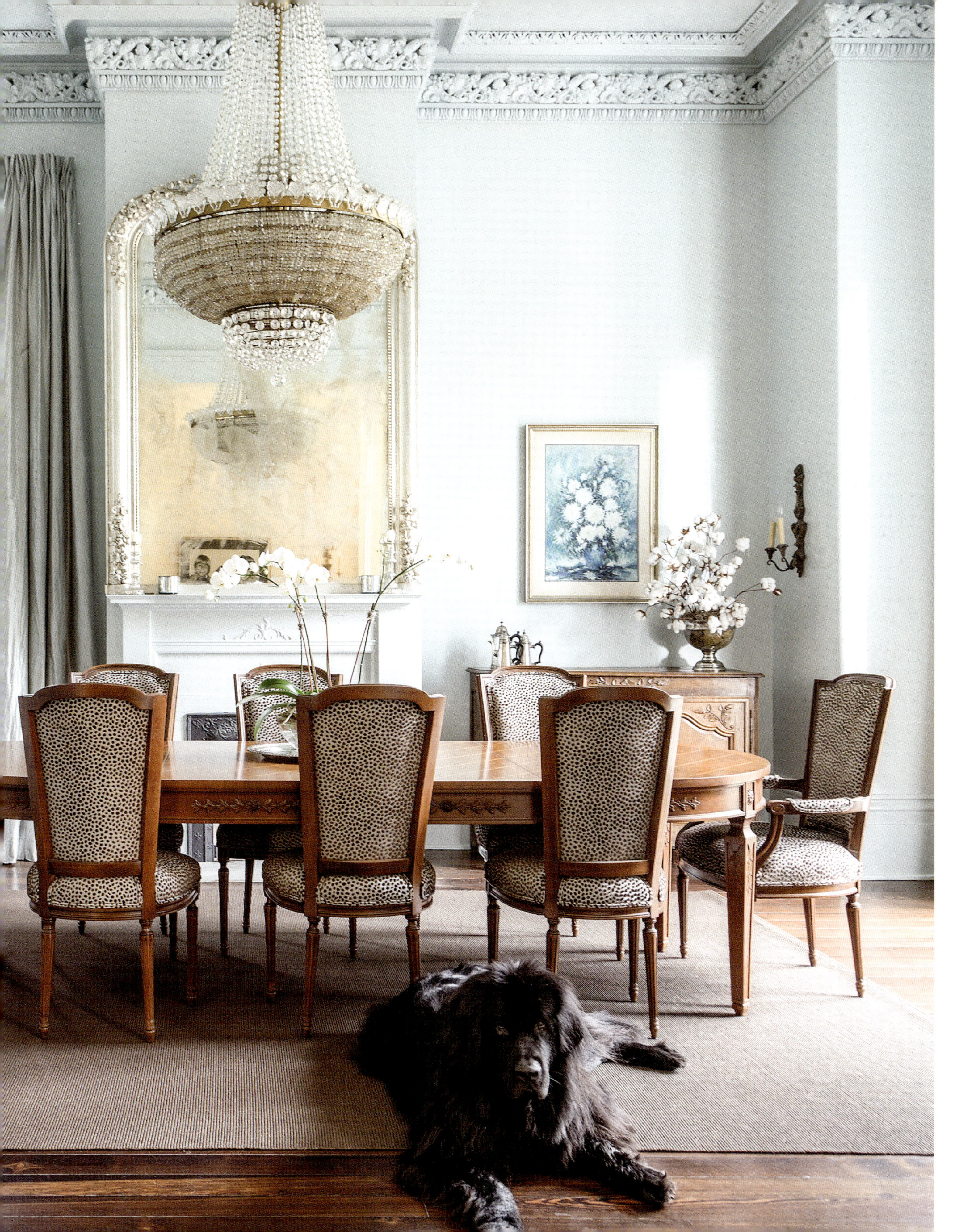

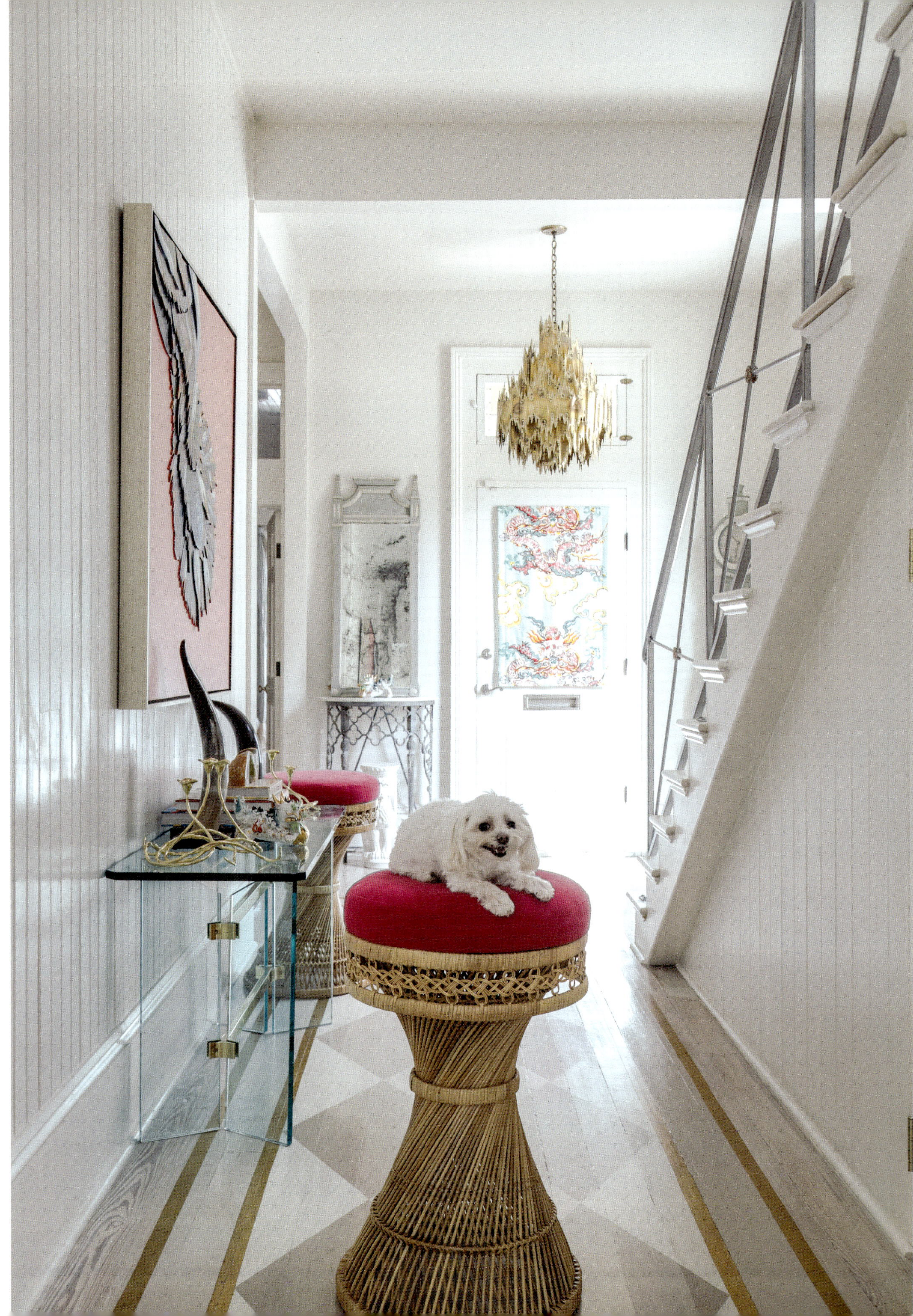

Chloe

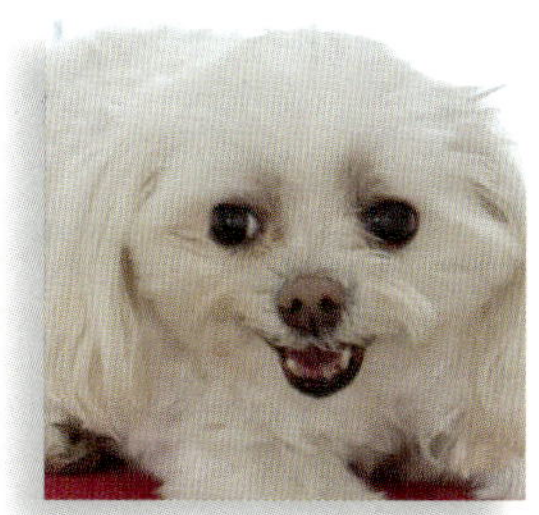

"I am an eleven-year-old, spoiled and lovable Maltese, and I'm pretty sure I'm human (look at my smile!), as I consider myself an equal, if not superior member of Emily Walker's family. My favorite pastime is watching TV, and I insist on watching animal shows. If I happen to be in another part of the house and hear an animal on TV, I'll run to the den and have a nice, barky conversation with whoever is on the screen.

Here I am perched on a vintage rattan barstool, purchased at Emily's favorite antique store in Charlotte, North Carolina. The chandelier was the 'find of the century,' from Sterling Provisions. The sculptural painting on the left is by Louisiana artist Ed Smith, and the floors were hand-painted in a harlequin design by Gretchen Howard. Emily collaborated with designer Chad Graci for the décor throughout this delicious house."

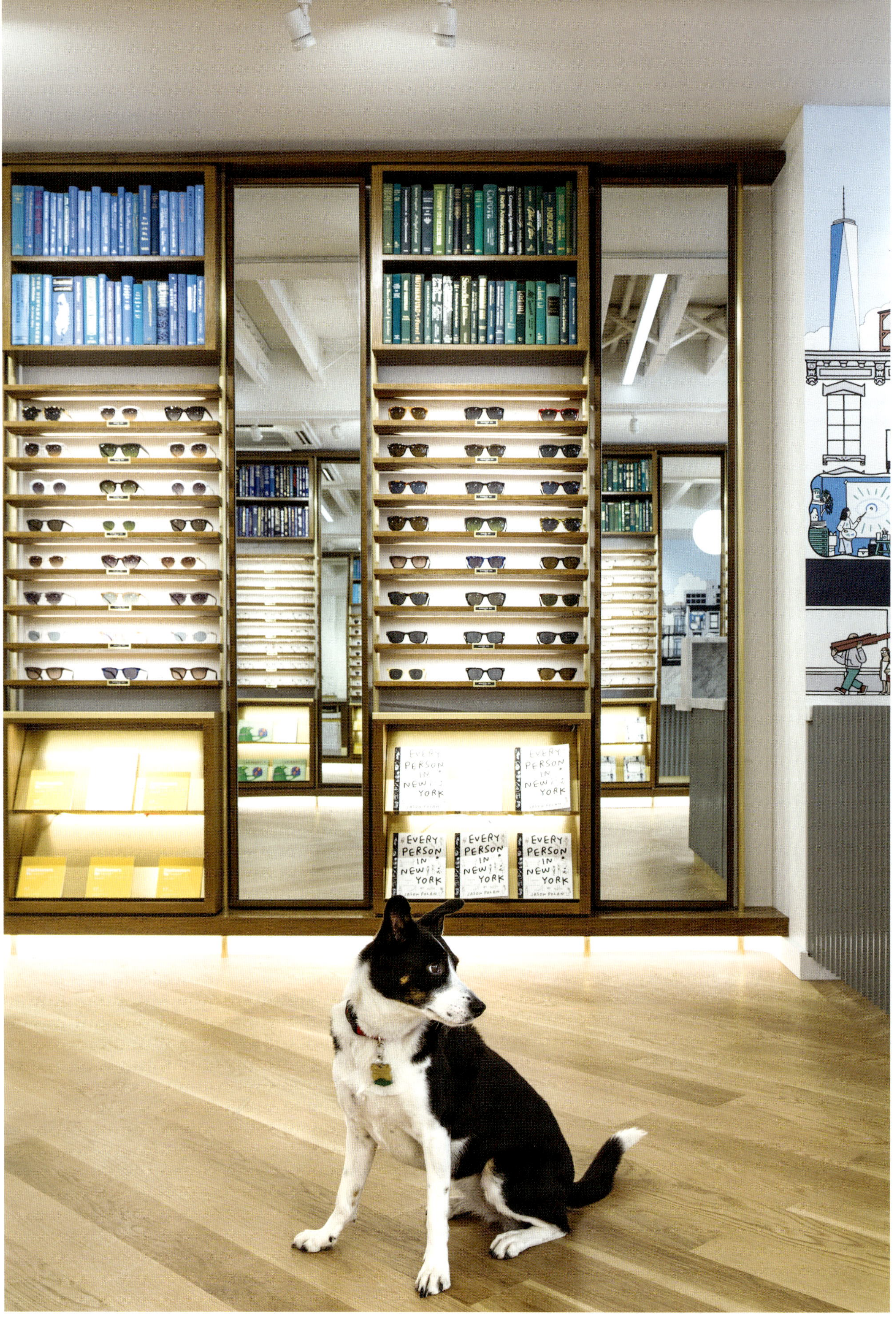
EVERY PERSON IN NEW YORK
EVERY PERSON IN NEW YORK
EVERY PERSON IN NEW YORK
JASON POLAN
EVERY PERSON IN NEW YORK
JASON POLAN
EVERY PERSON IN NEW YORK
JASON POLAN

Cheeseburger

"I live in Brooklyn with Cathy Begien, visual director of Warby Parker. I received this noble moniker because a friend suggested that if Cathy ever got a dog, that would be a good name. Cathy agreed, and now I bear the responsibility of personifying a delicious sandwich.

I am a very lively, curious, and sweet dog, and I rarely take my eyes off Cathy. Here I am, enjoying some time in the Cobble Hill (Brooklyn) store, which features custom art installations by Pete Gamlen, Adrian Tomine, Shantell Martin, and Jim Rugg. Cathy chooses designs for the stores that are clever, sophisticated, and tailored to the neighborhood where they're located. She hopes each store will inspire a sense of discovery.

Dogs are welcome in the stores, and the chain hosts a 'Warby Barker Day,' offering dog-friendly events in their stores. It began as an April Fools' joke in 2012 when the company created a website (warbybarker.com) purporting to sell glasses for dogs. My vision, happily, is 20/20, so I have no need for the hip stylings of Warby Parker."

Dakota

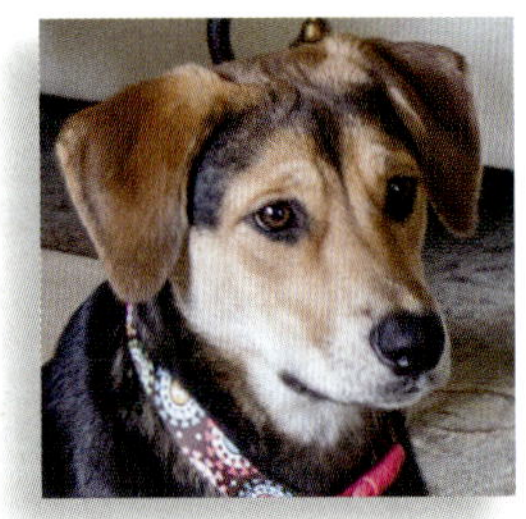

"I started out as a box of envelopes. Susan Peterson was heading to Office Depot to buy envelopes when she got distracted by a box of Lab-mix puppies from the Saint Francis Animal Sanctuary. So smitten was she by a certain puppy that she abandoned her original mission and came home with me instead of the office supplies that she needed in the first place.

I have grown into a loyal and affectionate pet, lavishing all with kisses so prodigiously that I have been nicknamed the 'Italian Lover.' I live in a grand home in Mandeville, Louisiana. The home's interior was meticulously designed by Connie Seitz Interiors."

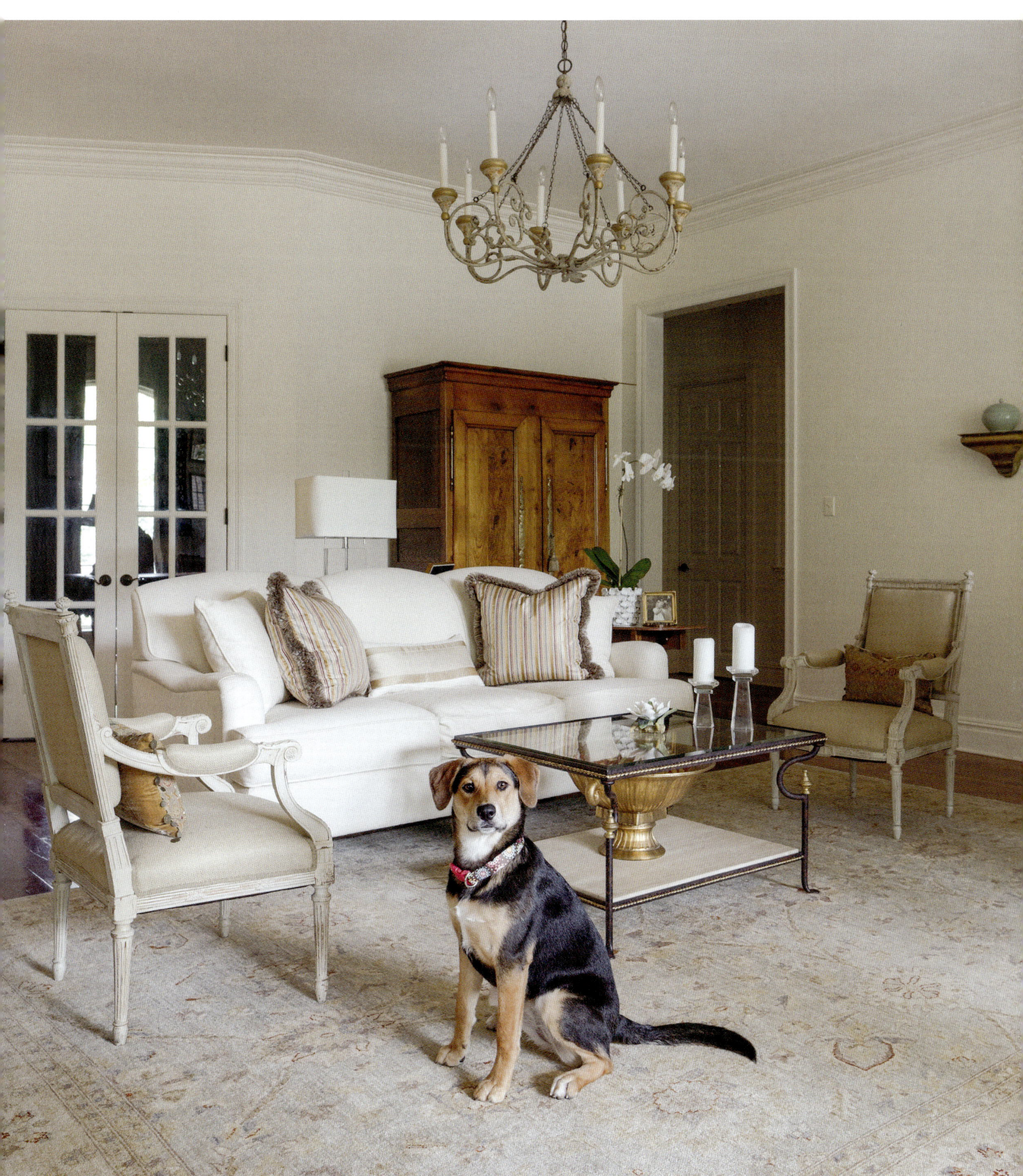

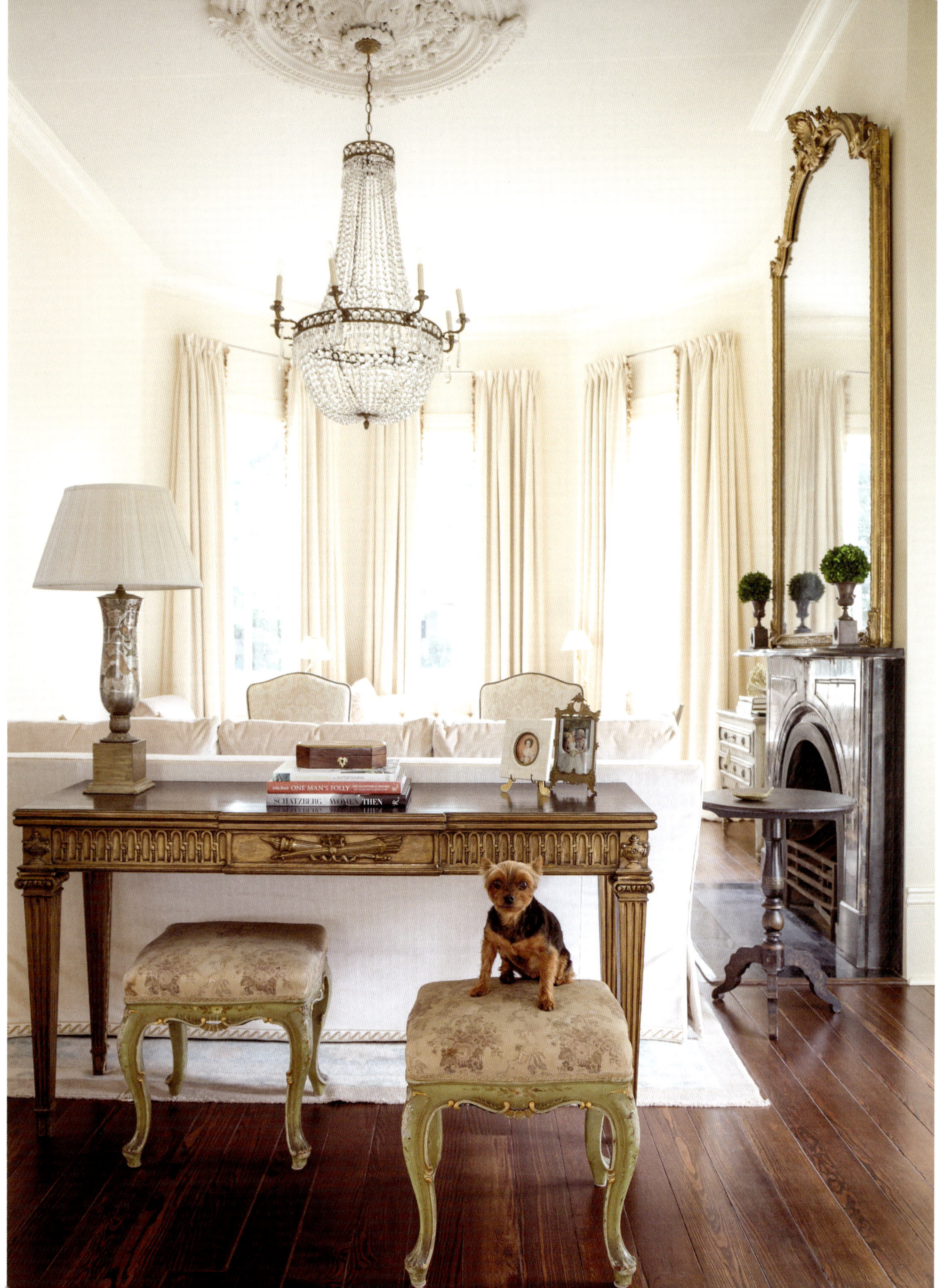
ENTERTAINING
ONE MAN'S FOLLY
SCHATZBERG
WOMEN THEN

Lulu

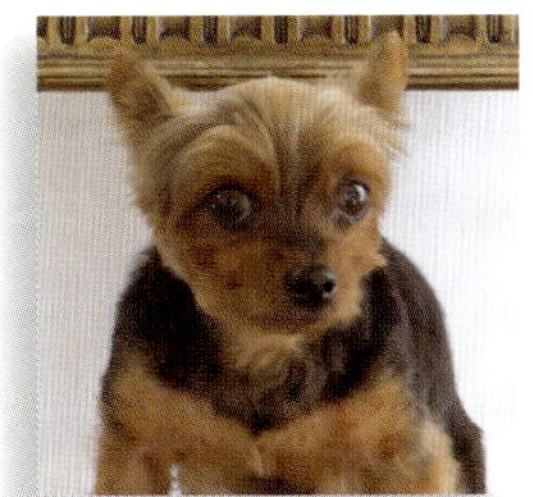

"People refer to me as a 'small dog' but I don't know what they are talking about. I was born in Aspen, and I am mighty and fearless—I have climbed mountains in Alaska and taken on dogs four times my size. Despite my formidable ego, I am a sweet, affectionate member of the family.

Designer Chad Graci worked with the family to choose a bright, modern palette to compliment the antiques and fixtures on which I like to perch. And they compliment me too! The Sherwin-Williams 'White Wool' paint, as well as the similar colored silk drapes, provide a soothing, and stylish backdrop for me and for all the furnishings, too, but that's really a secondary consideration."

Tyson

When Donna and Tom Russell found their home lacking a canine presence, the gods of dog placement did what they usually do, and filled that void in a surprising way. Donna, an interior designer, had done some work on a home in Dallas. As a reward for her services, her clients offered her the pick of their purebred litter. Tom was initially excited for the new puppy, but he became reticent when he learned the breed: American Pit Bull. He had the reaction so many uninformed people have to Pits, and was not so keen on the puppy anymore. Donna, however, was smitten with the runt, and scooped him up to bring home.

Fast-forward a few years. The Russells now truly understood the breed, and also realized that the adage is entirely true: there are no bad dogs, only bad owners. Tyson became a loving, friendly, and vigilant member of the family. He exhibited all the traits of his breed. He was extremely loyal and wicked-smart. His vocabulary was vast. So vast that they often wondered if there was more than just a dog inside of him.

Sadly, Tyson "the Boy" passed on, but the Russells know that the only option for his replacement is the American Pit Bull.

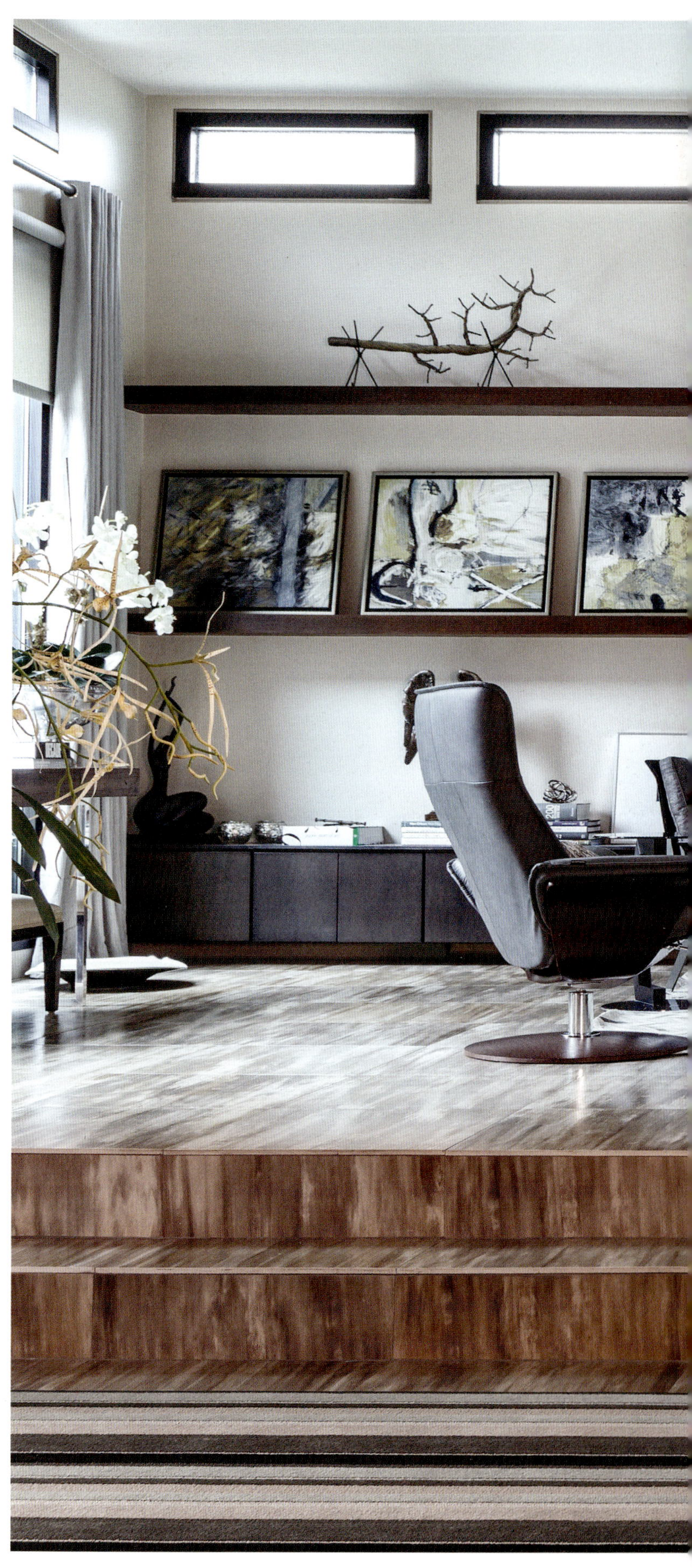

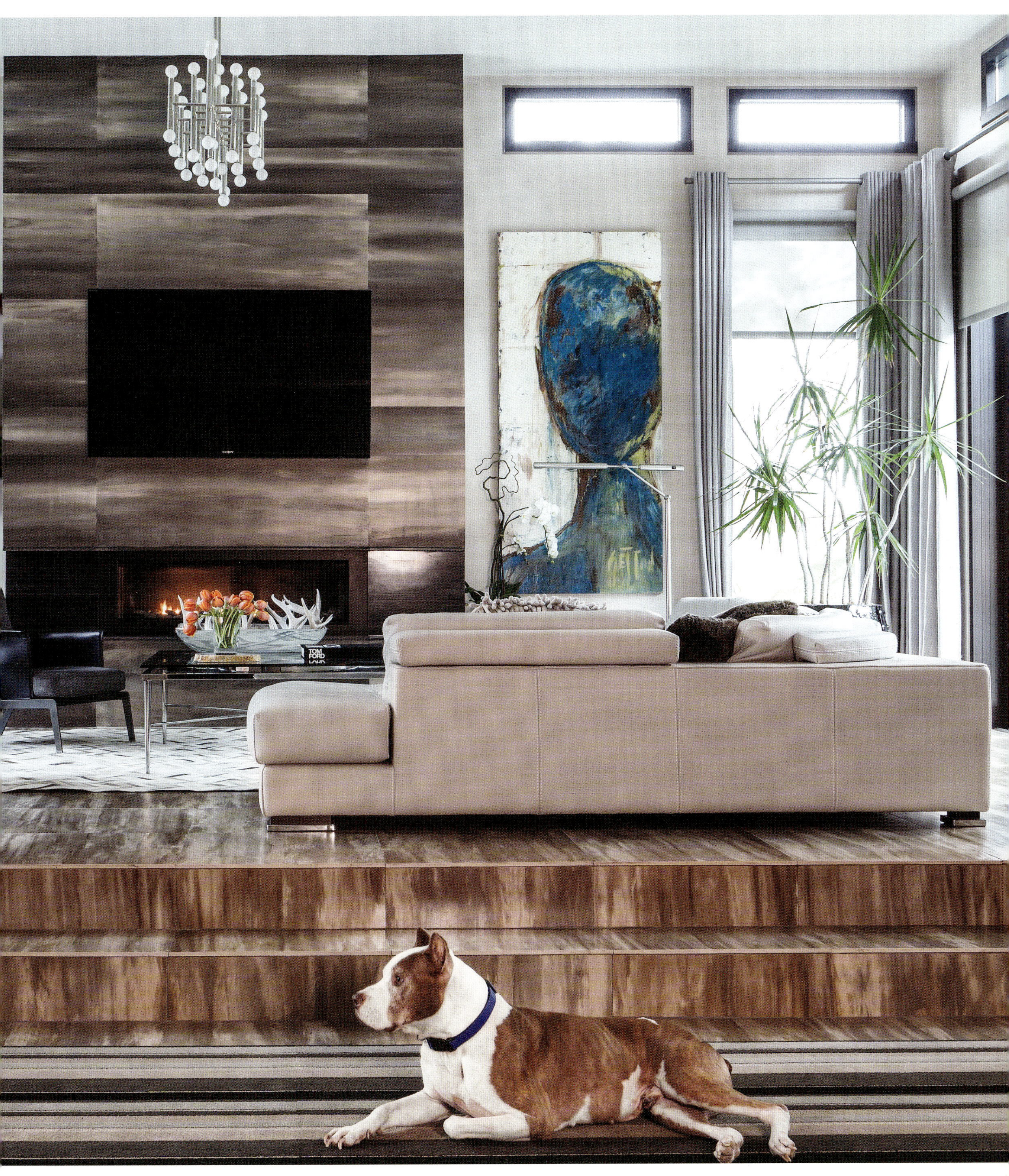
TOM FORD

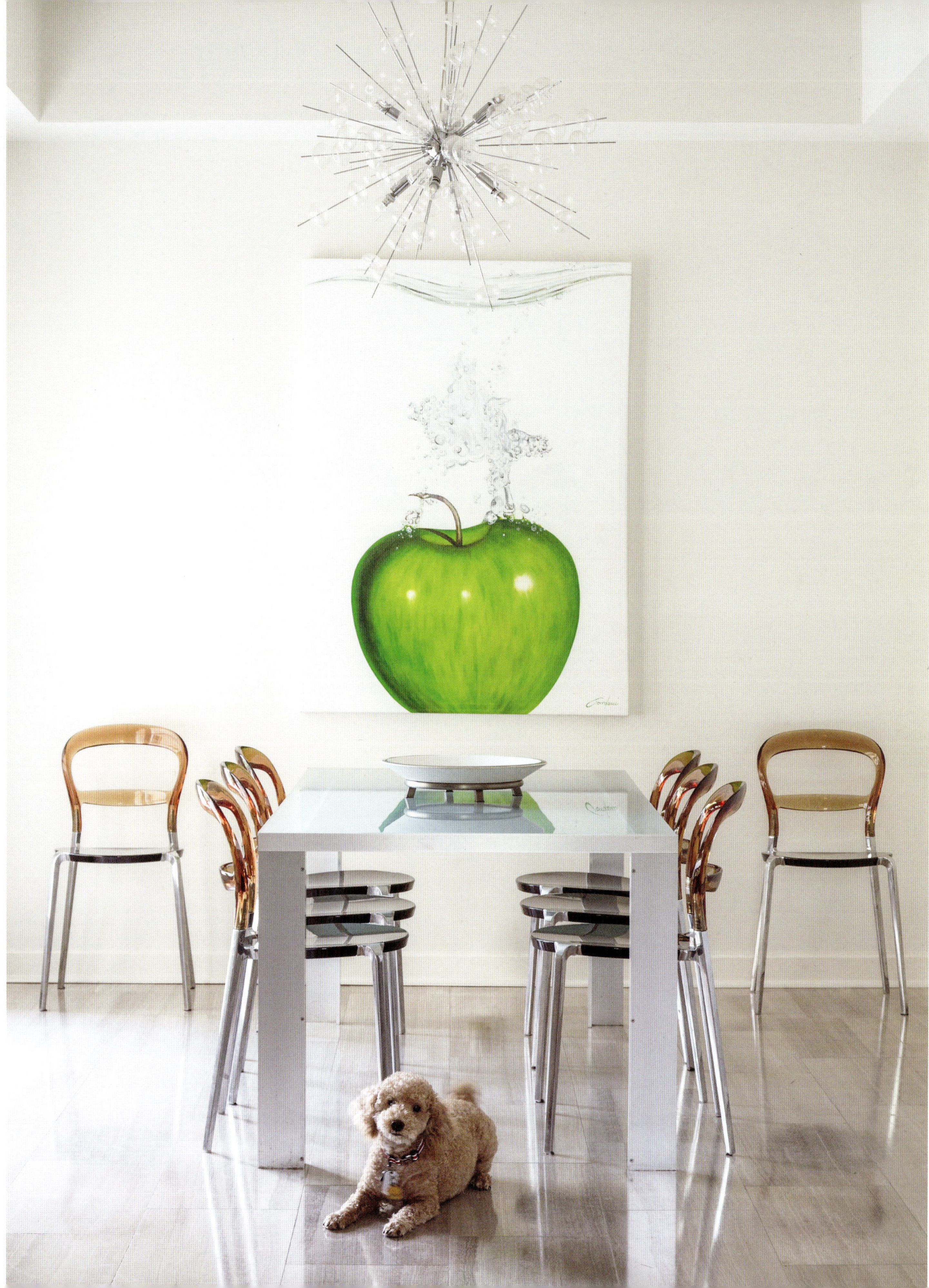

Drew Brees

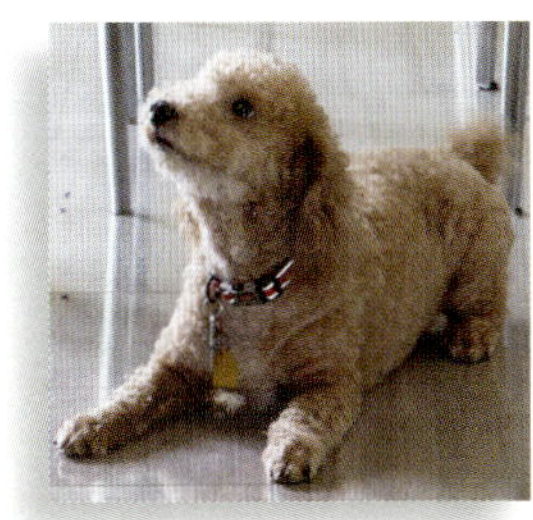

"When Penny Francis's daughter was two years old, they acquired a toy poodle and named her Sugar because she had the sweetest face. It soon became clear that the baby was too small for this energetic dog, and sadly, they returned her to the breeder, telling them to please keep them in mind in the future if Sugar ever had puppies.

Ten years and one Super Bowl victory for the New Orleans Saints later, they returned to the breeder and chose me, Drew Brees Francis. Drew Brees seemed like the perfect name for me. Like my namesake, the star quarterback of the New Orleans Saints, I am friendly, but dominant. I may not be able to throw a perfect spiral, but I excel at hiding. I love to play hide and seek, and when no one is available to entertain me, I'll instigate a game by hiding one of the family's socks. They never know when an errant sock will turn up behind a sofa cushion or curtain.

Penny Francis is a well-known New Orleans designer, and also owns the décor shop Eclectic Home on Oak Street. The table is from Design Within Reach, the chairs are Calligaris, and the glass bubble chandelier is Solaria, each of which were acquired through Eclectic Home. The painting is by Gardani."

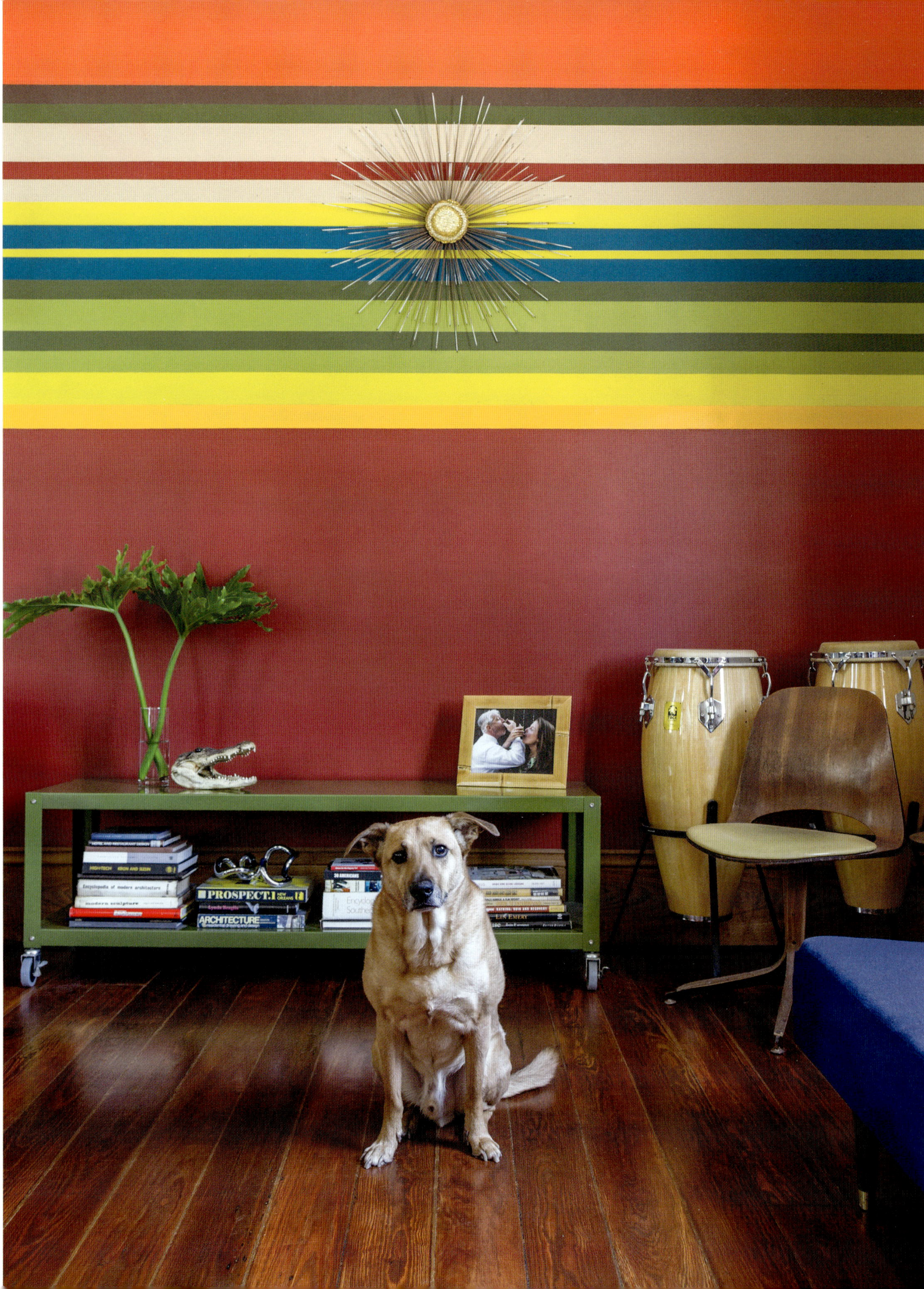
HOTEL AND RESTAURANT DESIGN
HIGHTECH
KRON AND SLESIN
Encyclopedia of modern architecture
modern sculpture
PROSPECT.1
NEW ORLEANS
ARCHITECTURE
residential drafting and design
30 AMERICANS
KATRINA: RUIN AND RECOVERY
LIN EMERY

Dude

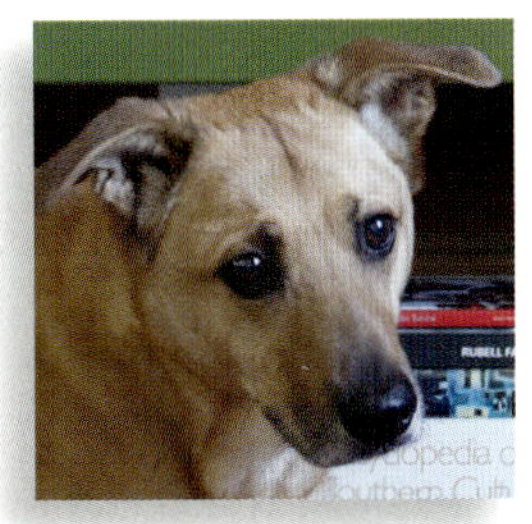

"I came to Lindsay Ross Owens in the spring of 2005 via the LASPCA, where I had charmed all the volunteers into preferential showings. Lindsay liked my Caribbean street-dog looks right away, but my mellow disposition prompted her to name me Dude. Not 'the Dude,' just Dude. I rode home that day in Lindsay's bright red 1975 Cadillac Eldorado, arriving at Lindsay's eclectic, cool, and art-filled New Orleans home. Lindsay handled all design and décor choices with a well-defined point of view and took extraordinary pains to get every detail to her liking.

One of her last challenges was creating an interesting, unexpected visual impact for the focal point of her living room wall. Lindsay found inspiration at the beach when a friend popped out of the water wearing a brightly striped bikini on a red background. 'That's it!' she exclaimed, subsequently heading to Helm Paint & Decorating with bikini bottom in hand. After managing to match all the colors in the suit except the red, Helm custom-mixed a color and named it 'Bikini Top Red'—the formula is still available in the store's database, as Lindsay discovered while doing repairs following Hurricane Katrina.

The decorative items are mostly vintage finds, with the exception of the shelf from CB2. In the frame is a photo Sara took of Lindsay and her husband (and my other best friend), comedian Matt Owens, on their wedding day, feeding each other oysters instead of champagne."

Evie and Coco

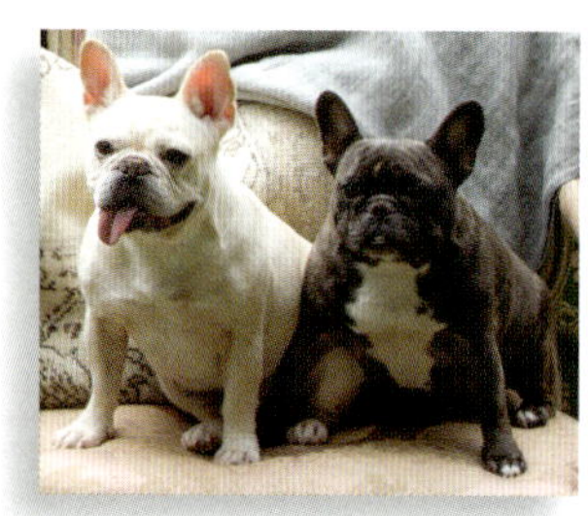

"Stephen Sonnier and Roy Duynn have a talent for creating luxurious space in any environment. As you can see, antiques and flowers from their shop, Dunn and Sonnier, in New Orleans, transform their elegant but modest backyard into the perfect set for Evie (left) and myself, Coco (right). Let's face it: We are the stars of the family and any environment.

We came to Stephen and Roy by way of a bitter divorce of some friends, and they tell us we have grown to become 'The best dogs we ever had.' We think that possibly everyone believes this of their dog, but we'll take the compliment. Along with our dog housemate, Crook (camera shy so not seen here), we report to work each day at the store. We spend our days happily greeting visitors, posting selfies on Instagram, and hanging out among the beautiful antiques and flowers. We think, 'They are the best parents we ever had!'"

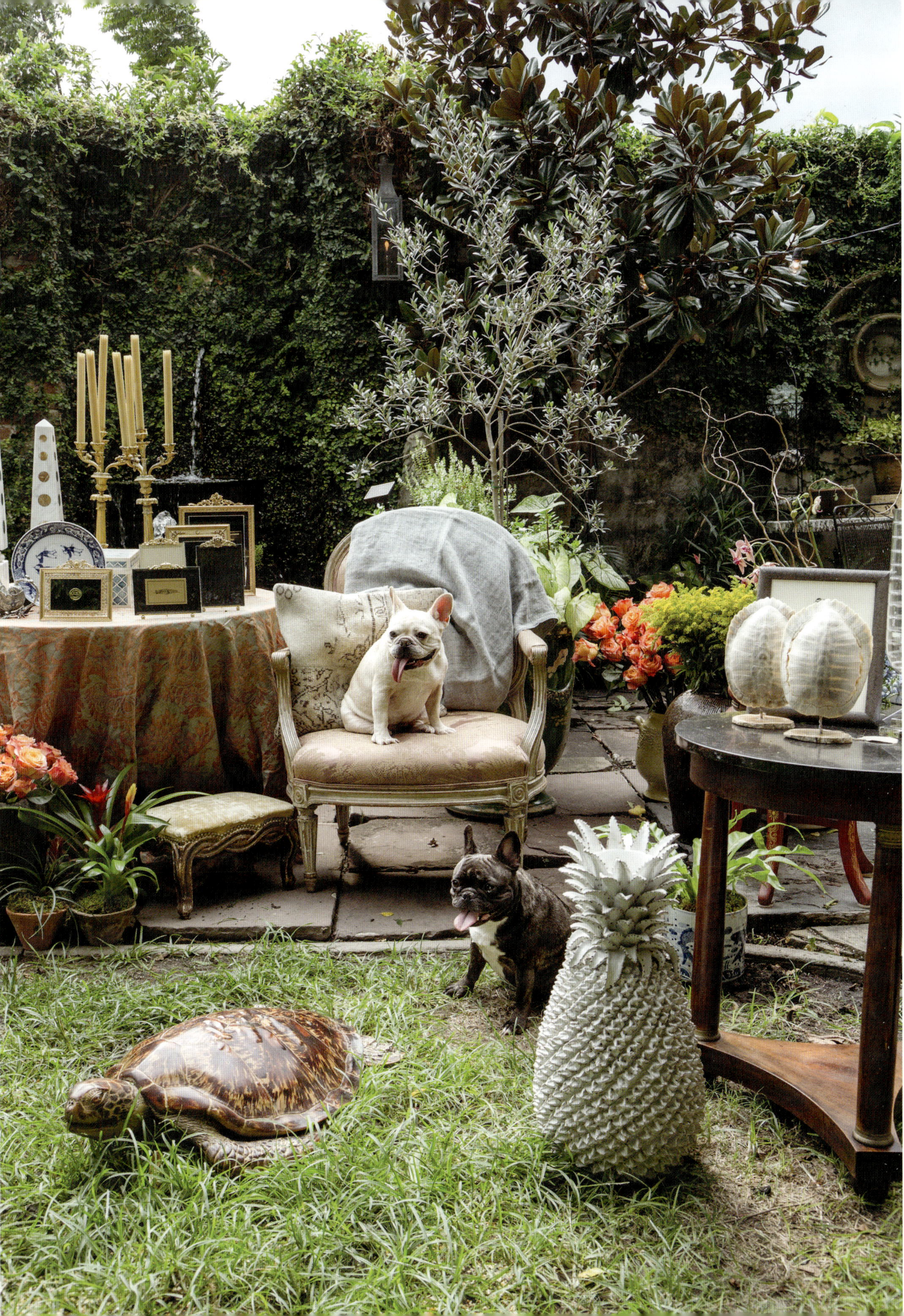

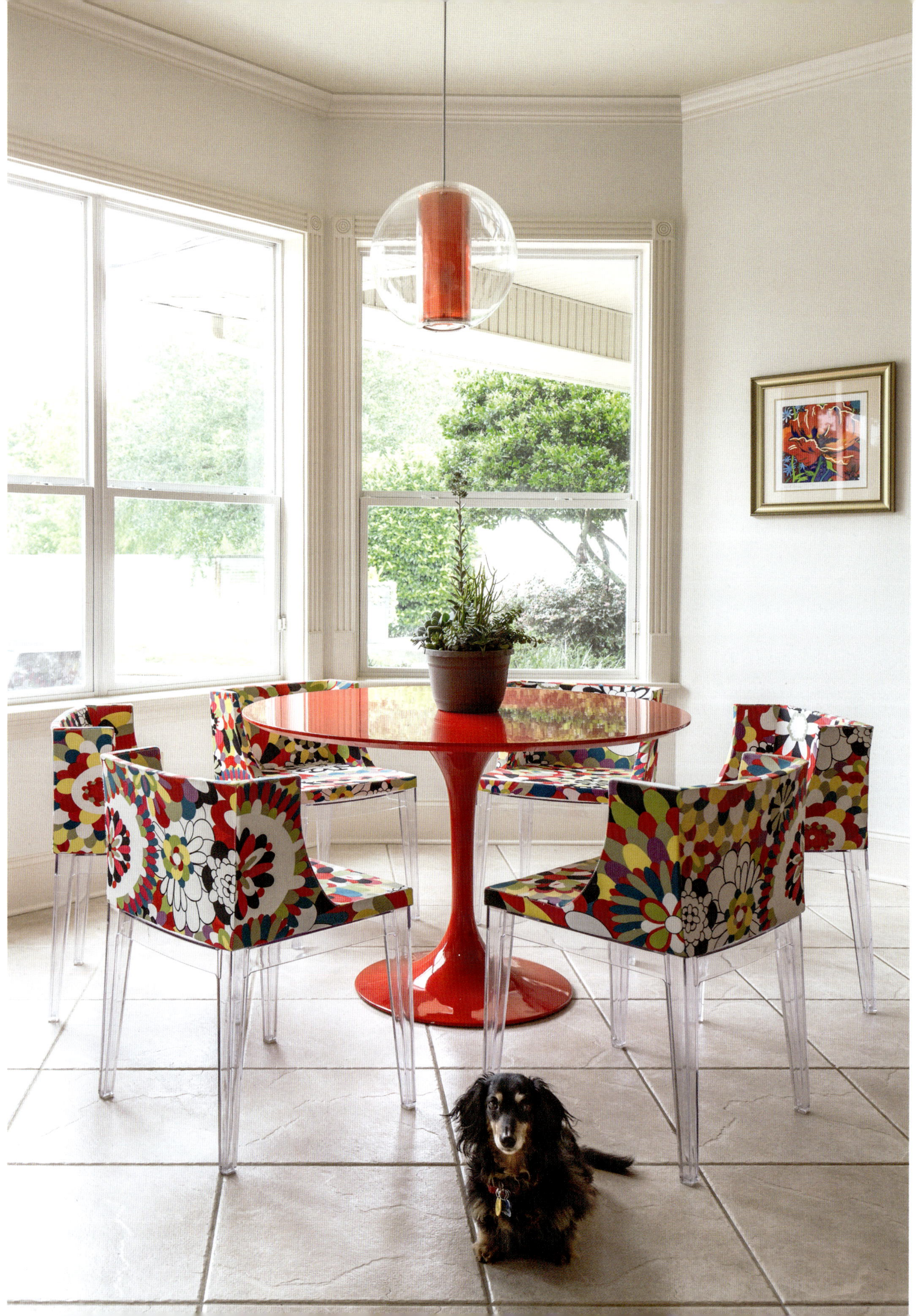

Ringo

"I am named Ringo for my mop-top hairdo, and I'm a lucky dog twice over. I was adopted by Michelle Edelman and Don Dykshorn from a foster home, having survived the mean streets of Escondido, California. I had been diagnosed with a rare heart disease that Michelle's other dog suffered from, so she figured why not? She knew how to deal with that. Turns out, I was misdiagnosed all along and I'm perfectly healthy.

I repay my saviors daily, patrolling the house and monitoring the kids. I have even stepped in to break up fights, pulling one daughter by the sock until she backed away from the brouhaha.

I'm rather a dandy, and enjoy nothing more than a trim and a blowout, prancing around after to show off my new 'do.' But I still have a little street left in me. Left to my own devices, I will scavenge for tasty garbage in the trashcans I can reach.

Michelle and Don employed the talents of designer Nomita Gupta, who appointed our house with finishes and furnishings from her shop Spruce, on Magazine Street in New Orleans. Spruce specializes in environmentally friendly products and practices."

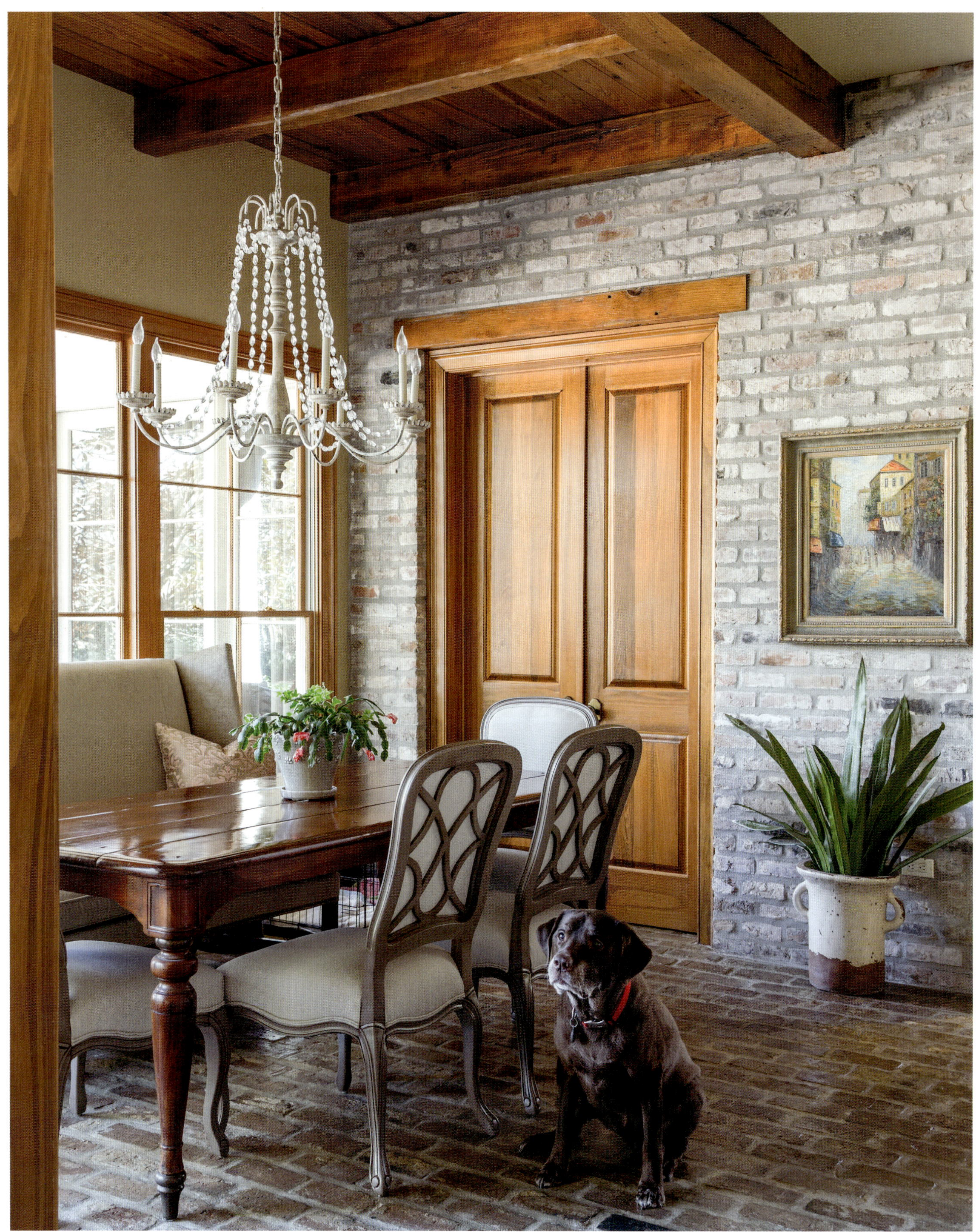

Roux

"To give their home a fresh look, the Evans family enlisted the help of designer Jennifer DiCerbo, who also owns the Covington, Louisiana, housewares shop the French Mix. Jennifer helped them combine existing family pieces with stylish new acquisitions.

One existing family piece that did not need updating was me, Roux, their eight-year-old chocolate Labrador Retriever. In my early, feistier years, I was infamous in the family for 'counter surfing,' scouring the kitchen countertops, devouring everything in my path—whole bags of apples, entire pizzas, platters of barbecue shrimp, a box of cupcakes. I am not a picky eater. These days I stay closer to sea level. I'm a gentle, kind, and patient fellow, tolerantly enduring the annoyances of the other dogs. Here I'm obediently posing in the kitchen, obeying the command stay, knowing a treat is in the offing."

Rooney

"I am an English-bred Golden Retriever and a fine and loyal girl. Named for English footballer Wayne Rooney, I am a docile, introspective charmer. I am also a bit of a shoe and sock thief, and will hoard them in my bed for safekeeping. I am perfectly comfortable in my beautiful new home in Covington, Louisiana, designed by architect George Hopkins. Connie Sietz Interiors handled the décor. I am shown here in the master suite, which features a chandelier and two bedside lamps of Murano glass by Jan Showers. The bedding is from Leontine Linens, and the headboard is custom. The custom bench is upholstered in Aegean velvet."

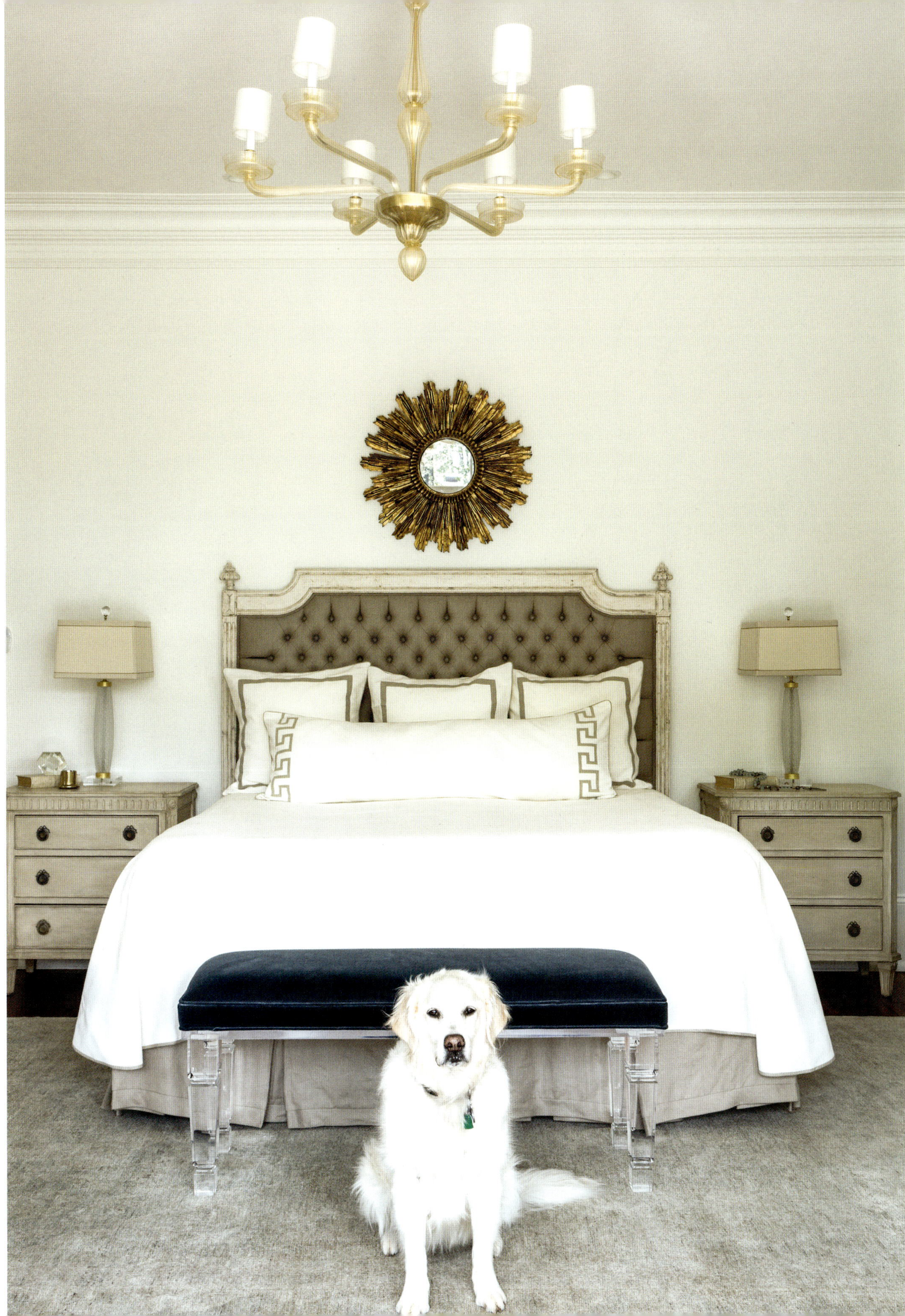

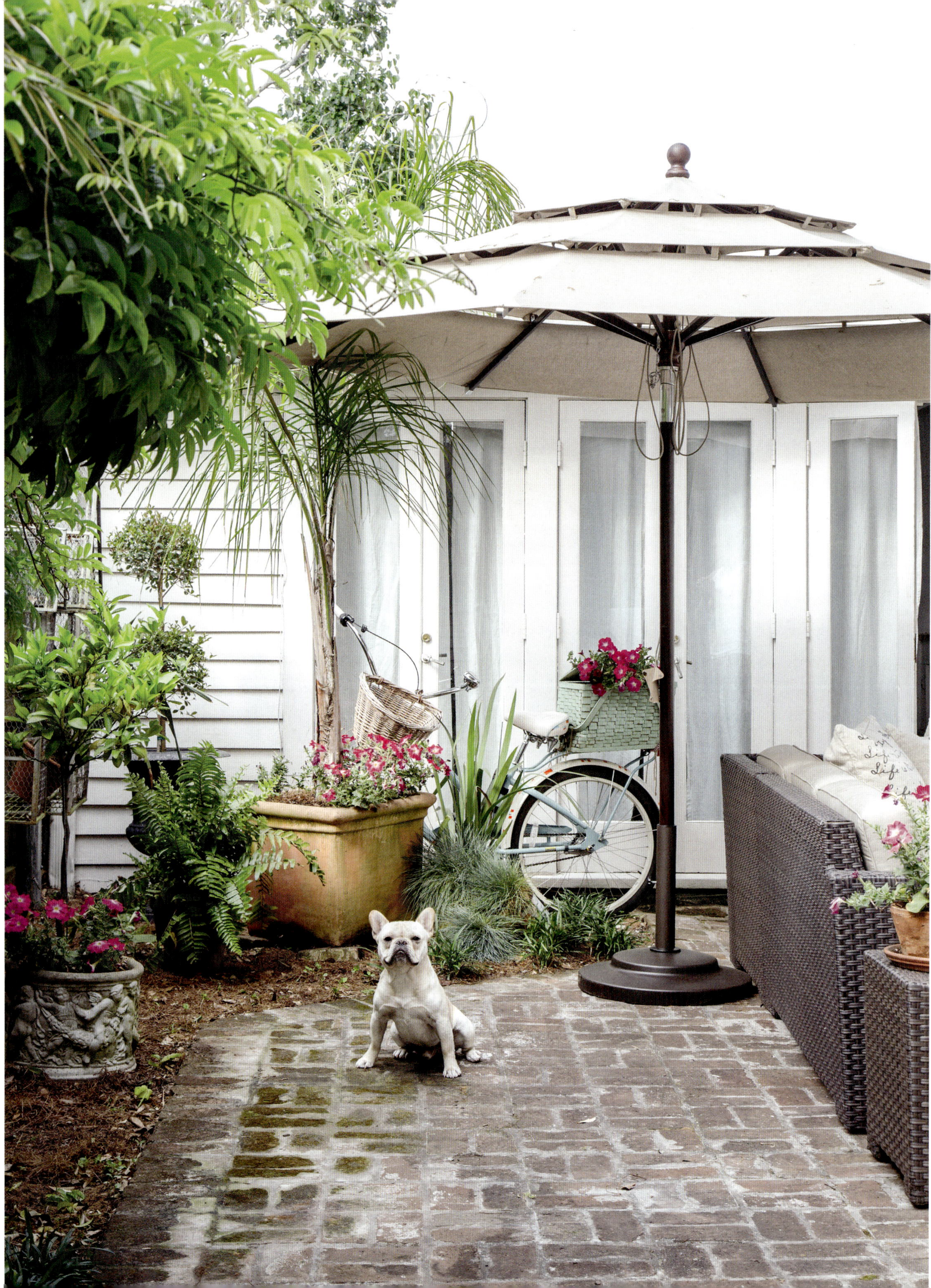

Poppy

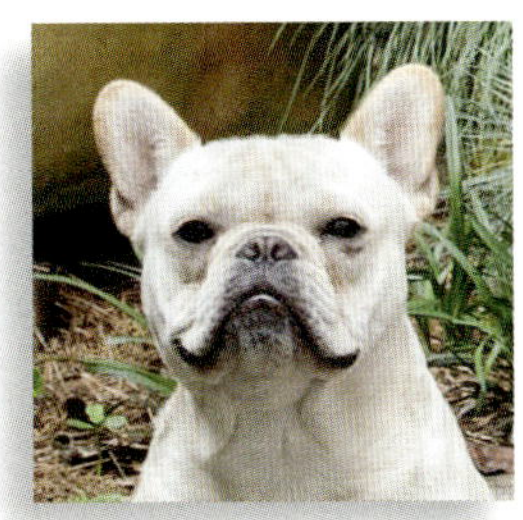

"Dianna Knost moved to New Orleans for the same reason so many have become ensnared: it felt right. She adopted me, her French Bulldog, at eight weeks old, and I have been her constant companion ever since. I accompany Dianna daily to her store, AKA Stella Gray, a unique and lovely shop on Magazine Street that caters to the 'Bohemian Luxury' aesthetic. I am well known amongst the shop's regulars, who sometimes pop in just to give me a belly rub. When not belly-up for my adoring fans, I enjoy playing on my patio, which features an eclectic mix of comfortable contemporary patio loungers and garden vignettes composed of vintage architectural salvage, vessels, and potted plants. This is my favorite location to chase lizards, lie in the sun, and, of course, snack on yummies."

Shiva

You were either in or you were out with Shiva; there was no gray area for her. She would sum up her guests instantly, either cuddling or barking. This dog was decisive. Shiva, named for the goddess of creation and distraction, truly lived up to her moniker. She was a unique spirit, and when she sensed that her owner, designer Natasha Shaw, was feeling blue, she would place her little head on her lap and look at Natasha reassuringly with big brown eyes.

Shiva survived many health hurdles, and made it to the ripe old age of sixteen, going to sleep for the last time next to Natasha in bed. Natasha is so grateful for her time with Shiva.

Here, Shiva lounges in a sun spot, next to a Saarinen tulip table. The chair frames were found on eBay, and custom upholstered in black leather and zebra. The wooden carved bowl was purchased in Botswana. The chandelier is by Ingo Maurer and is called *Birds, Birds, Birds*.

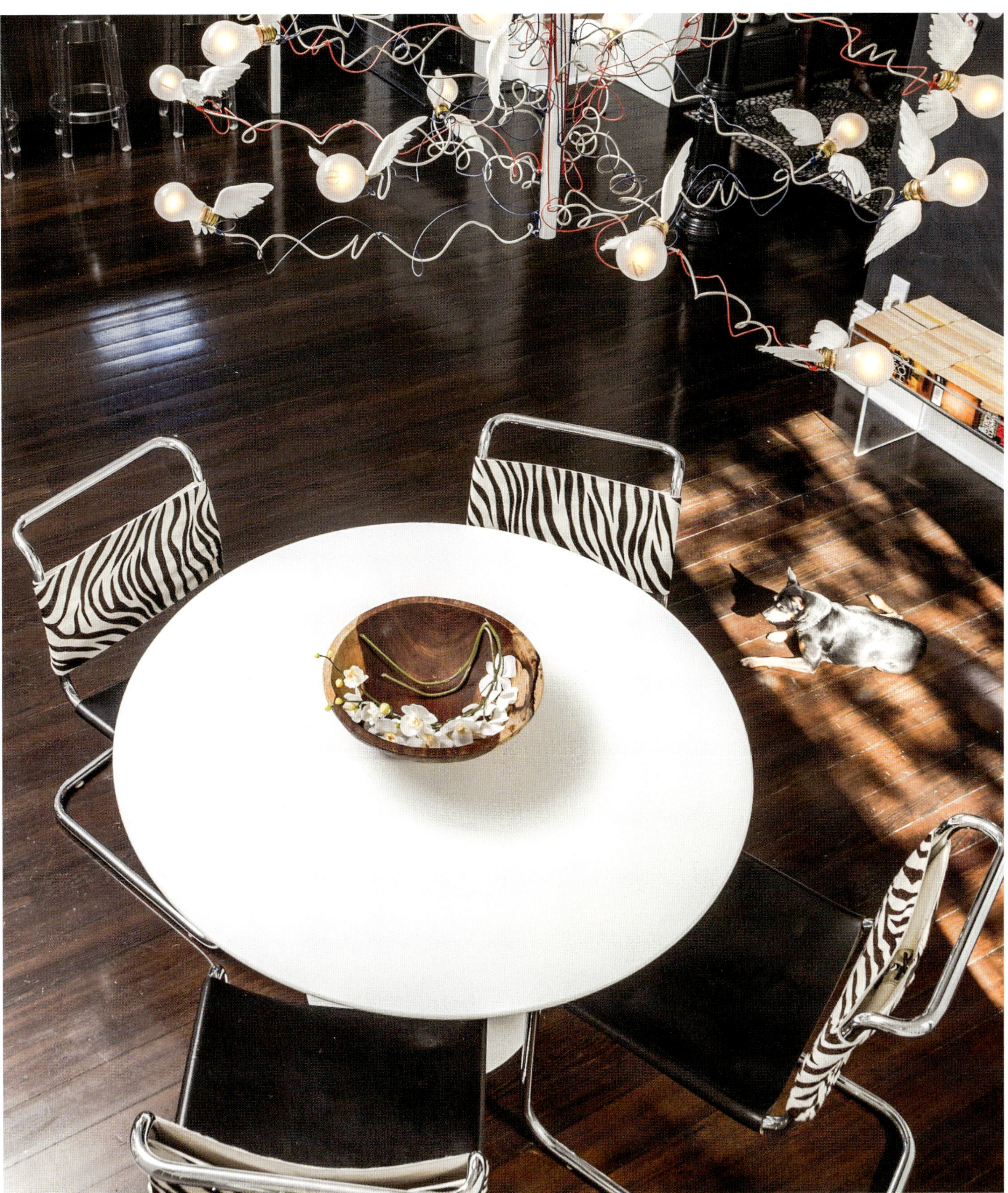

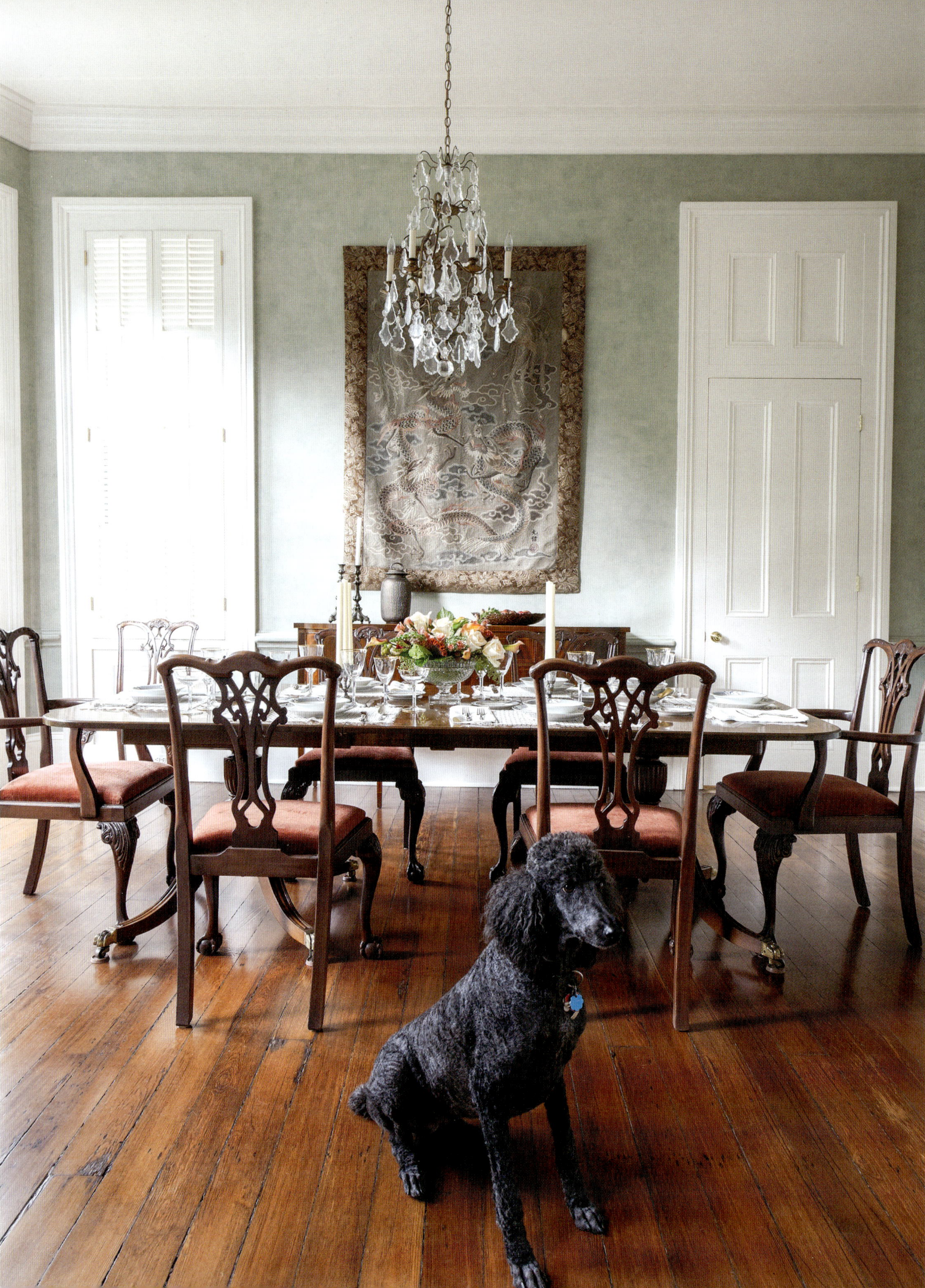

Sophie

"I have a job to do, and I will not rest until I have rid the world of all cats. As an American Standard Poodle, I am vigilant and vibrant, even at the ripe old age of fifteen. Highly intelligent, I think of myself as another human in the house. I will reveal my dog side, however, for the beloved belly-scratch.

My owners, Kay and John Colbert, bought this gorgeous, Italianate-style home in New Orleans' Garden District in 1992, and have carefully and lovingly restored and maintained the home in period style. I think I fit right in being pretty gorgeous and elegant, myself. Along with many custom-built furnishings by Rubert Kohlmaier, the Colberts collect antique oriental tapestries, as seen above the dining table."

Boomer

Carole and William Troutt purchased their Garden District gem in 2007. Their décor choices aspired to blur the lines between inside and out, with a palette of olive greens, tans, and blues. Their appreciation of Greek mythology is evident in the mural on their dining room wall. Carole layered antiques with contemporary pieces for a cultivated effect.

Amidst the finery is Boomer, their Old English Sheepdog. Boomer was a jolly, exuberant chap. He was especially fond of the grounds of Rhodes College, where William is president. Mention taking a walk there, and Boomer would leap into the air with joy. He was also excessively fond of riding in the car, and was know as "the Buddha in the back."

Boomer unfortunately passed in 2010, and was so beloved that he is buried at the foot of the obelisk in the parterre in the backyard.

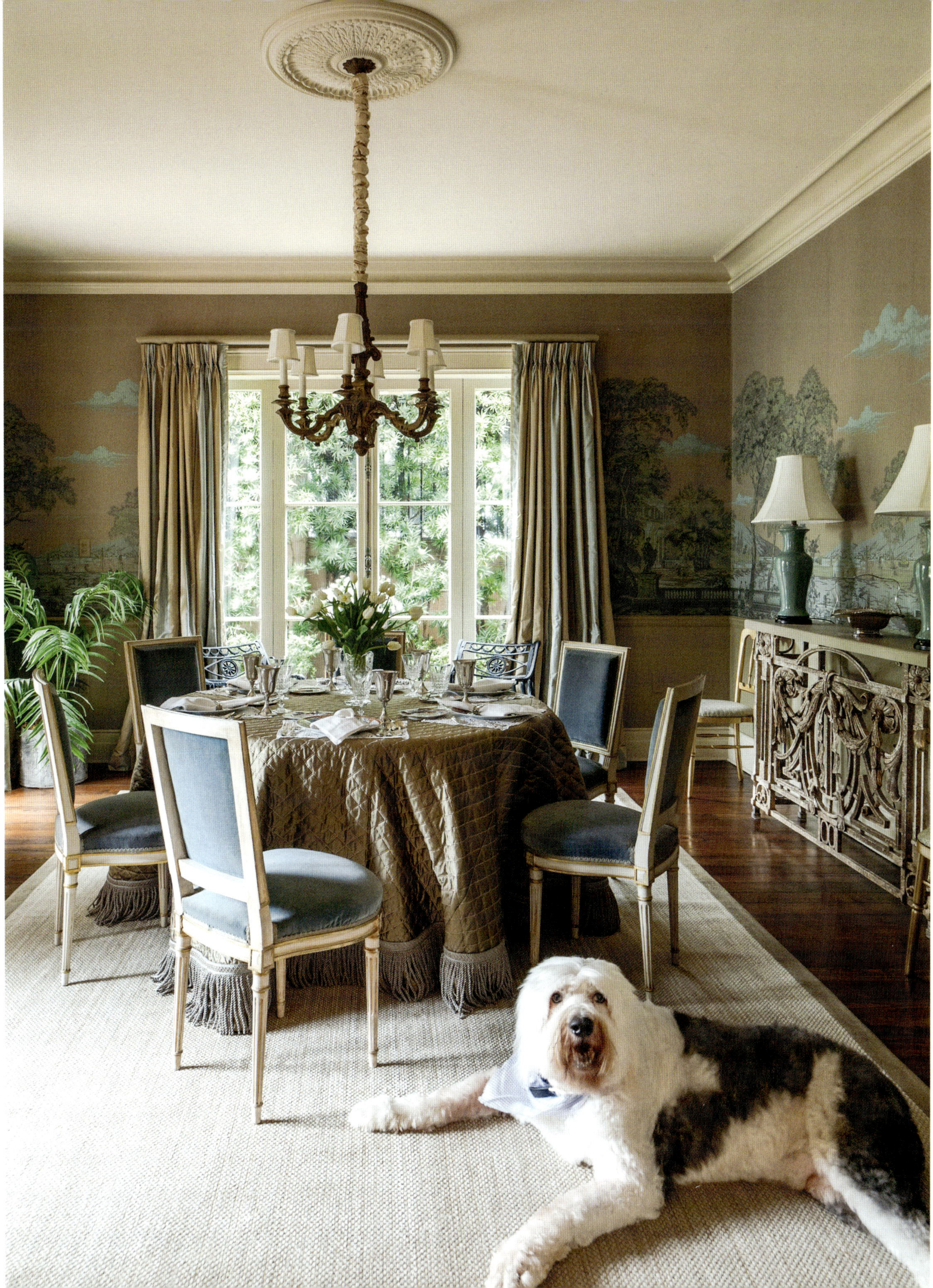

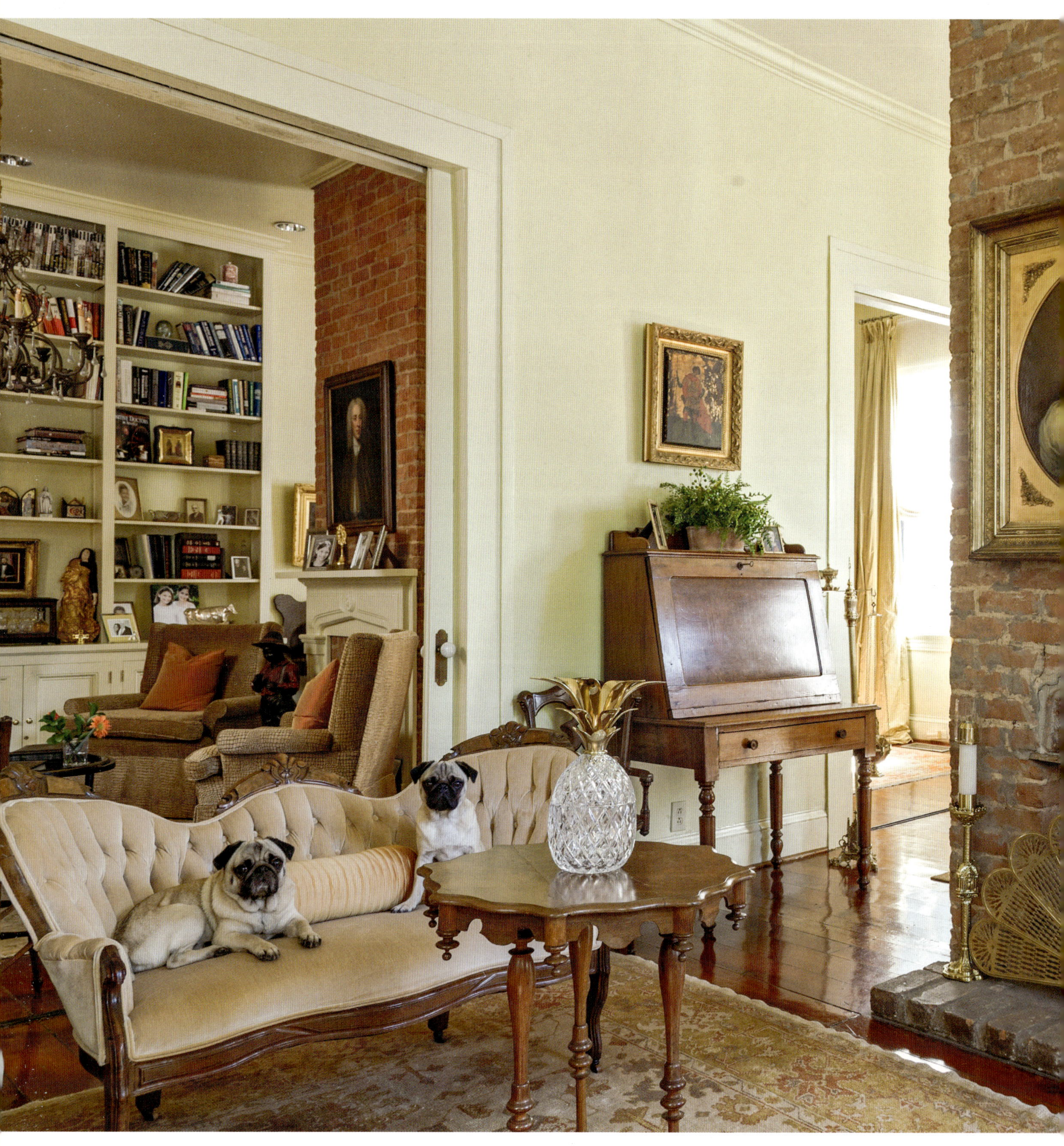

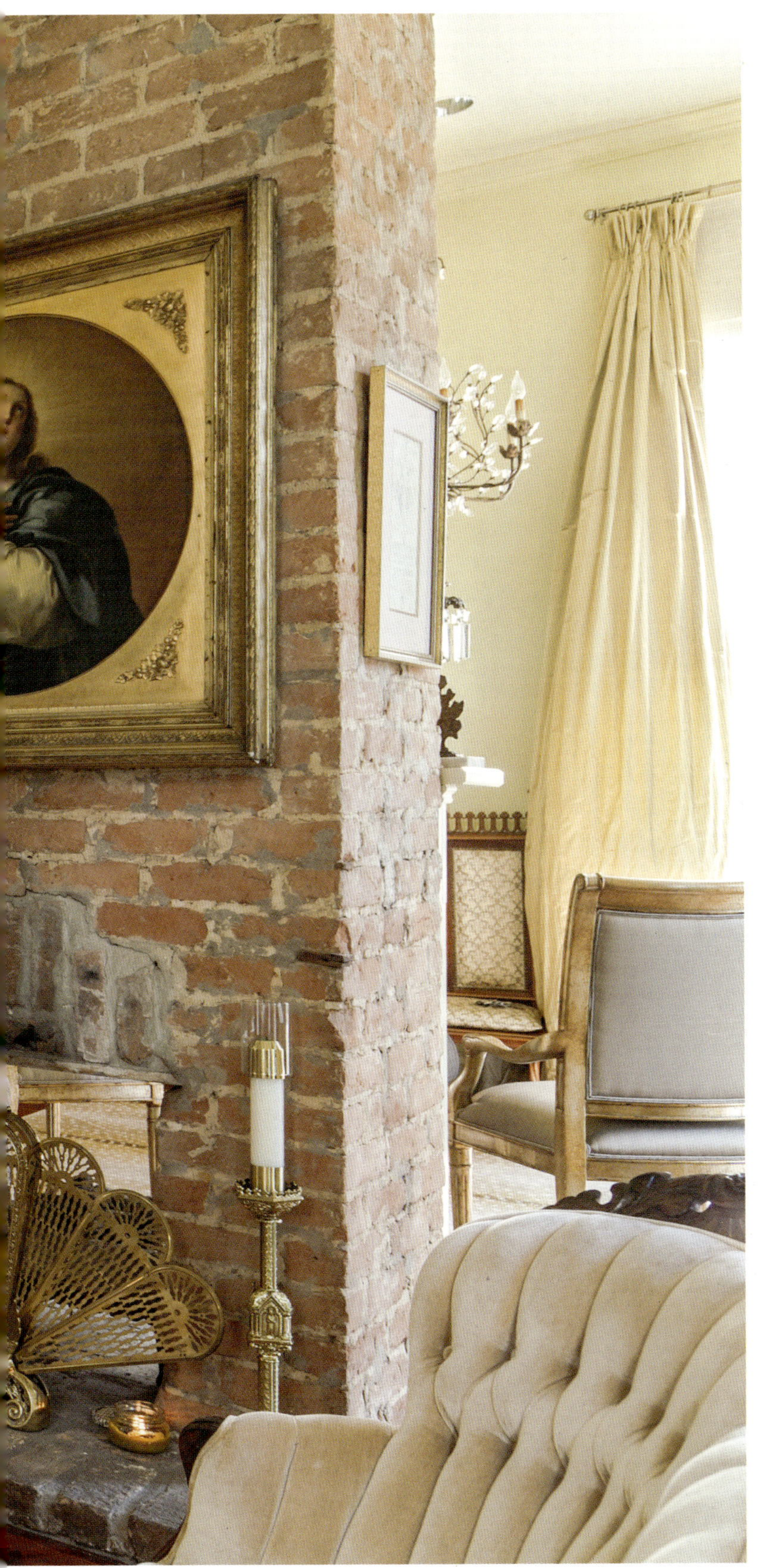

Ernie and Bob

"My brother Bob (left) and I came to the home of Sandra and Ted Borgman when we were each small puppies. With a five year age difference, Bob being the elder, we share the same father. Though we look strikingly similar, our personalities are completely different. Bob is the serious one: stoic, concerned, and quiet—a bit of a worry-wart, especially when it comes to food. As feeding time approaches, Bob becomes more and more distressed, his little brow furrowing deep, convinced that this is the day that the food will not come.

I, however, haven't a care in the world. I expect food, love, and happiness, and return affection gleefully. I am a wiggly, cuddly companion, and when I do slow down, my preferred napping pillow is Bob's ample bottom.

Sandra furnished the house mostly with family antiques. The Madonna painting was a gift. Sandra had admired the painting in a New Orleans Auction Gallery catalog, and Ted surprised her by purchasing it."

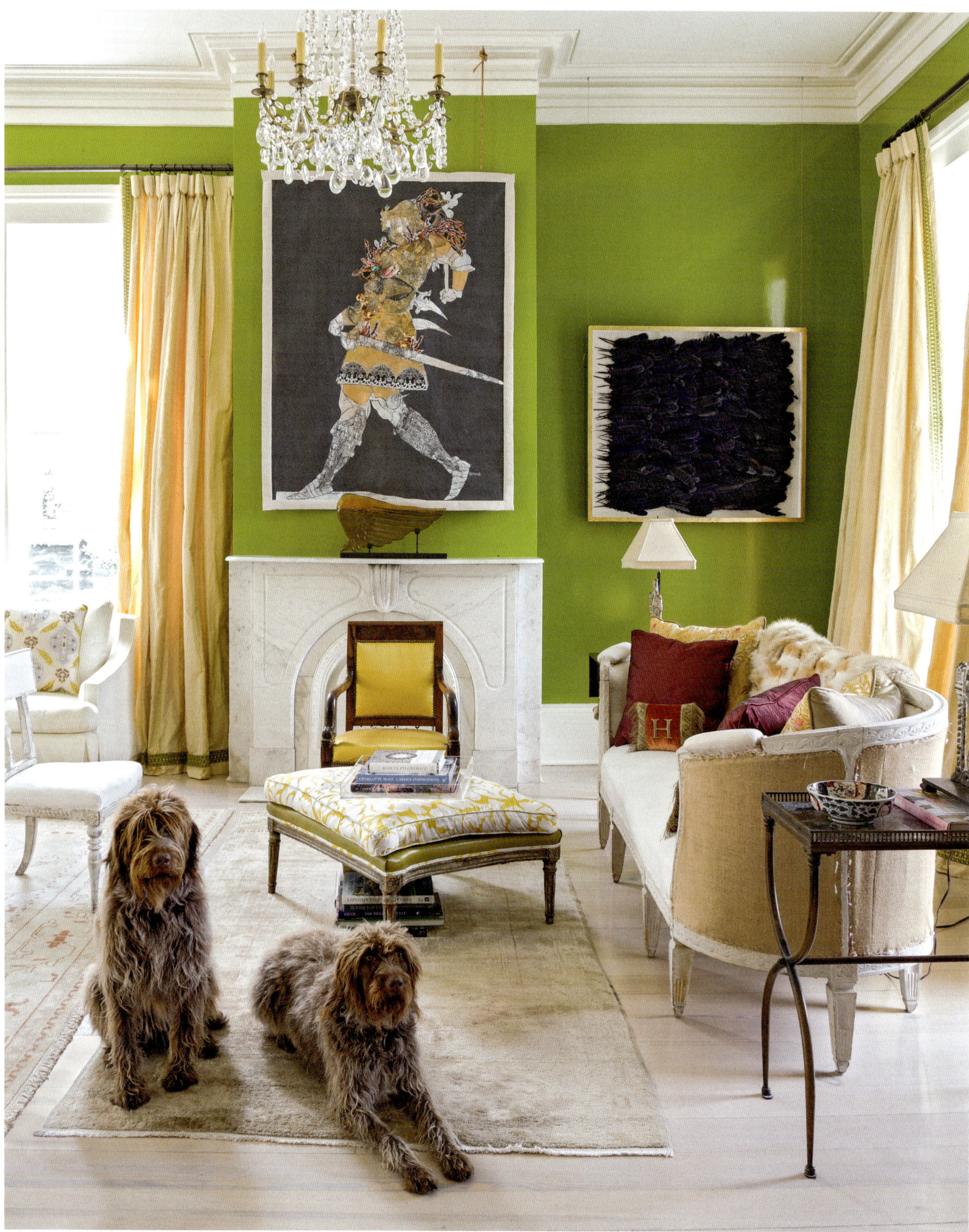

Coco and Dulce

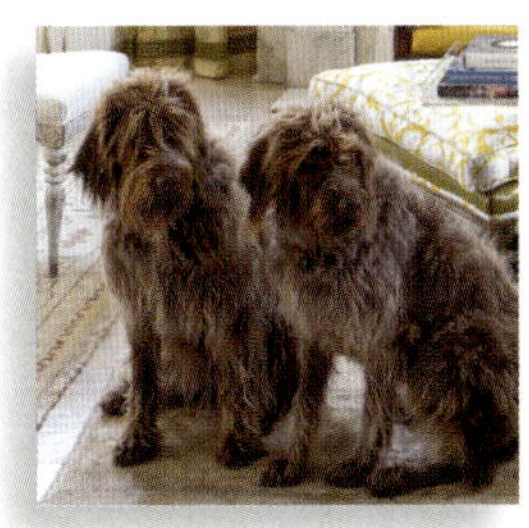

"While I and my sister Coco (right) appear serene in this photo, we would not be accurately described as mellow dogs. Raised as country dogs in Kentucky, we had a much different experience than our dog neighbors in New Orleans, where we now reside, with textile designer Jane Scott Hodges, and her family. Before moving to our elegant Garden District digs, we enjoyed frolicking in the country with donkeys, chickens, goats, and a horse. We faced some challenges assimilating into city life but have adjusted well, replacing chickens and goats with squirrels and lizards.

We have an audacious streak, and a couple of years ago, I took a little adventure of my own. Eventually, my owners found me celebrity-stalking in Sandra Bullock's yard down the street. Fortunately, Ms. Bullock was out of town, and I was retrieved, but without an autograph, I am sorry to report.

With Jane Scott's children grown, she wanted to create a home that was elegant, fun, and inviting for her family to hang out. The result is captivating and delightful. Bright colors and funky art are layered with exquisite antiques and classic pieces."

Stilts

"When decorator Jeannie McKeogh took on this design project in Old Metairie, near New Orleans, she may have been influenced in part by me, Stilts, the tan and white Welsh Corgi who lives in the house. Whatever the provenance, Jeannie had the idea to match my color palette specifically to the stone walls of Sienna, Italy, which is a much warmer tone than those of Provence. She designed a floor pattern that was custom painted, as well as designed and fabricated all of the other custom items in the room.

I am an extremely friendly and social dog. While Sara Essex Bradley was photographing in the house, she dubbed me her assistant. I accompanied her from room to room, staying close by her side. If I had pockets, I would have gladly held her lens caps."

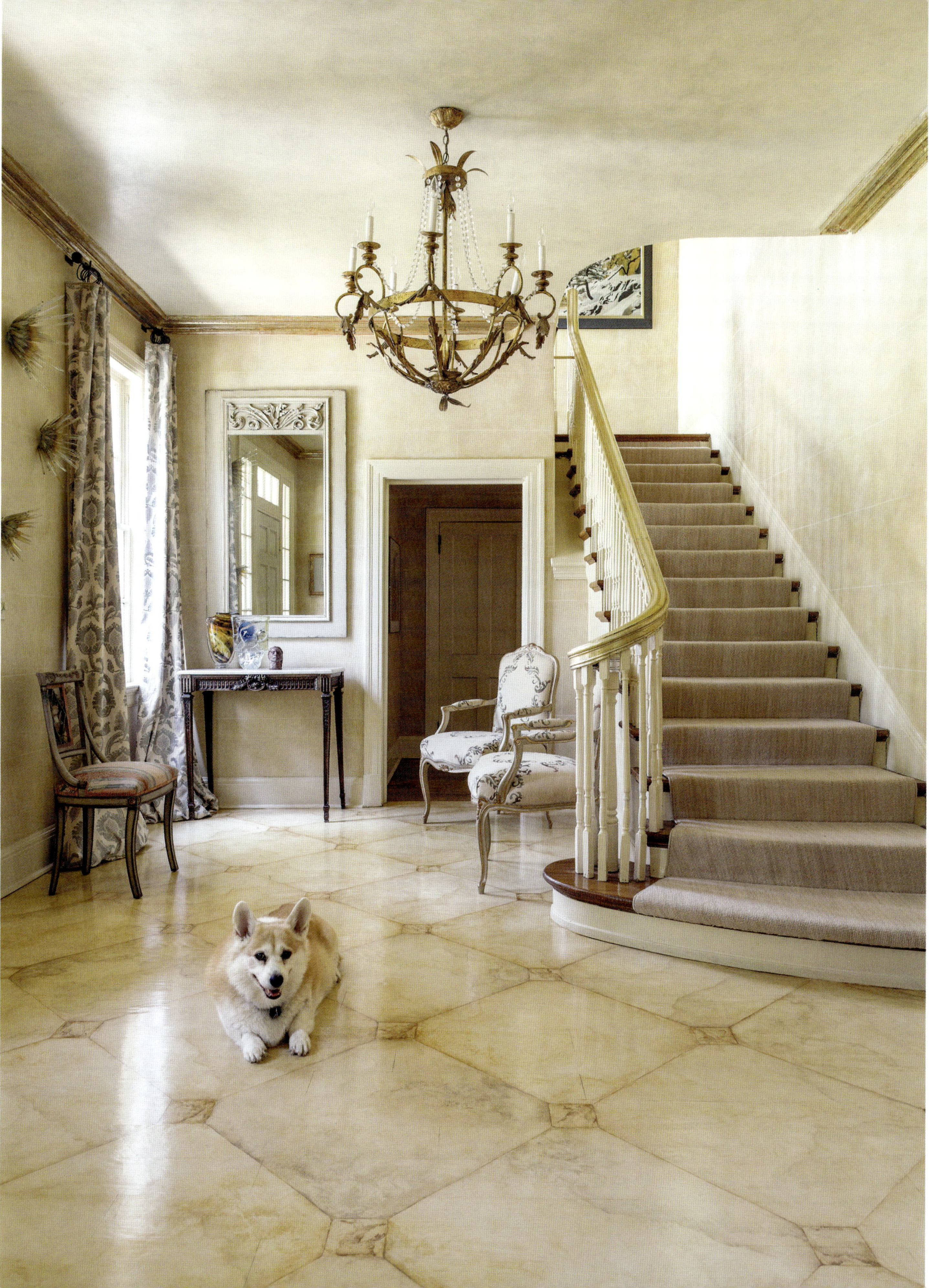

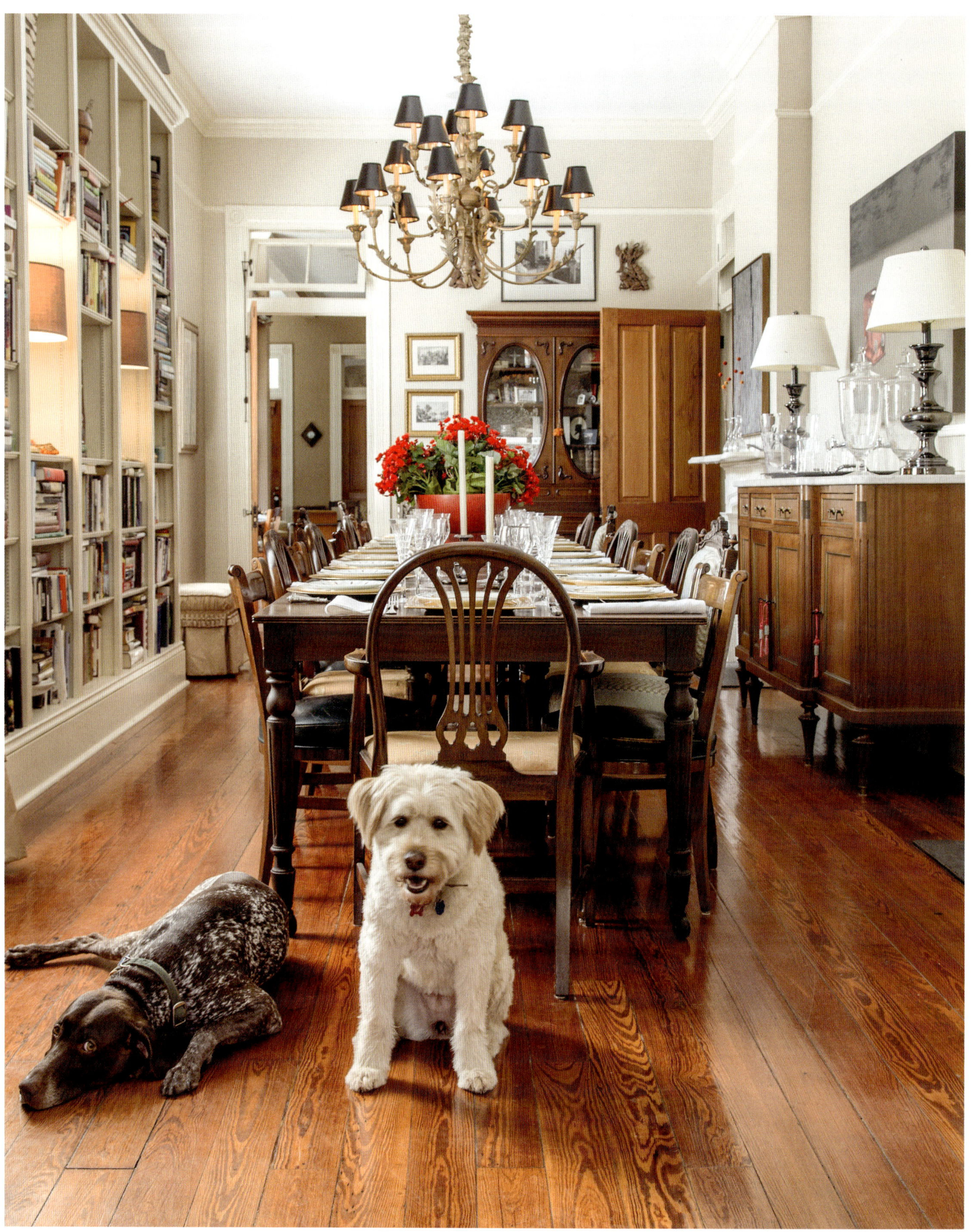

Tucker Anthony and Lottie Leona

"I am Tucker Anthony (left), and this is Lottie Leona on the right. We live in the beautifully curated home of Pamela and Seph Dupuy. The shotgun double in Uptown New Orleans is one of the more interesting conversions from double to single.

The long, narrow dining room was originally intended as a double parlor, but after seeing little use in that capacity, Pamela decided to use it as a dining room, replete with a very long antique table from Crescent City Auction. The table comfortably seats twenty, and Pamela did not concern herself with finding twenty matching chairs. The mix of seating and styles adds to the bohemian salon feel of the room.

Madame Lottie reigns supreme in the household, making her wishes known and respected. She is a soft-coated Wheaten Terrier mix, but in her mind, she is a thoroughbred. I am a German short-haired Pointer and kind and humble as Saint Anthony, from whom I got my middle name. We are both loving and gentle dogs, and enjoy sitting for the lens, especially Lottie—a natural supermodel."

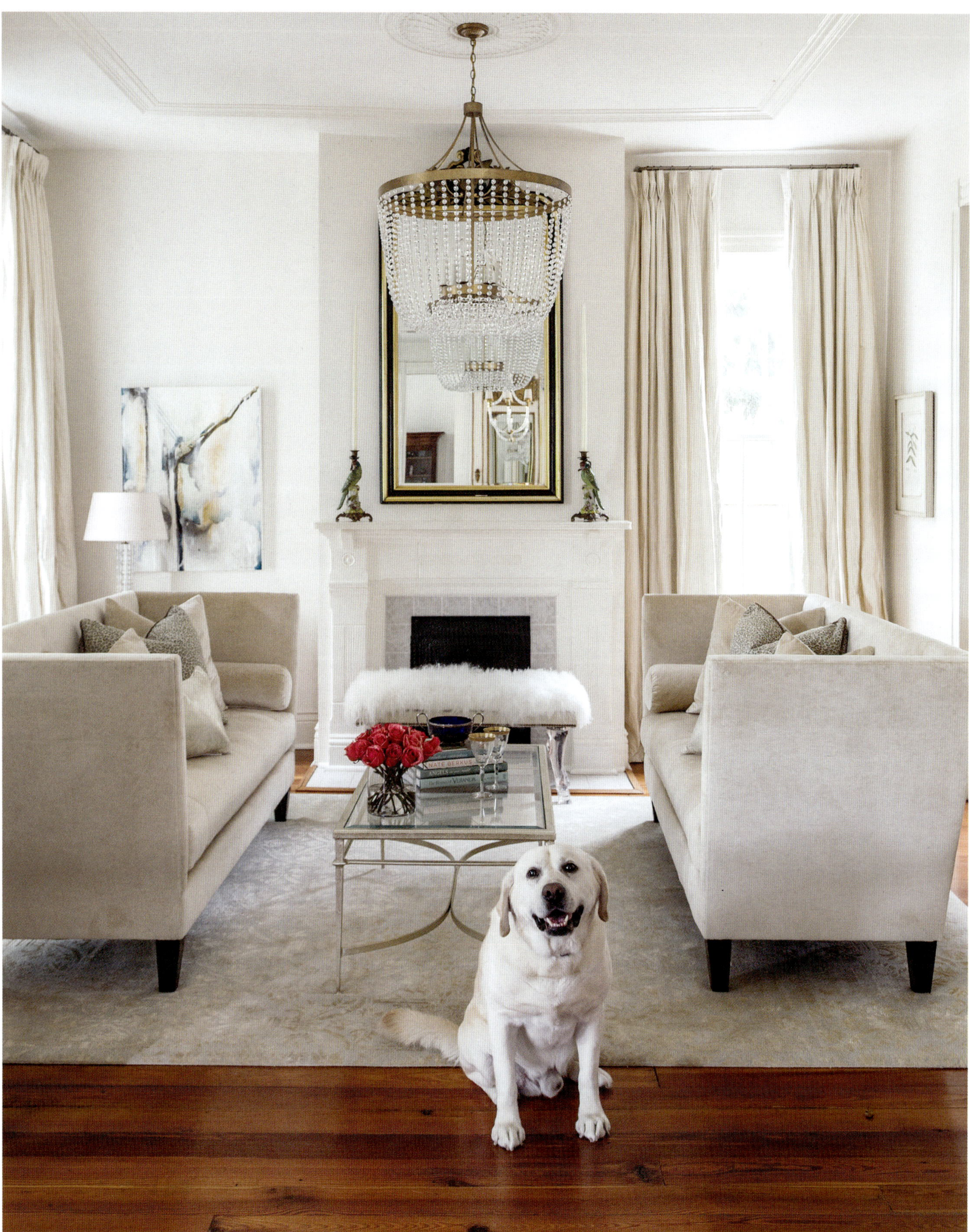
NATE BERKUS

Beignet

"I could tell that Sara Essex Bradley was instantly drawn to my down-to-earth demeanor and unassuming attitude from the moment she met me. In fact, after meeting me (while photographing our home for designer Jennifer DiCerbo and stylist Chris Piazza), she joked that I seemed like someone one might share a beer with. Chris nicknamed me Larry, and some say you could almost see me in a blue work suit with a red 'Larry' nametag.

In reality, I live in a refined home in Uptown New Orleans, and my name is Beignet. I am a sweet and affable guy, just happy to be in the middle of things.

Jennifer chose furnishings that would evoke a sophisticated and chic feel, while maintaining a serene and welcoming environment. The matching shelter sofas, iron-glass coffee table, and Tibetan hair-upholstered bench were all sourced through her store the French Mix. And did I mention that I fit right in with the calm, serene, and beautiful décor?"

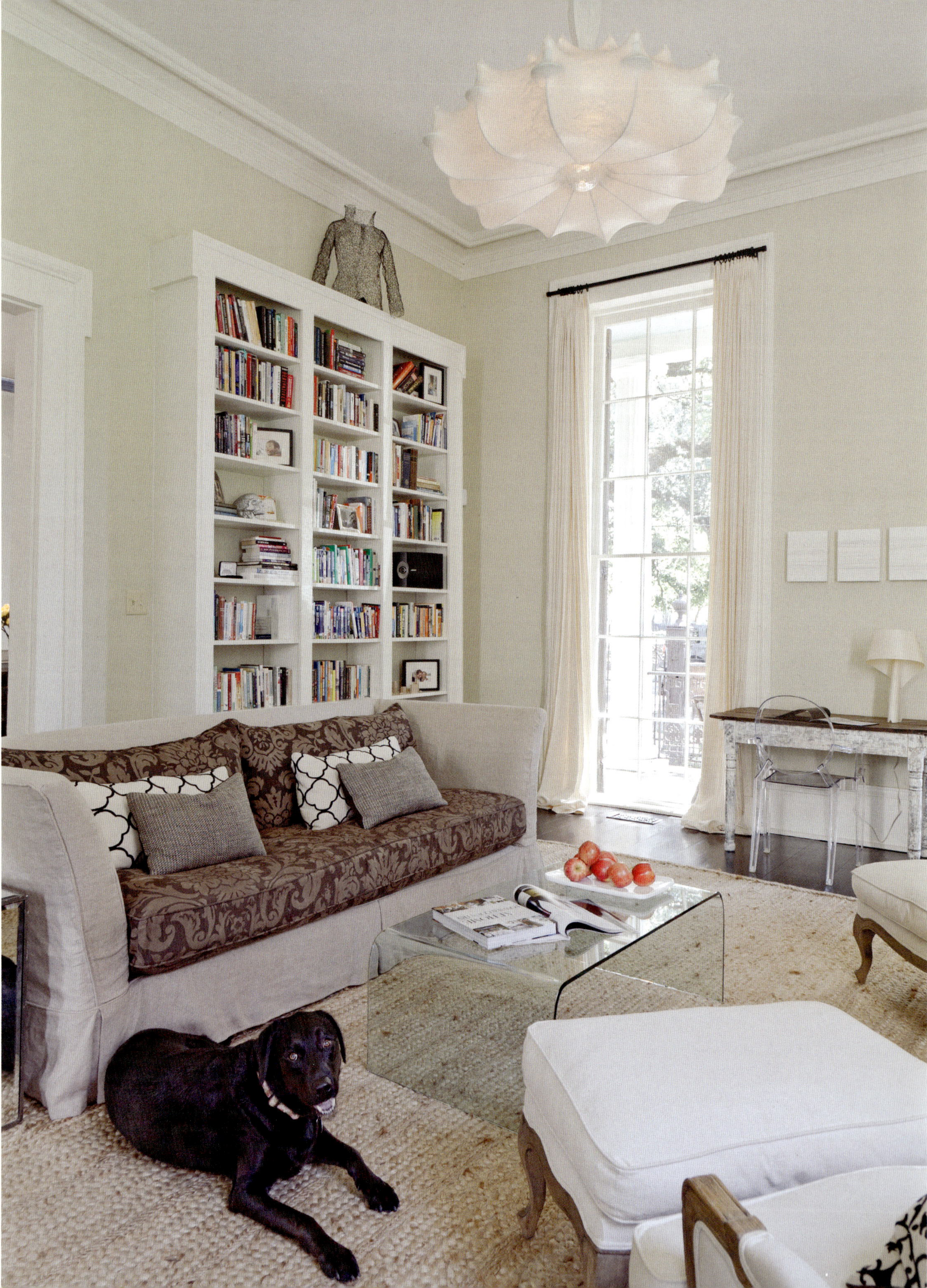

Lucy

While Nick and Jessica Bride were in the final phases of completely renovating their historic home on Coliseum Square in New Orleans, the gods of dog placement intervened with a final decorative touch. A full-bred AKC registered Black Labrador had been found in the park across the street by a friend, and they wondered if the Brides might take her in. Dubious at first, Jessica and Nick thought they should at least take the dog for a spin around the block before saying no. On that walk, they bought a new leash and collar, and came up with a name, Lucy, for their new family member.

From Lucy's embedded chip, they learned about her breed status, and that she had been slated for euthanasia at one point. They also learned that the last person to adopt her had surrendered her, so she was free and clear to live with them.

And what a life she has had! A month after being adopted by the Brides, she went with them for a month of skiing in Switzerland. Lucy took to the snow like she was born to it, frolicking up and down mountains and swimming in half-frozen lakes. Lucy was the perfect dog for the Bride family; she was loving and gentle with the children, even sharing her bed with their daughter when she was small. She had boundless energy and spirit and a voracious appetite that somehow did not extend to children's toys or shoes. There is a beloved picture of Lucy sleeping with a Lego figure just inches from her nose.

Here, Lucy is flopped out under a chandelier by Marcel Wanders, and the triptych on the back wall is by New Orleans artist Sidonie Villere. The Brides worked with designer Bruce McNally of BKLN Designs.

JET

"When Carli and Josh Gertler moved in after completing the renovations on their midcentury home, they still felt as though something was missing. Carli was certain a black shaggy dog was just the thing the décor (and their souls) needed. She searched adoption sites until she saw me and fell in love at first sight. Although I was riddled with the myriad of ailments one sees in so many rescues, I was nursed to health by a foster family and was soon ready to move into my forever home in New Orleans (and Carli and Josh's hearts).

I have an affectionate and cheeky personality, jumping into neighboring fountains and bayous and returning triumphant for belly rubs. I even managed to arrange payment of a hot dog in exchange for this portrait, eschewing the lowly dry dog treat.

Our home was stylishly designed by Logan Killen Interiors, which is run by Jensen Killen and Katie Logan in New Orleans. They selected warm greenish-blue hues to create a relaxing breakfast nook that feels as much outdoors as in. The rattan bar cart is by Serena & Lily, and the swag pendant lamp is a vintage find. The seating is a Coventry Sectional in Buffalo check by Ballard Designs. The paint color is Teresa's Green by Farrow & Ball."

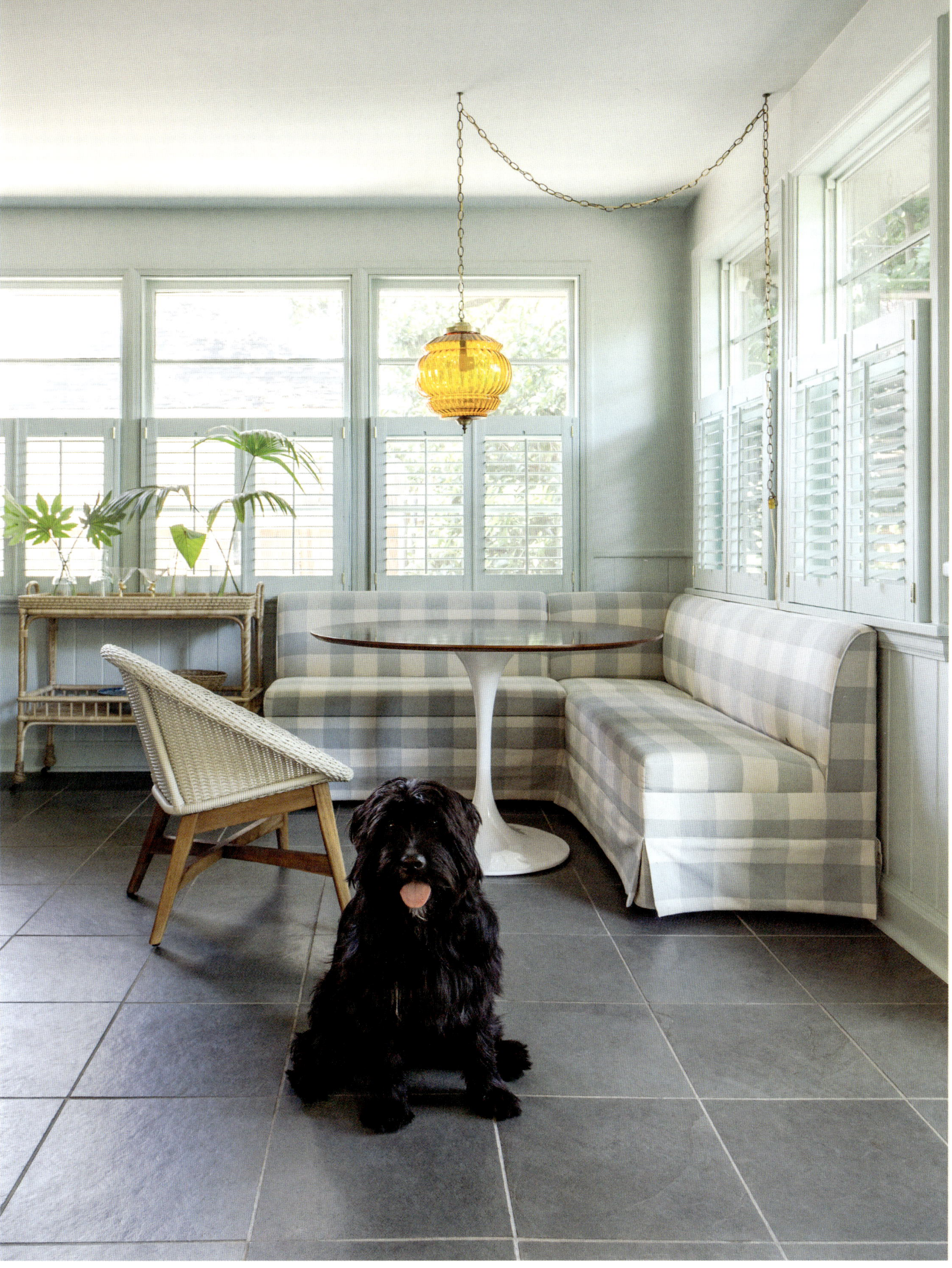

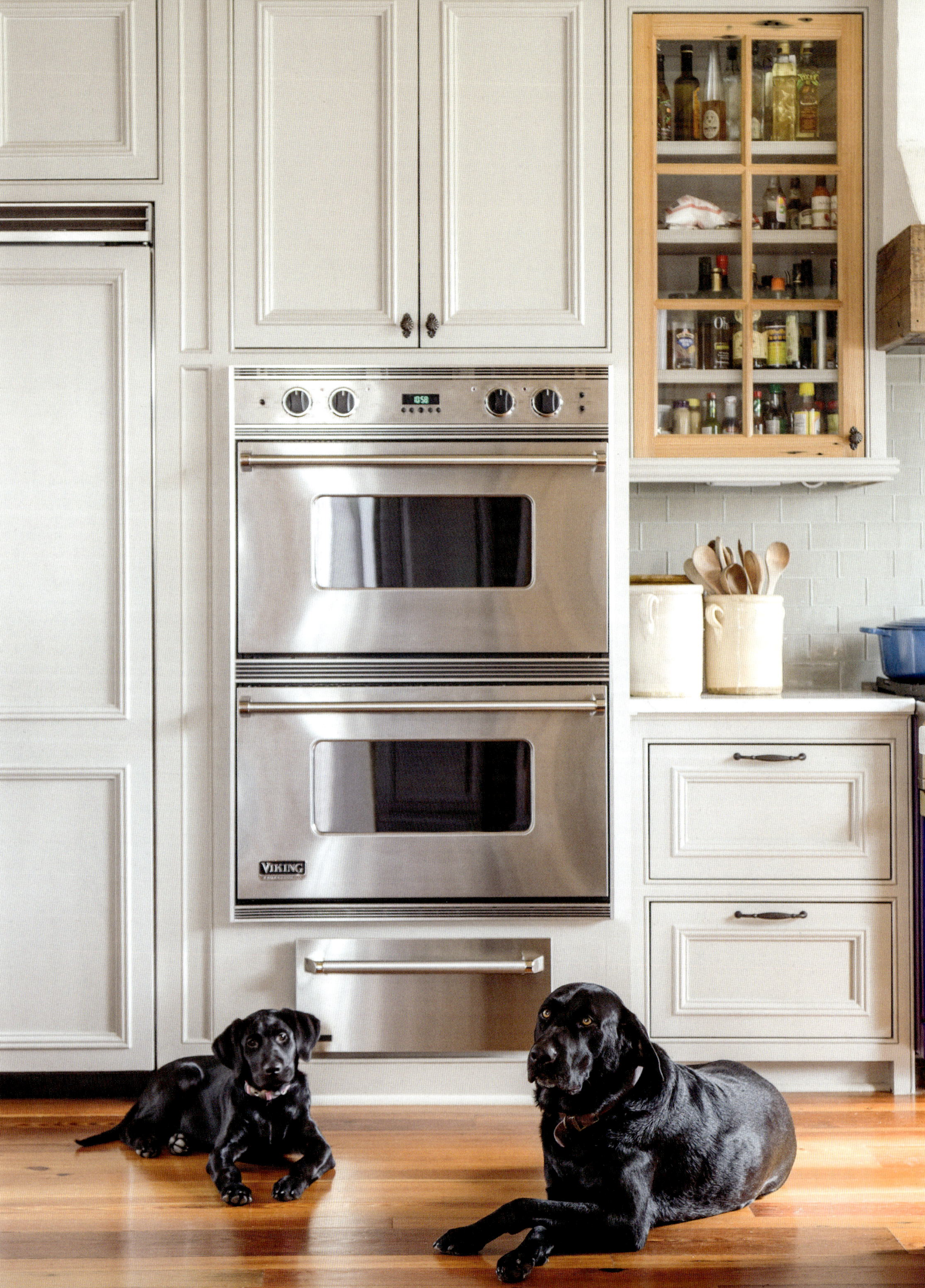
VIKING

Morgan and Shatzi

"Louisiana chef John Besh is happiest when he's at home cooking in the kitchen of his Creole-style home on the bayou, a quick forty-five minute drive from downtown New Orleans. His main goal in renovating the kitchen area was to create a bright, welcoming space that would accommodate not only his family for daily meals, but also could serve as the gathering place for larger holiday family meals.

Mission accomplished. The space is large but cozy, well-appointed but not cluttered, and most of all, warm and welcoming, and not sterile.

I'm Morgan (left), shown here with my companion Shatzi. We're typical labs—loyal, gentle, intelligent, and charming. I have to admit that I idolize Shatzi, and I follow his every move.

We look calm in this wonderful photograph of the two of us in the kitchen in repose, but the truth is that we always enjoy being underfoot while John cooks (Who knows, some food might see its way to the floor in front of us!), when we're not running, playing, and hunting with John's sons."

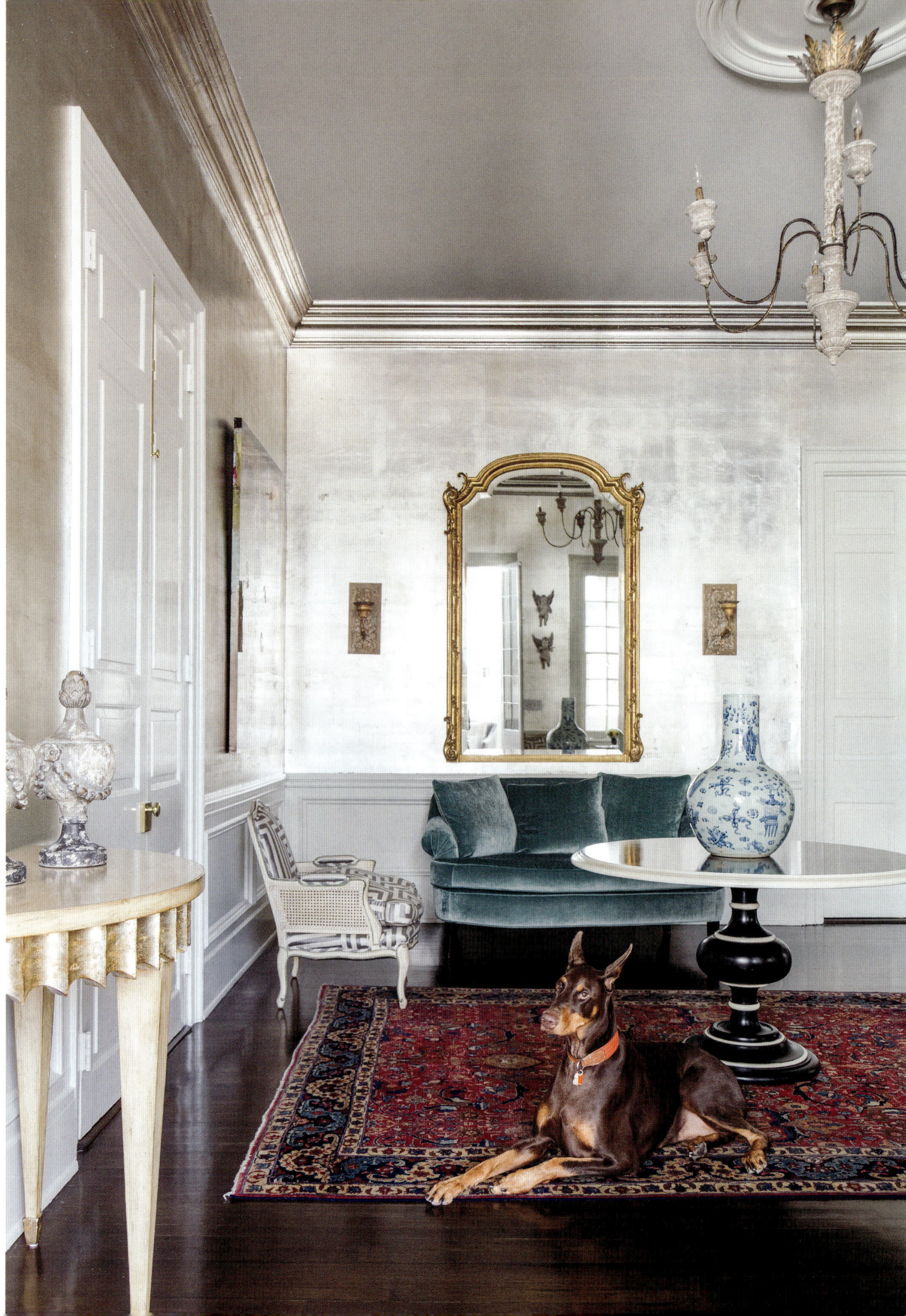

Momus

"I, Momus, consider myself one of the finest brown Dobermans in the area, having been named for one of the most esteemed Mardi Gras krewes. By day, I hang out at historic Arnaud's Restaurant, one of the oldest continually operating restaurants in the country. Founded in 1918, it is nestled in the French Quarter and has been owned by my family, the Casbarians, for as long as I can remember.

I go to work with Jane Casbarian every day, and as the appointed 'Director of Arnaud's Bonding,' I take pride in my ability to connect with all comers. While I may appear fierce in stature, I'm truly a loyal, lovable pup.

I enjoy having downtime in the private quarters of Katy Casbarian, who, along with brother Archie, manages the day-to-day operations of the restaurant. I've watched her upgrade the finishes and fixtures of this upstairs apartment, which previously housed her grandmother, Ellen Casbarian. With the help of designer Jim Elzey, she has renovated the space to suggest an elegant stateliness that suits our family."

Boudreaux, Fu Dog, and Gris Gris

"Meet Boudreaux (left), Fu Dog (on floor), and me, Gris Gris, the canine contingency of art scene power couple Mitchell Gaudet and Erica Larkin Gaudet. Boudreaux was a pre-Katrina rescue by Mitchell. A renowned pug lover, Mitchell made it his business to keep up with all things pug-related, so when his mother saw a 'Found Pug' sign, she alerted him. It was fortunate someone was nice enough to take him in and attempt to find his owner, but unfortunately for Boudreaux, this man had a passel of Chihuahuas and they drove Boudreaux to the brink. He was a nervous wreck by the time Mitchell rescued him. Now, he enjoys the serene tranquility of their camp-like environs, on the shores of Bayou Sauvage just outside of New Orleans.

He is such a mellow, laid-back dog that Mitchell is convinced one day he will achieve some Herculean feat with all his saved-up energy. Fu Dog, so named for her uncanny resemblance to the Chinese guardian Temple House sculptures, is tiny in stature but fierce in nature. Like her namesakes, she is a true protector. She goes to work every day, and takes her role of studio dog very seriously, monitoring all visitors and watching over Mitchell and Erica as they work. They call me, Gris Gris, a 'Dachador'—part Dachshund, part Labrador. Mitchell's father found me running around on their land, and tied me to the house. Erica came home first, fell in love immediately, and called Mitchell to tell him the good news. Mitchell was less than enthusiastic, but when he got home and met me, he was converted. As my name suggests, I put a spell on them.

The three of us make for a lively, entertaining pack, running about the house and out onto the deck to watch passing fishing boats. Mitchell and Erica bought, and personally rebuilt, this waterside house after Katrina. It is rustic but well-appointed, simply but stylishly decorated. The red ceramic flowers are by Bradley Sabin. The fish head is a cast from a New Orleans family tomb."

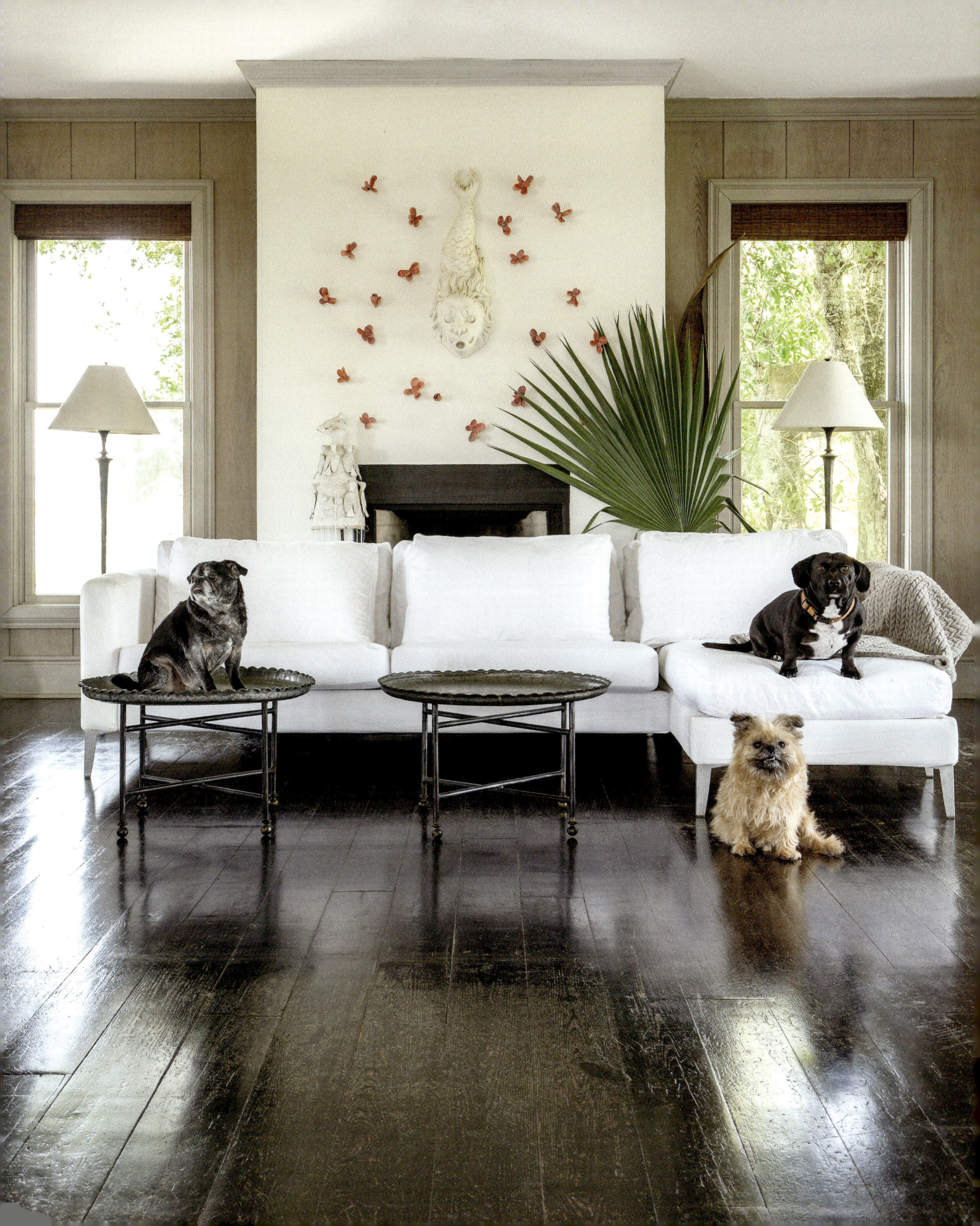

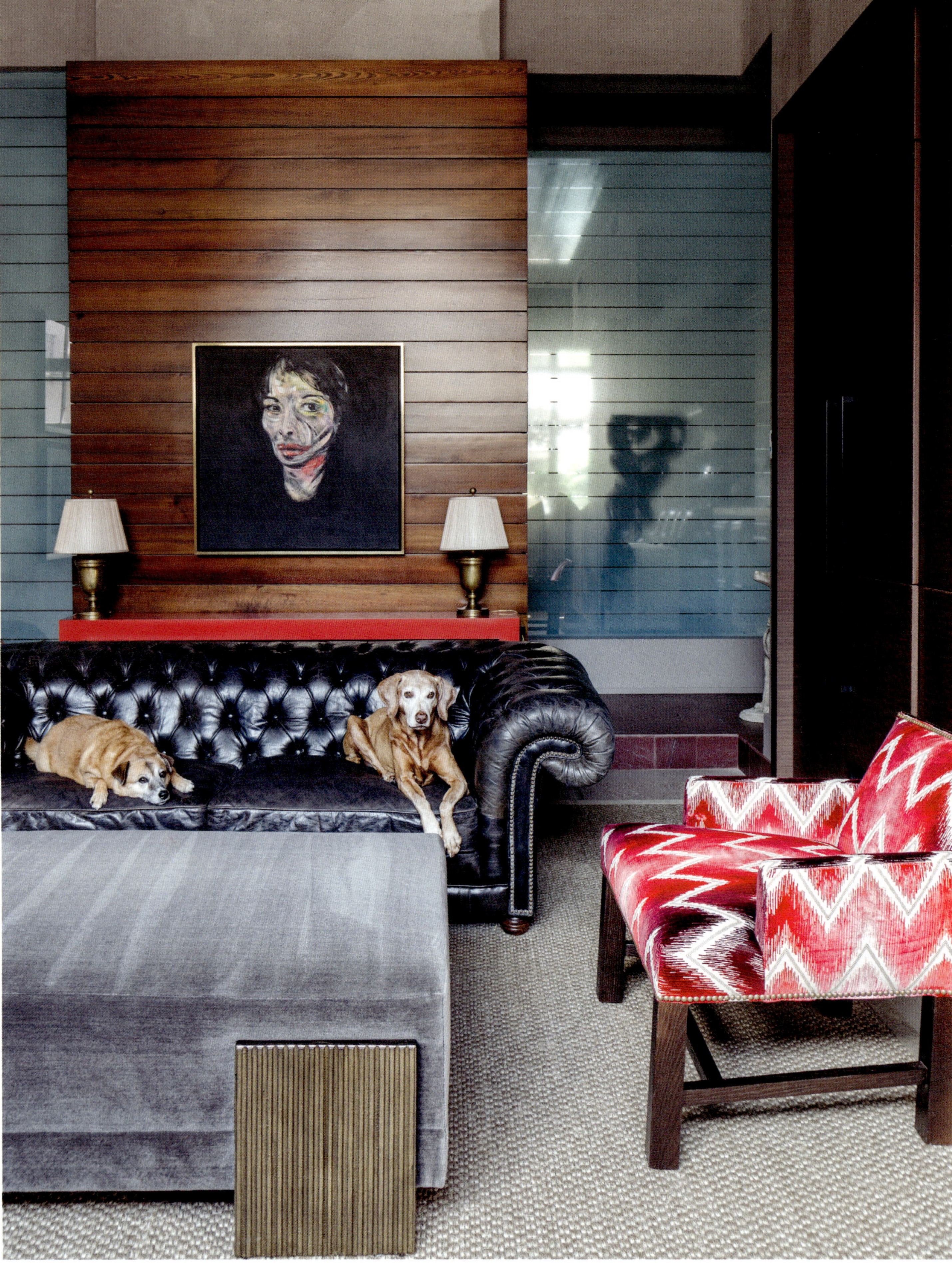

Zena and Indiana Jones

"A purebred Hungarian Vizsla, I had a good life as a puppy in Miami with my owner Linda Huffman. I loved going to the beach, playing in the ocean, and catching bait fish. But by the time I was about one year old, Linda sensed that I could use a companion. Linda turned to a local rescue agency, which suggested a Terrier-like mixed breed, roughly my age. They brought Zena (left) to visit, and I was smitten with her from the start. When the agent took Zee away at the end of the trial, I was so grief-stricken that I cried at the front door for half an hour. Needless to say, Zena returned the next day to be permanently united with me, and we have been living happily together since then.

Though Zena had been abused by her previous owner, she soon settled into her new life and has become a protective, adoring member of our family. Where I am all hyper energy, Zee is laid back and thoughtful, the exception being her equal enjoyment of the beach, where she preferred digging for crabs in the sand, away from the tumultuous ocean. The two of us have both slowed a bit as we've aged, but we continue to provide joy and limitless love to Linda and her family.

Linda now resides in the French Quarter, in a modern loft-like conversion. Shaun Smith helped her select furnishings and finishes. The painting is by Bill Dunlap."

Buddy

"I had a rough beginning, since I was adopted from an abusive home, but you wouldn't know that now. I have become a loving, faithful, and intelligent companion. I am nineteen years young and still going strong. I'm an active member of the family, and I serve as ambassador to visiting guests.

Whether it be lap-sitting or bed-sharing, I do not discriminate. I give my love freely.

Valorie Hart helped Terry and Jay pull their décor together throughout their Old Metairie home just outside of New Orleans. This room features a vintage bed, lamps, and nightstand from Eclectic Home. The dresser peeking in the left side of the frame was painted with a custom finish by Mitchell Settoon."

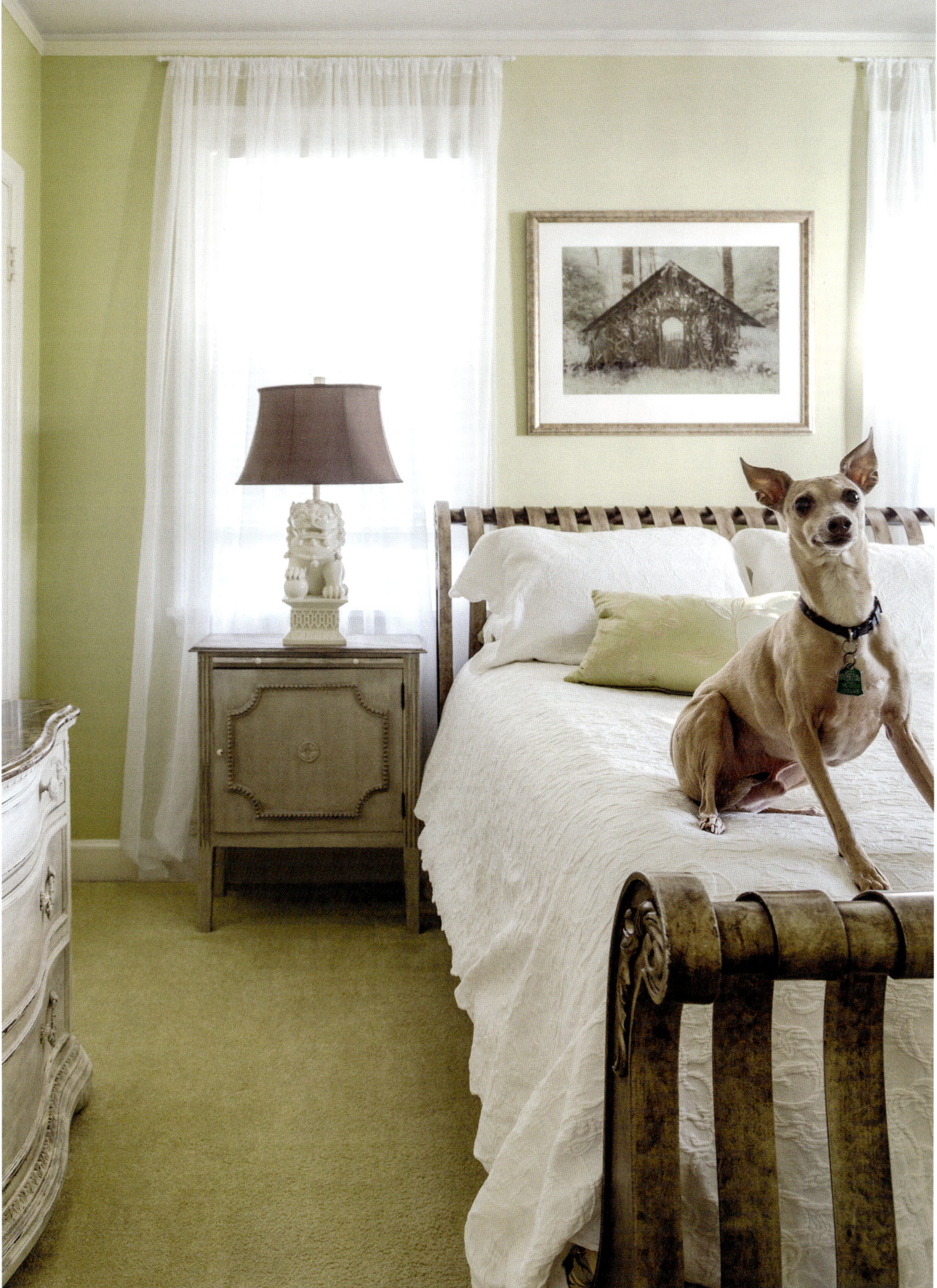

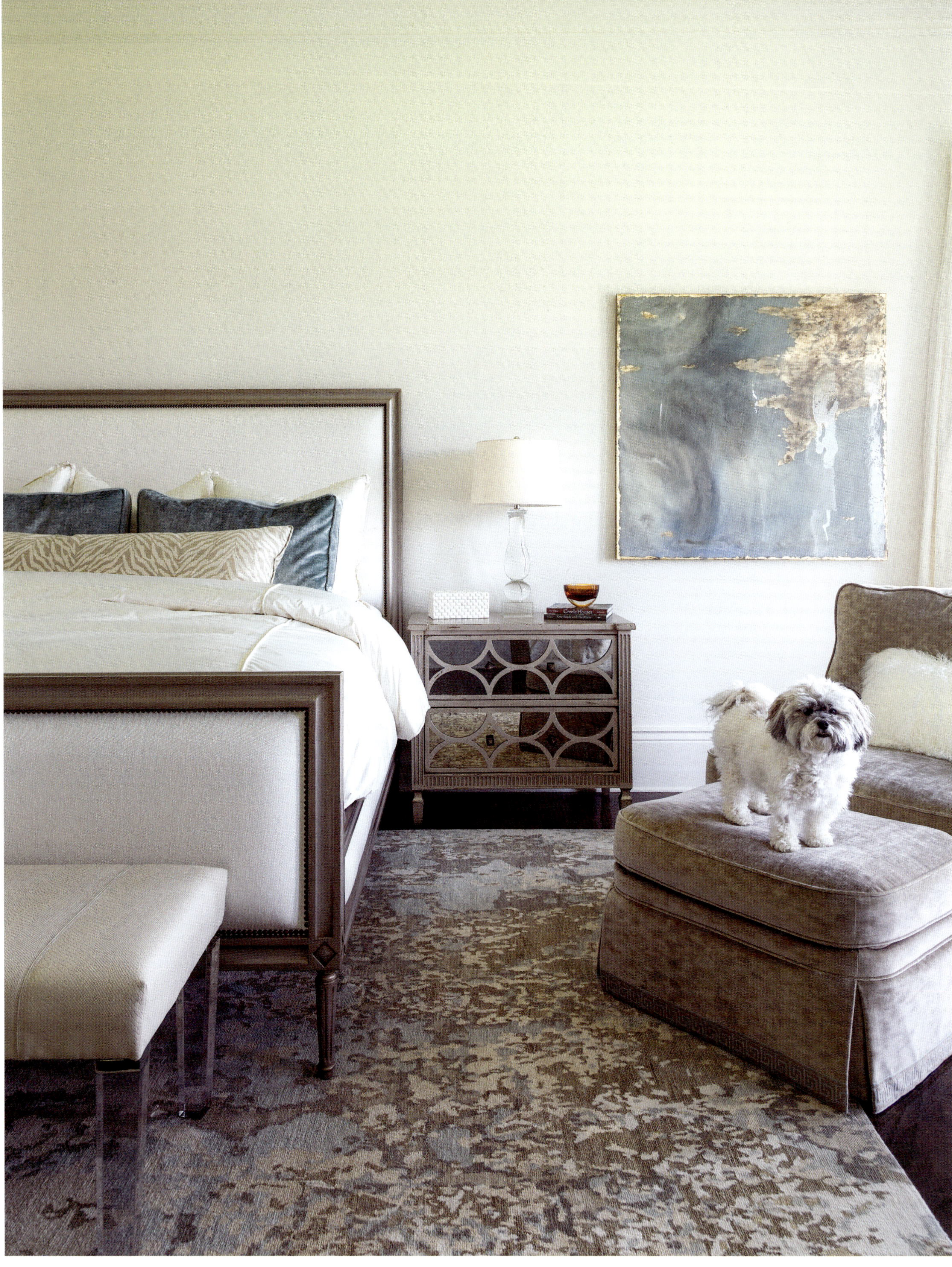
Creole Houses
New Roads and Old Rooms

Mitch

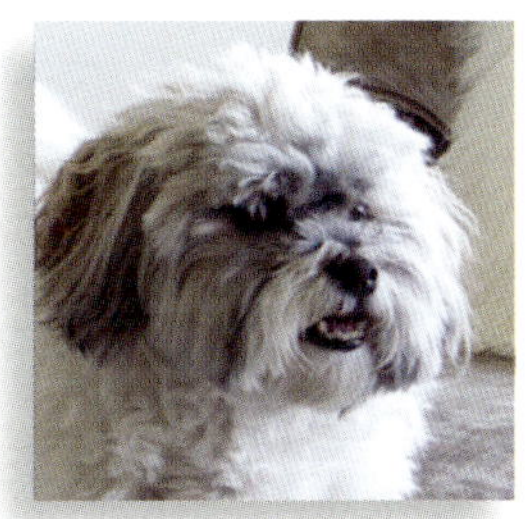

"A four-year-old Havanese, I am a funny and intuitive fellow. From the very beginning, my charming ways and mop-like good looks won the hearts of the Van Hook family. I am not fond of alone time, and earned the nickname 'Velcro dog' because of my desire to consistently stick right by their sides at all times. I fly across furniture and have a mischievous streak. No need to buy a machine—shredding paper is my favorite past time.

Lisa Van Hook worked with designer Jennifer DiCerbo to pull the master bedroom suite together. The room enjoys a beautiful view of Lake Pontchartrain, in Slidell, Louisiana. Jennifer picked up the blue tones of the water for accents in her tranquil creamy white setting. A mixture of textures and tones creates the layered look, with wools, silks, satins, fur, and leather. Lisa wanted the room to feel like a sanctuary, and now she and I relax there together."

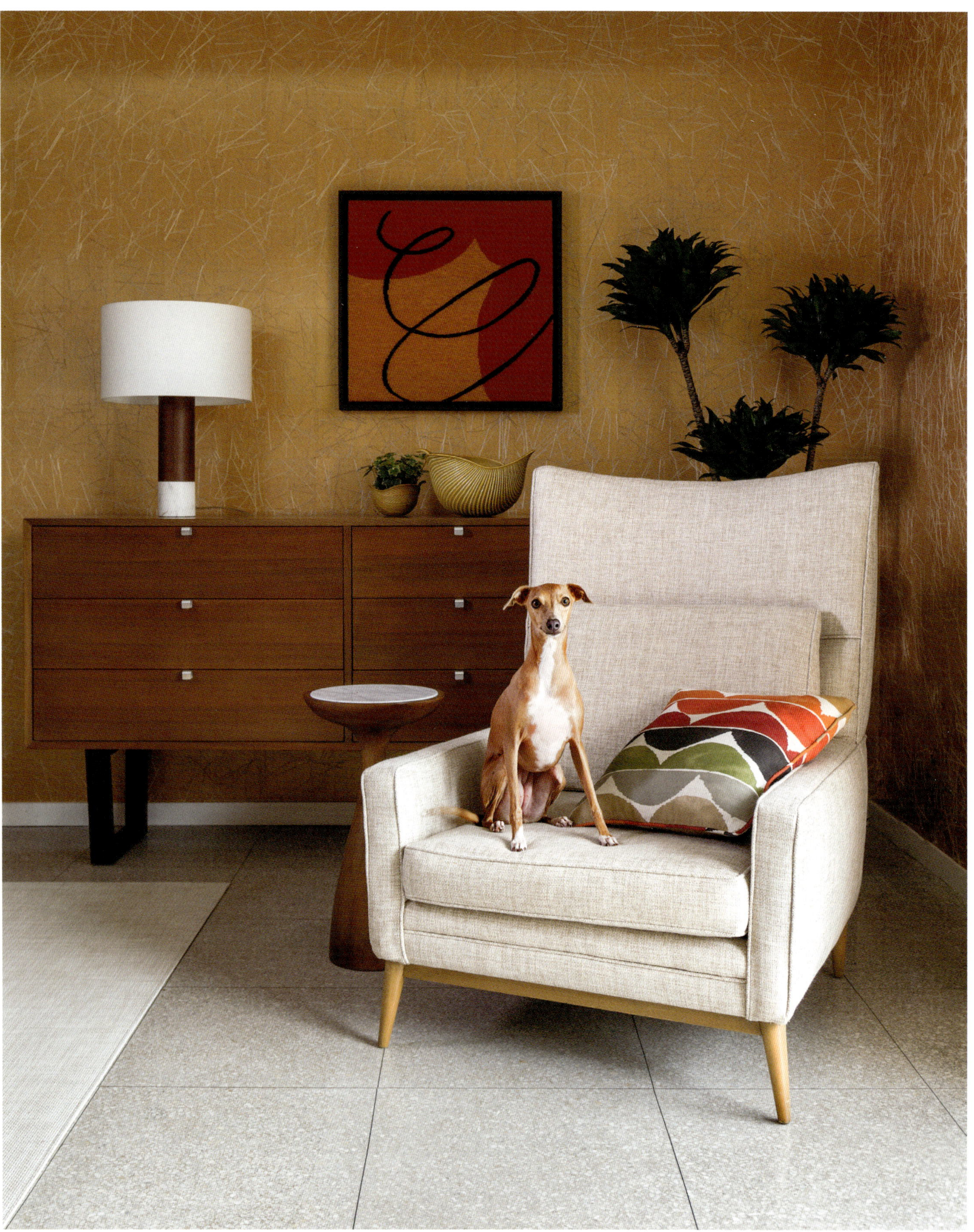

Gia and Lola

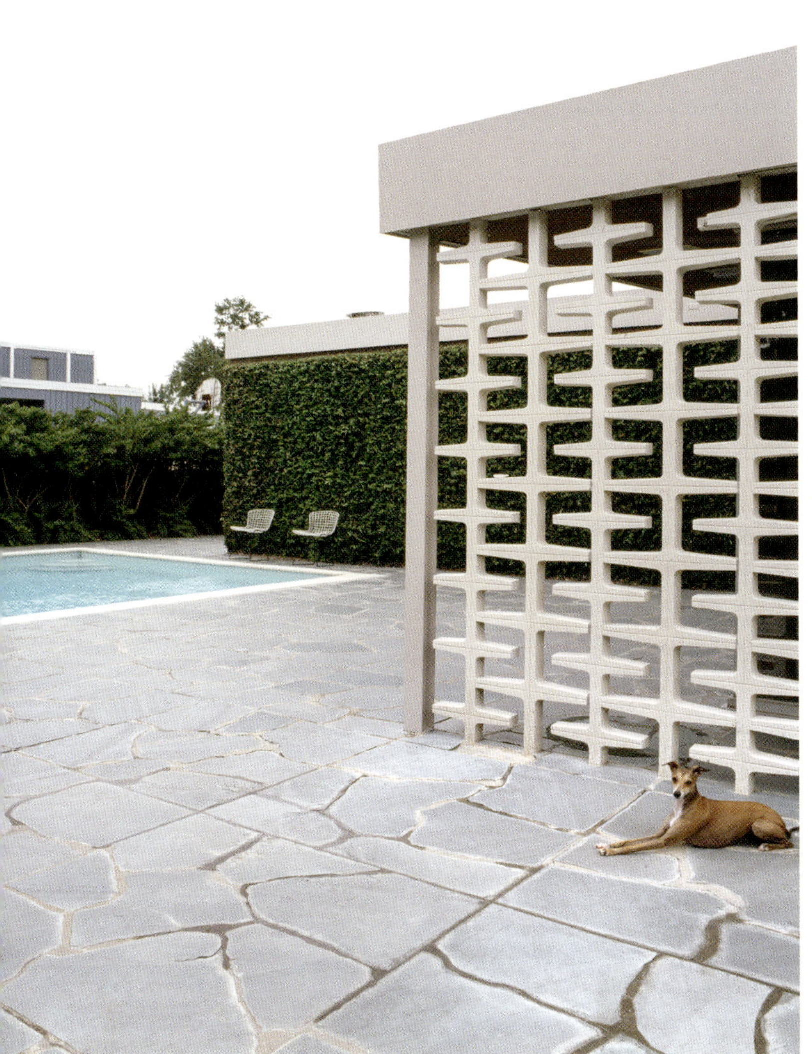

"Stylist Lisa Tudor has a thing for midcentury modern design and Whippets. After living in two other midcentury jewels in the Lakeshore neighborhood of New Orleans, Lisa and her husband Michael Sichel have settled in their dream house, designed by renowned architect and New Orleans native Albert J. Saputo. Lisa enlisted the help of design team Bockman+Forbes to pull the interiors together.

I'm Gia, a feisty, friendly three-year-old girl, who loves posing—in this case on a vintage high-back Paul McCobb armchair covered in Designers Guild basket-weave upholstery. The console is Herman Miller; the side table and Baton lamp are Jonathan Adler from Design Within Reach. The framed tapestry is by Native American artist Ramona Sakiestewa. The sustainable natural textured wall covering is by Phillip Jeffries. I love high design and I love that Lisa and Michael have provided me with such a delicious environment!

Gia's predecessor, Lola, now deceased but recorded in this photograph, lounges by the pool in Lisa's first midcentury home, built in 1957. Designed by August Perez III, it was featured in *Architectural Record* and restored by Lisa Tudor and Fritz Stoller in 2002."

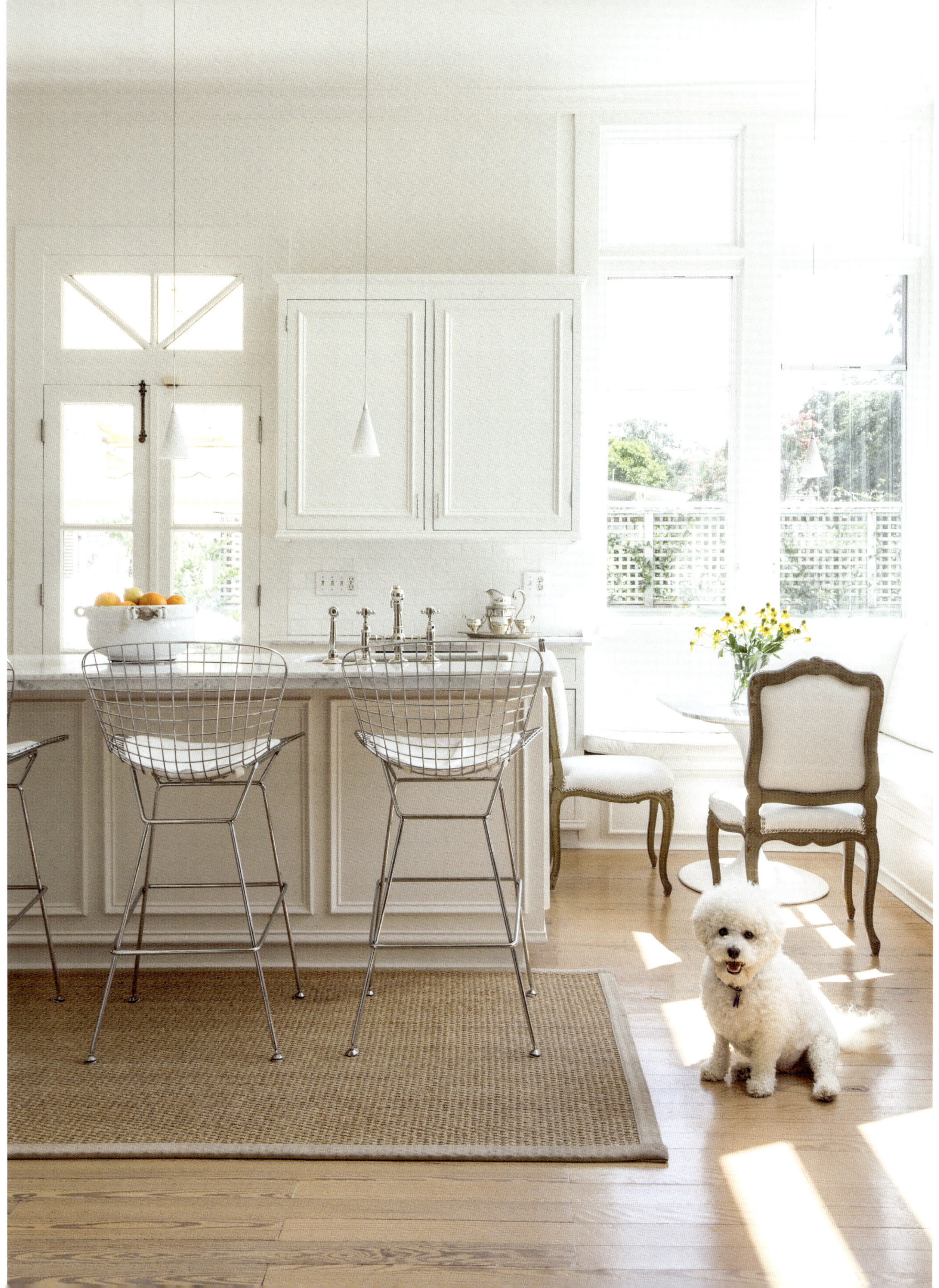

Louis

"True to my French heritage, I love cheese, but then again, I love pretty much all food. If my owners are even five minutes late with a meal, I will pick up my food bowl and drop it at their feet. *Excusez-moi!* My other French quality is that I am told I can be rather aloof, preferring to sit in the front window where passing neighbors can admire me. Donna and Joe Maselli are certain more people know my name than know theirs.

After the unexpected death of Joe's son, I have become Joe's only boy, and I live up to that role exceptionally well. My happy, and let's admit it, funny face is a welcome distraction from life's daily stresses. I am a true bon vivant, and yes, I have a Louis Vuitton collar from Saks Fifth Ave. *Naturellement!*

Donna is an interior designer by trade, and our uptown New Orleans home is a showcase of her style. Clean lines, bright whites, and crisp accents create an inviting, polished look."

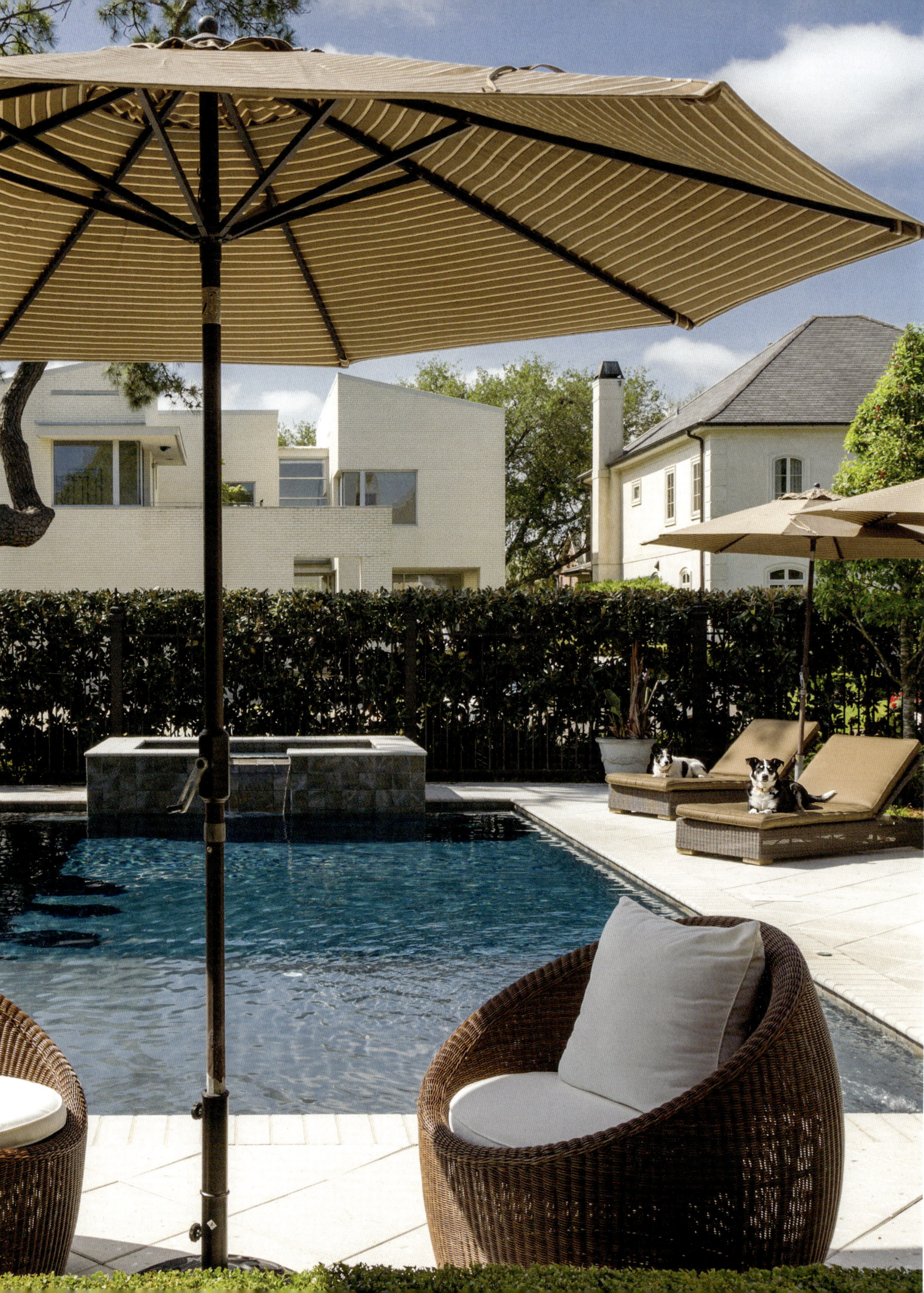

Moki and Winnie

"Hanging out in Jackie and Vincent Palumbo's backyard in Lakeview in New Orleans feels like stepping onto the grounds of an Italian villa. A koi pond leads to a fountain with a bench grouping to the left and to the right; a large rectangular pool segues to an outdoor dining area and a sheltered outdoor kitchen with a seating area.

Just as you're settling into your lounger, cocktail in hand, you are suddenly not alone. Jumping into the chaises on either side of you are the two of us, Moki and Winnie. Moki's auspicious beginning was the side of a road in Austin, where Jackie's son rescued him, and brought him back to live in the dorm until she was too big to hide. Seventeen years later, she's as bright and bubbly as ever, hopping up on furniture like a little mountain goat. I'm her buddy, Winnie. I'm five years old, and weigh in at a hefty sixty pounds—but that doesn't stop me from wedging myself onto any willing lap. We both like to hang out at the pool—on our own special chaise lounges of course—all day."

McKenzie and Chico

"Husband and wife design team Kendall and Patrick Schindler have fostered at least seventy-five rescue dogs. And I've been through all of them. Nearly dead when rescued myself, I'm a Goldendoodle, and I've grown into a most patient, sweet, and mothering lady. In my hey-day, I was an athletic marvel, jumping eight feet into the air and twisting my body to catch tennis balls. These days I have slowed a bit, but I still retain my happy-go-lucky demeanor.

The only member of my busy household to try my patience is little Chico. Of unknown pedigree, Chico was the first dog Kendall took into her rescue group she calls 'Scruffy Mutt,' thinking he would be a temporary guest. I babied this older dog, licking him on his head until he developed a bald spot. Perhaps in retribution, Chico enjoys jumping on my head, which I begrudgingly endure.

With me as backup, Chico enjoys terrorizing other neighborhood dogs, but he is a sweet and funny dog. He's thought to be about fifteen years old, but the family swears he gets younger every year. Did Benjamin Button come back as a tiny wiry head-jumping dog?

The bathroom fixtures are from Restoration Hardware. Kendall designed the vanity, and contractor Stephen Cacioppo built it. The hanging light fixture in the office is Fortuny from Italy. The art is from French Mix."

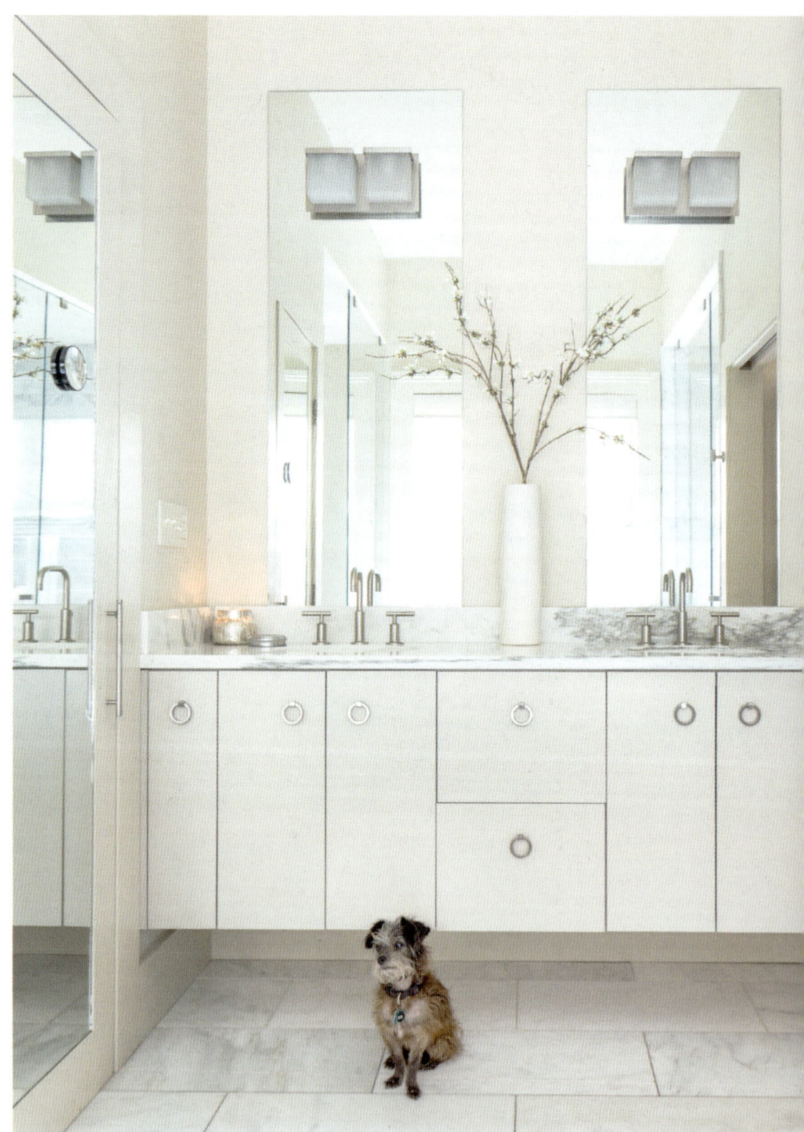

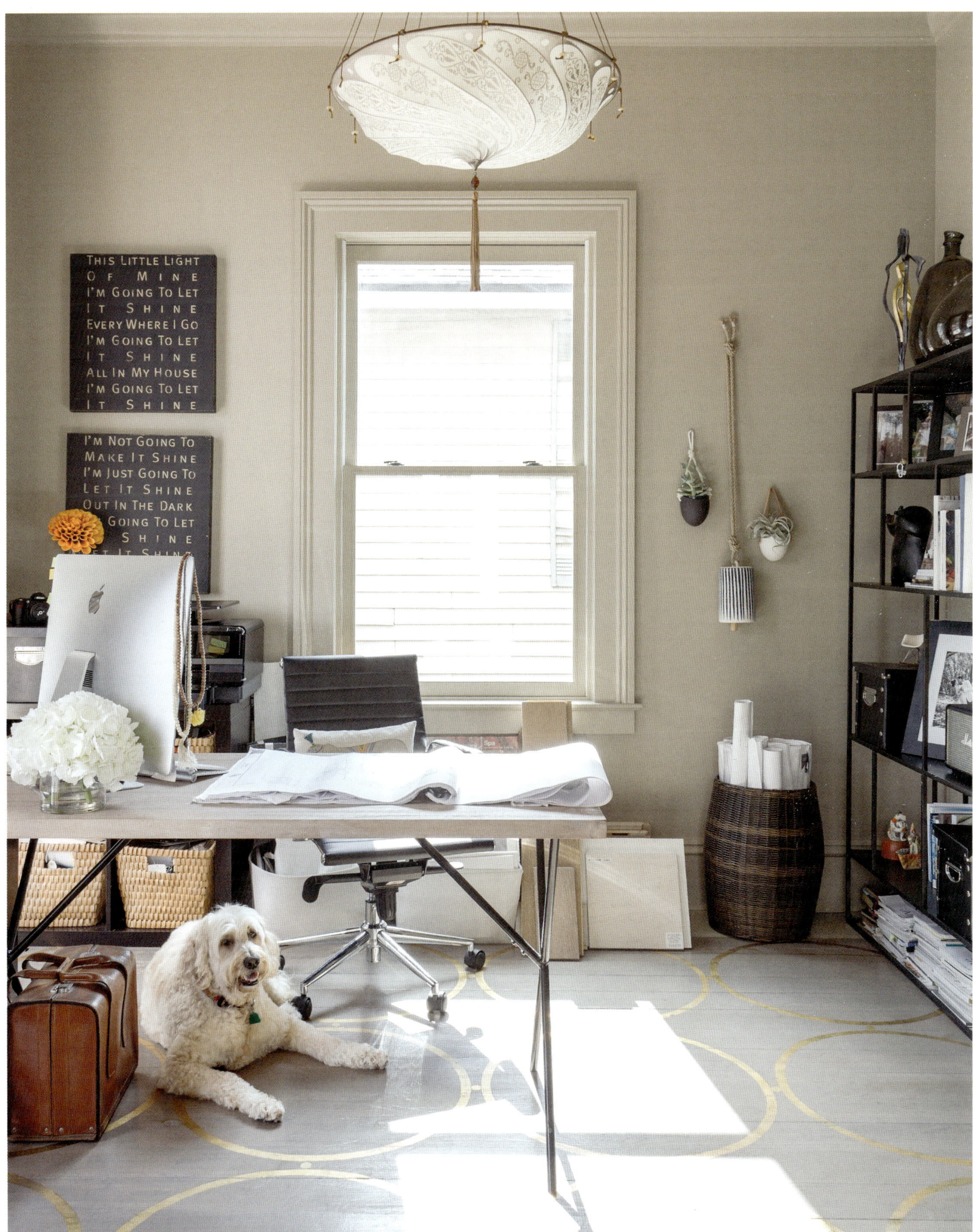
THIS LITTLE LIGHT
OF MINE
I'M GOING TO LET
IT SHINE
EVERY WHERE I GO
I'M GOING TO LET
IT SHINE
ALL IN MY HOUSE
I'M GOING TO LET
IT SHINE
I'M NOT GOING TO
MAKE IT SHINE
I'M JUST GOING TO
LET IT SHINE
OUT IN THE DARK
GOING TO LET
SHINE

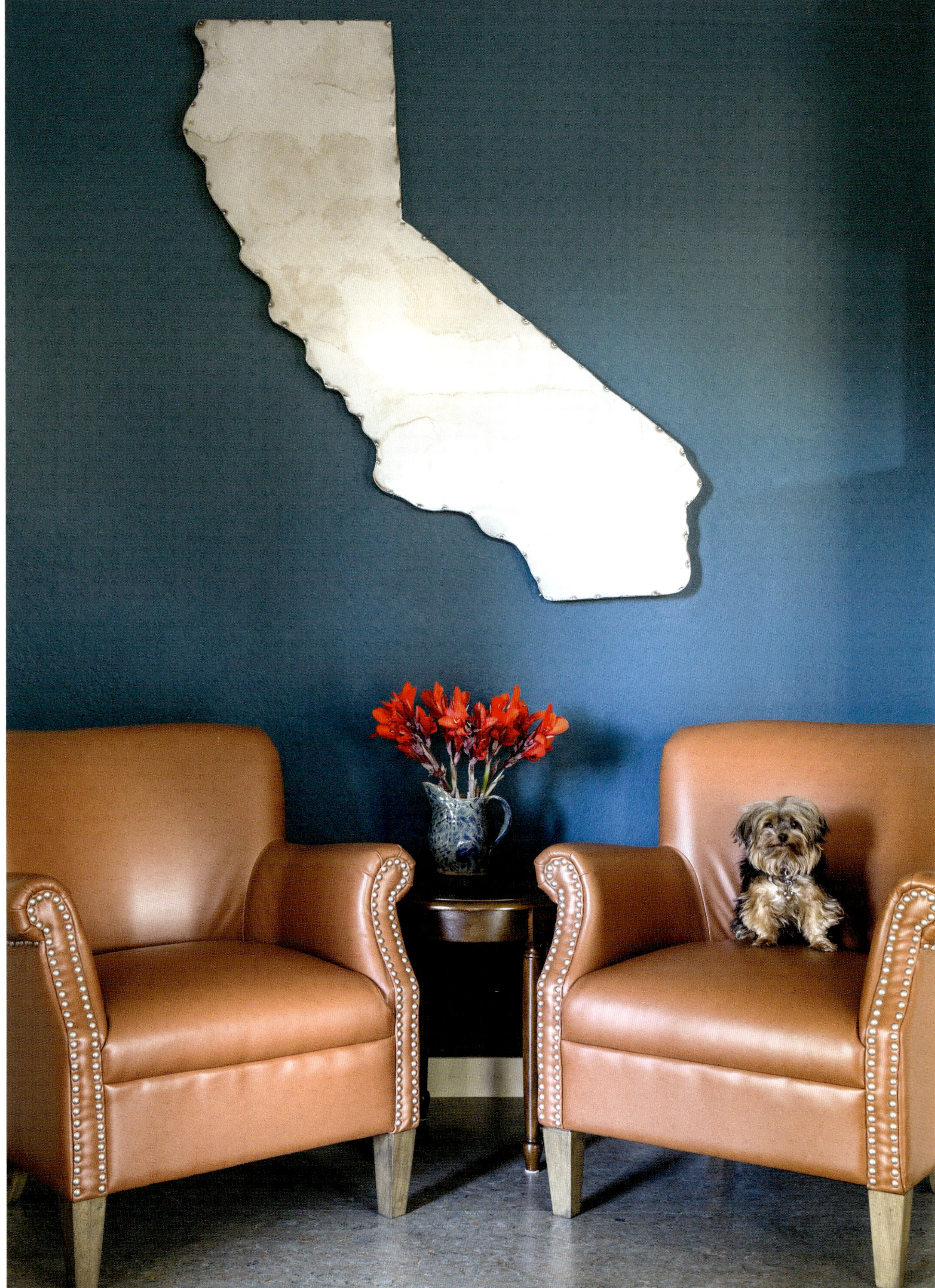

Mimi

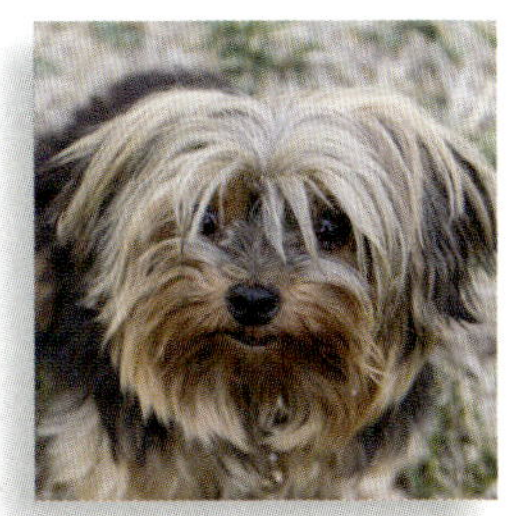

"I am one of two hotel dogs that Sara Essex Bradley has been lucky enough to meet and photograph. My name is Mimi, and I reside in the L&M Motel in Healdsburg, California, a hip haven for visitors to Sonoma wine country. I was adopted by Wanda Brester, the third-generation owner of the hotel, who lives in her grandparents' former bungalow on site. Wanda has creatively updated this classic horseshoe motor court, and you will often see her working on projects all around the motel grounds, which feature beautiful gardens hidden in every corner and brightly painted Adirondack chairs around a fire pit (for enjoying local wine in the chilly evenings).

Wanda bakes the best blueberry scones from scratch every morning, and I spend most mornings in the communal lobby greeting motel guests who stop in for them and some coffee. By afternoon, I make the rounds with housekeeper Maria (who spoils me rotten)."

Bear

"Jen and Chris Lyman renovated their home to retain the look of a traditional New Orleans cottage, but designed the space to provide a comfortable and accessible environment for their young son, who has cerebral palsy and is visually impaired. The result is subtle, bright, and modern, with modifications being concealed within the architecture. The glass back doors open onto a patio and pool, and fold away almost completely to create an inside outside feel in nice weather.

I'm Bear, a Newfoundland mix, and I came from a Native American reservation just outside of Durango, Colorado. I'm now fourteen years old and try periodically to strike the intense look of a wise Native American chief, even though I am somewhat diminutive for my breed. But that makes me less clumsy, right? I'm very well behaved and like the bear Baloo in *The Jungle Book*, I am a careful and protective compaion to the young son in the family, who I love very much."

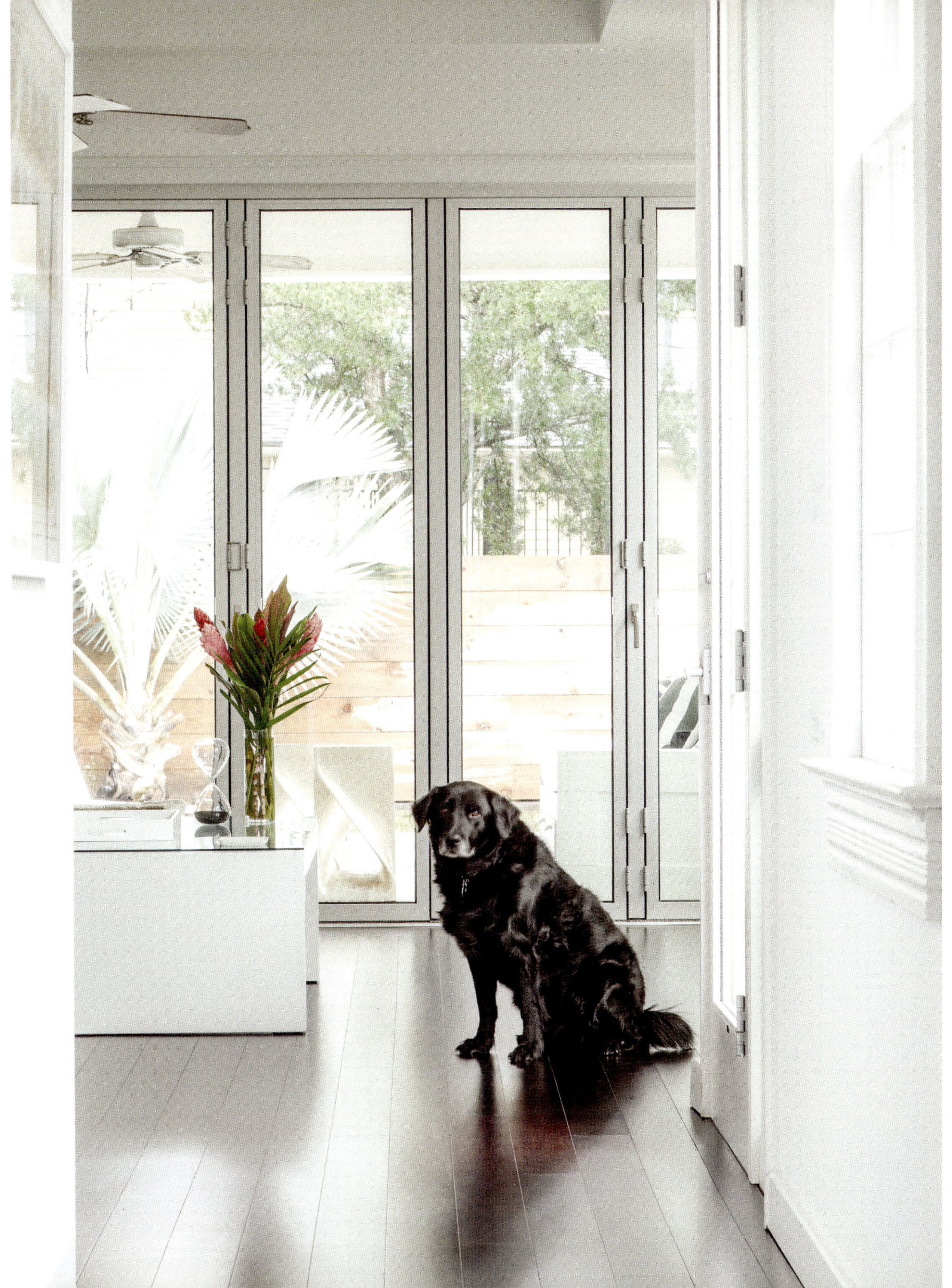

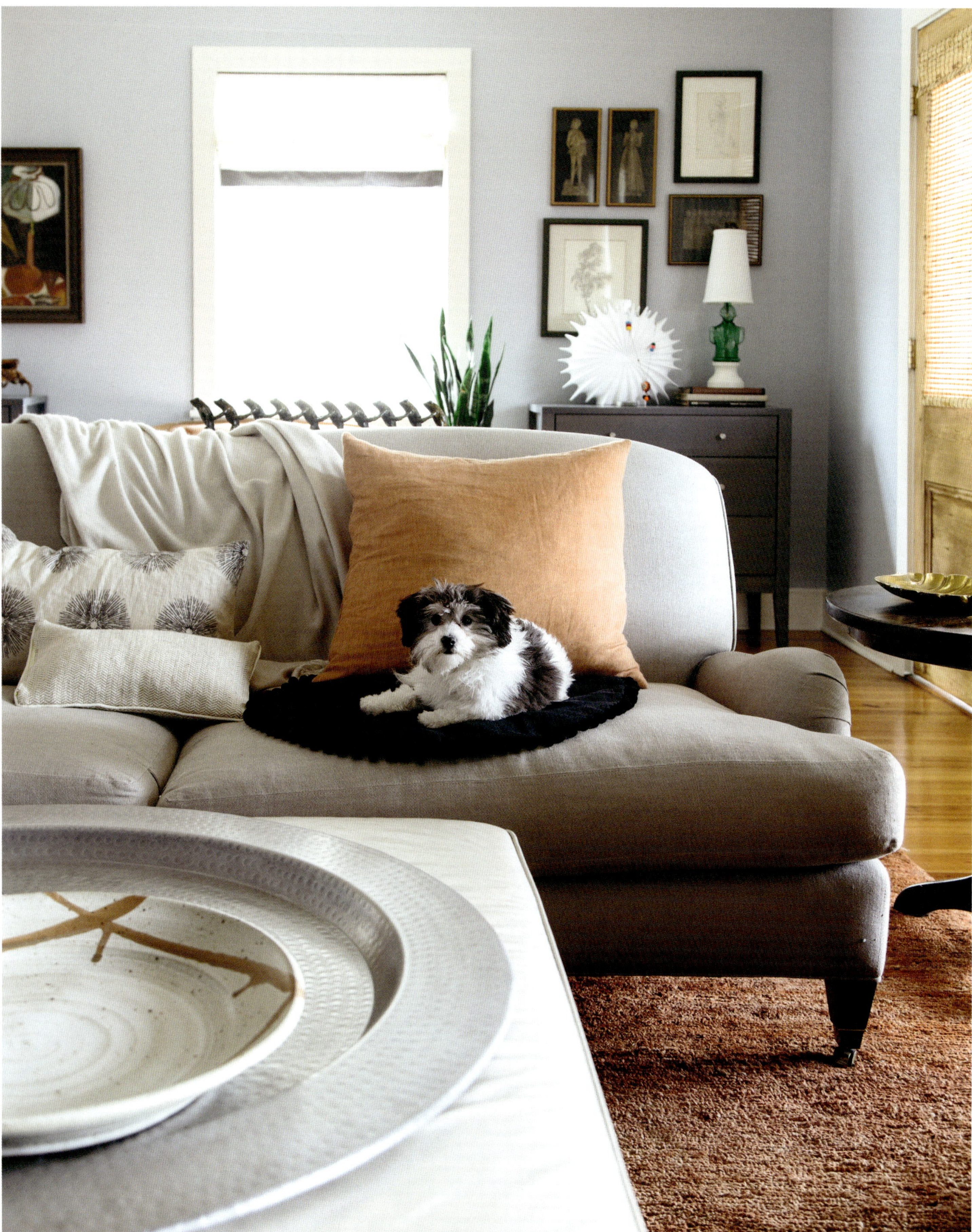

JOSEPHINE

"When Amber and Jacob Donnes bought their first home together, in the Broadmoor neighborhood of New Orleans, they knew to enlist the help of professionals when it came to decorating the quirky split-level cottage. Enter LKI Interiors principals Katie Logan and Jensen Killen. Katie and Jensen helped the couple create a warm, inviting space, combining vintage finds with carefully selected investment pieces to create a curated, layered look.

I love lounging on the sofa in the living room, being mellow and cool. I'm Josephine, also known as Jojo, and I am a Havanese who comes from Thibodaux. I still have a little country left in me; witness my rolls in the grass, preferably grass that has a pile of worms.

At the end of the day, though, I like to snuggle up to Amber and David, unless I feel 'stretchy' and want to take up the whole couch."

Otto and Inky

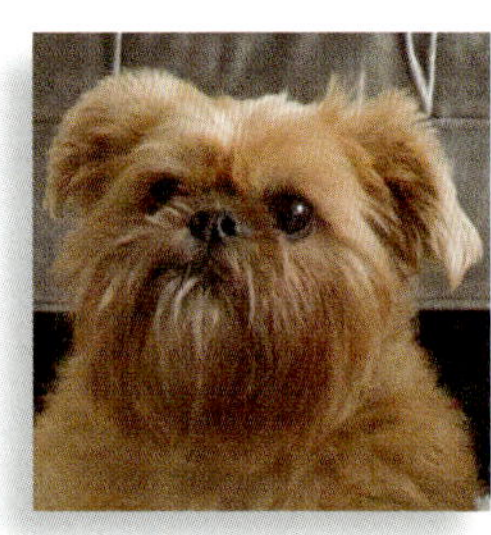
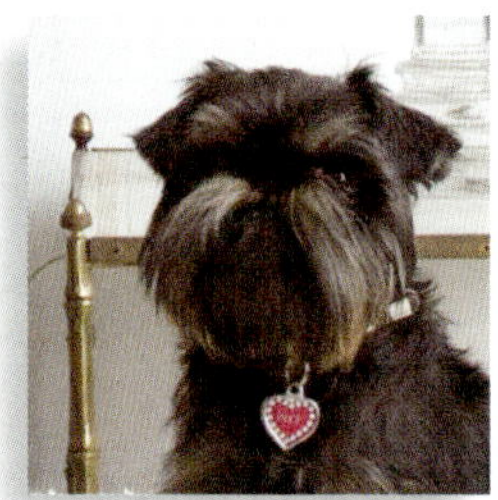

"We're Otto (left) and Inky (right) and we live in the tony Tudor City apartments in New York City, on Manhattan's East Side, with dramatic views of the United Nations building. Constructed in 1927, Tudor City was the world's first residential skyscraper apartment complex—I bet you didn't know that!—topping off at thirty-two stories.

Our parents are Mary and Michael Millea and we're Rough Brussels Griffons. Inky is the diva of the house. I'm very cuddly and more subdued and reflective—and I like to read a lot. We both welcome visitors and are known to be exuberant when they appear in the breezeway, where we set off a pandemonium of joyous yelping and copious licking.

Mary, a former fellow at the Metropolitan Museum of Art, specializes in classic Italian paintings of all vernaculars, while Michael (along with his twin brother) operates Millea Bros. Ltd., which conducts auctions and appraisals of fine furnishings. Their impeccable taste is evident in the furnishings and finishes in their fully renovated prewar apartment.

Above the Jonathan Adler sofa hangs a textile of Senufo mud cloth from the Ivory Coast. On top of the brass table sits a Chinese archaic ritual jade ax head from the Han dynasty. The floor lamp is Cedric Hartman, vintage late seventies. The Louis XVI bronze and marble gueridon in the corner supports a polychrome wood serpent from the Baga tribe of Africa."

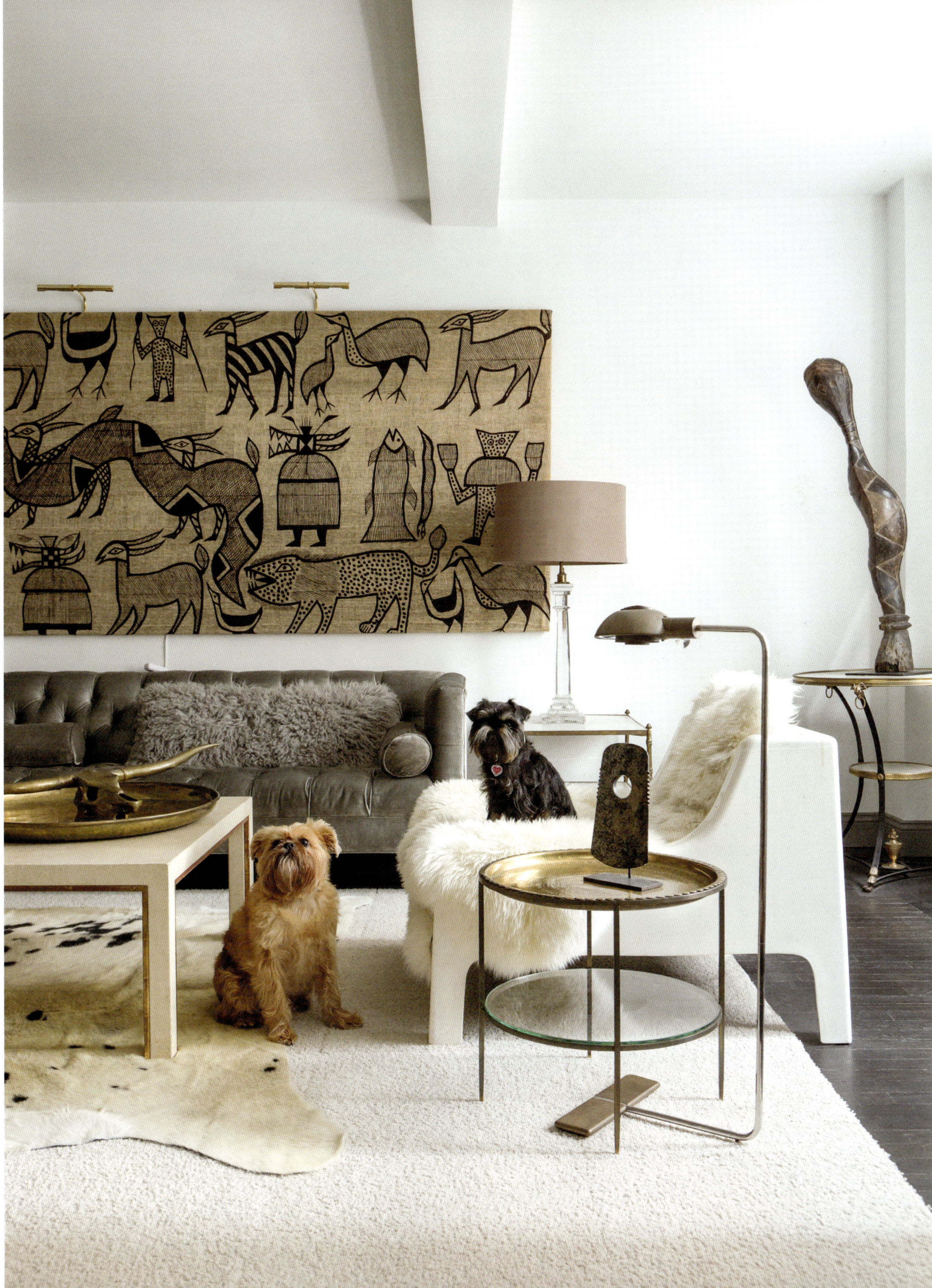

Patches

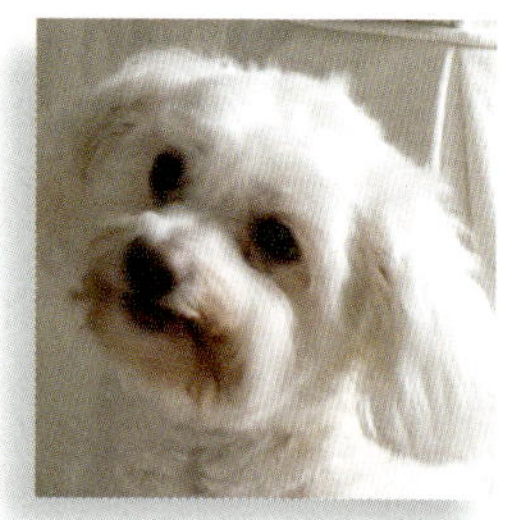

"I arrived in the wake of Hurricane Katrina, bringing a little happiness in an otherwise challenging time. I am a friendly, sociable little dog, and I'm very eager to sit for treats. I am fanatically devoted to the daughters of the family, so much so that I insisted they not abandon me for a high-speed tube ride behind a motorboat—I joined them on the lake, ears a'flapping at forty-five miles per hour.

Connie Seitz Interiors, along with associate designer Christine Diggs, handled the elegant design of this dining room, where I wait patiently as meals are served for food to somehow fall nearby, for me to rescue. The wall finish was created by New Orleans Decorative Finishes, which hand-painted multiple glazes on the walls and ceilings. Gold leaf was applied to molding throughout the room. The Oslo chandelier was designed by E. F. Chapman for Circa. The drapes are an opalescent damask, and the linen slipcovered chairs feature a custom two-color monogram.

Isn't this a glorious place?"

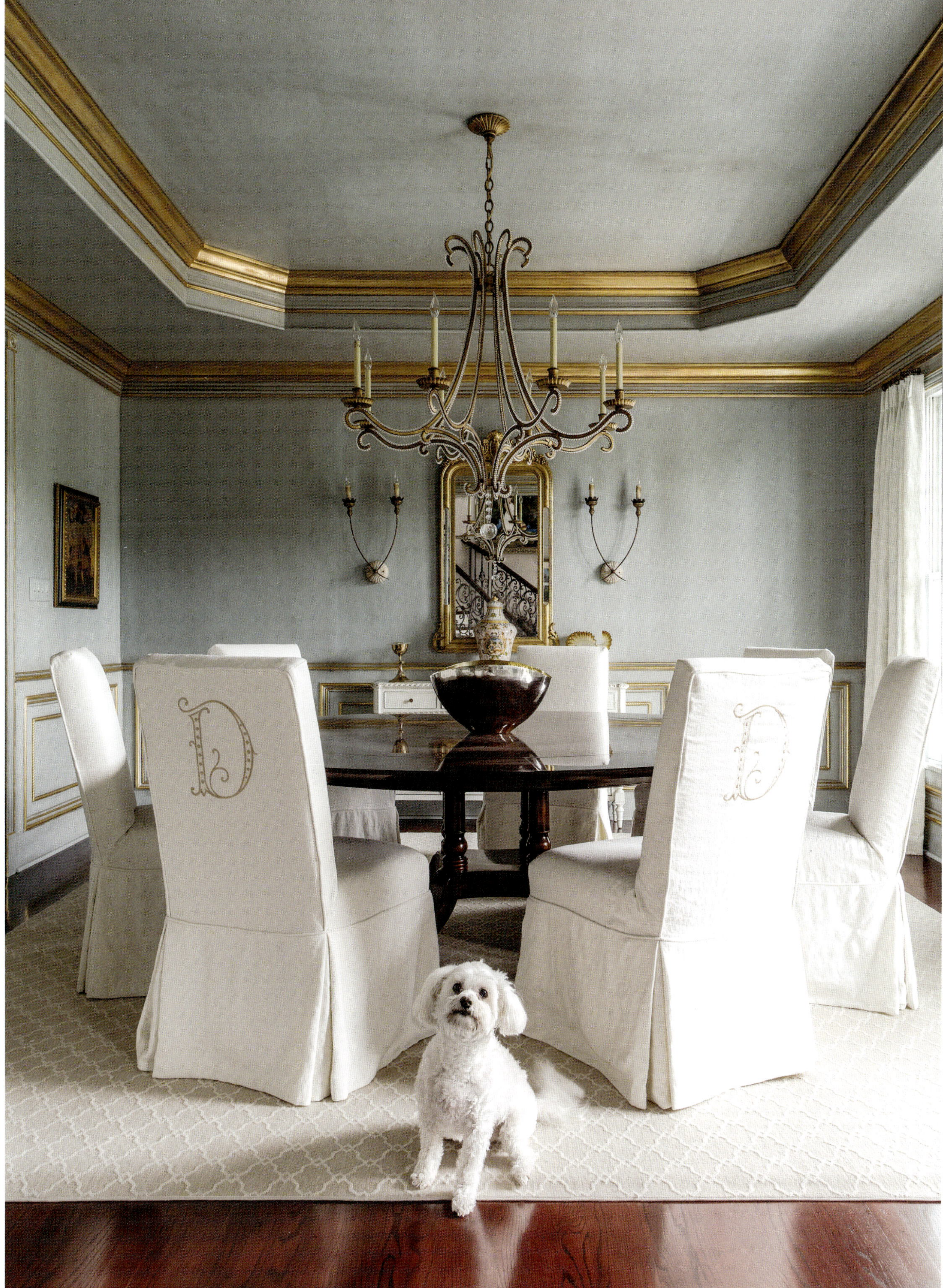

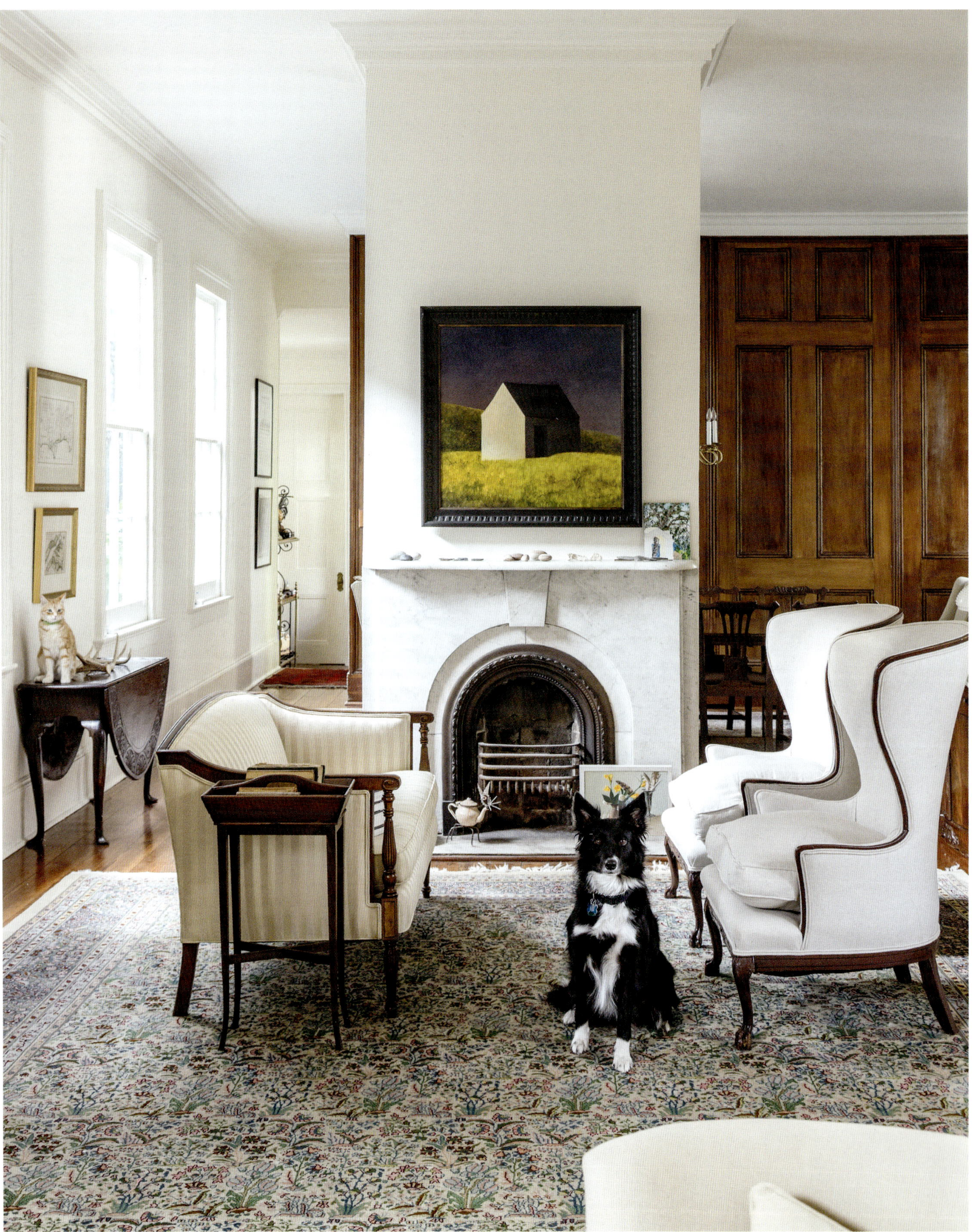

Luna and Flag, the Cat

"You could say physician Michell Thurmond is a dog person. And a cat person. Throughout her life, she has had many dogs and cats, mostly Border Collies, for dogs and strays for cats. Fifteen years ago, she acquired a Border Collie, but that dog was getting on in years, and Michell feared she would not live much longer. Since a house without animals is unthinkable, Michell began to ponder a second pet who would fill the void when she lost her cherished Border Collie. A second dog would be too stressful on her older dog, but she thought a cat might fill the slot perfectly.

That's when I showed up. I am Flag, the orange tabby cat, who found my way to Michell by way of her sister's yard. I appeared one day, covered in mud, and her sister knew I would make a great pet for Michell. When the time came, Michell sought another Border Collie, this time via a Virginia breeder. Luna is the perfect companion, and I tolerate her as well. She is a true Border Collie, and tries to keep me in line, to no avail. But mostly she is a sweet, friendly dog, beloved by friends and strangers alike.

Michell dreams of buying Luna a sheep farm, but for now, we reside in the Garden District. By chance, Michell was able to purchase her grandparents' house, and has reunited many of their antiques with the home. The painting over the marble fireplace is by South Carolina artist Edward Rice."

Gladys

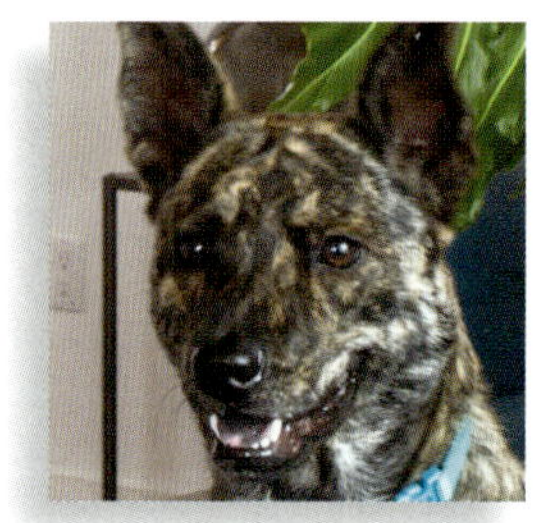

"Architect Ross Karsen had to jump through many hoops to build this award-winning modern home in the historic Bywater neighborhood in New Orleans. The Historic District and Landmarks Committee were not initially favorable to his plans to build a modern two-story home on a lot that once housed a one-story grocery store. But Ross prevailed, and he proceeded to create a thoroughly modern space that still respects the neighborhood's Creole sensibilities, in color and design.

I was adopted from the SPCA, after being found under a house at three months old. A dingo-like Shepherd mix, I consider myself unique and energetic. Not the worshipful sycophant, I hop up and down on furniture, monitoring the windows for outside activity. I adore Ross and his wife, Sarah Wiseman, but I am my own dog. My feline-like qualities extend to my looks—neighborhood children refer to me as 'cat dog' due to my markings.

Ross and Sarah, a fine artist, keep the décor simple, contemporary, and stylish, allowing the architecture to be the focus—just like me, simple, stylish, and contemporary!"

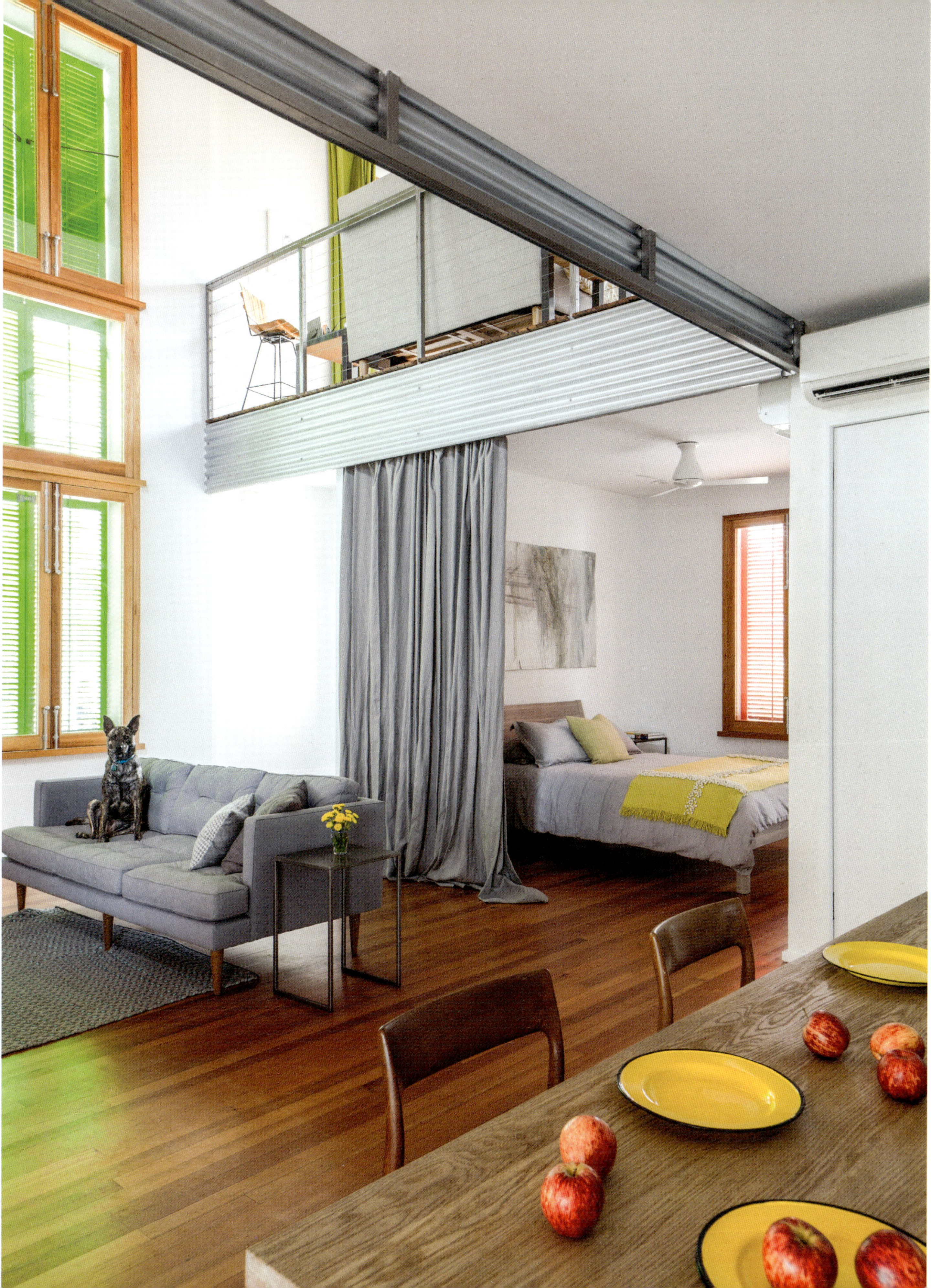

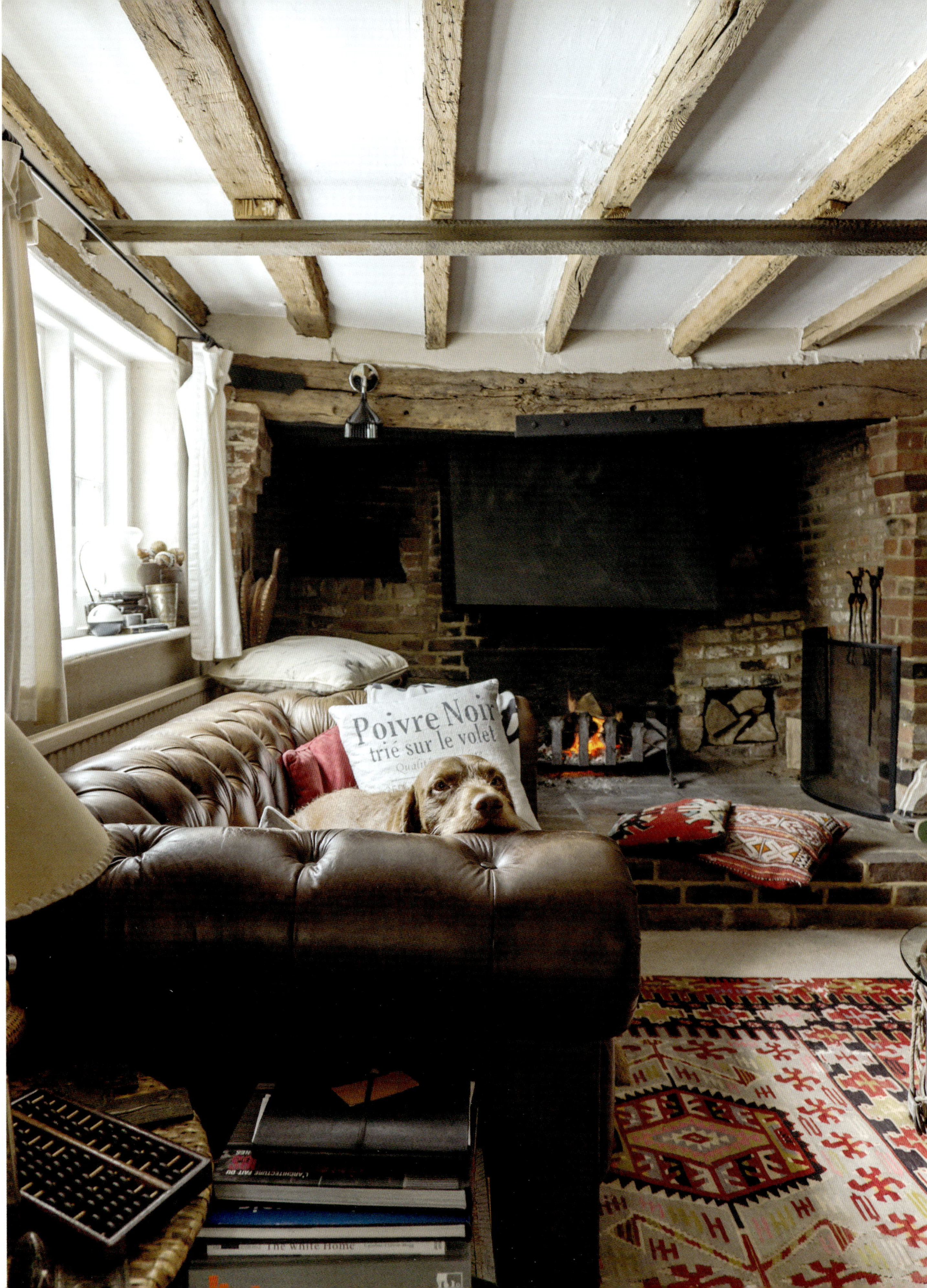
Poivre Noir
trié sur le volet
L'ARCHITECTURE FAIT DU
The White Home

Odie

"Most dog owners can't claim that their pet is a cross-dresser.

As a wirehaired Hungarian Vizsla, I'm typically recognized for my intelligence, obedience, and gentle nature. However, when it comes my attire, my tolerance is quite pronounced, as I willingly and patiently allow young Georgie, the daughter of my owner, Sarah Capp, to dress me in all manner of feminine costumery: hula skirt, fairy wings, flowers, and ribbons. I am indulgent and enjoy any kind of play.

Sarah, Georgie, and I make our home in the lovely countryside on the Sussex-Kent border in England. I take full advantage of country living—running, swimming, exploring, but not hunting, unless you count sausages as prey. After a walk in a nearby park, I was in despair, not having received my usual sausage from the park café. Sarah removed the lead to put me in the car, but I had other plans. I took off for the café, and retrieved my sausage.

A lover of rustic French antiques, Sarah appointed her home with finds from antiques markets and French brocantes, which suits me perfectly."

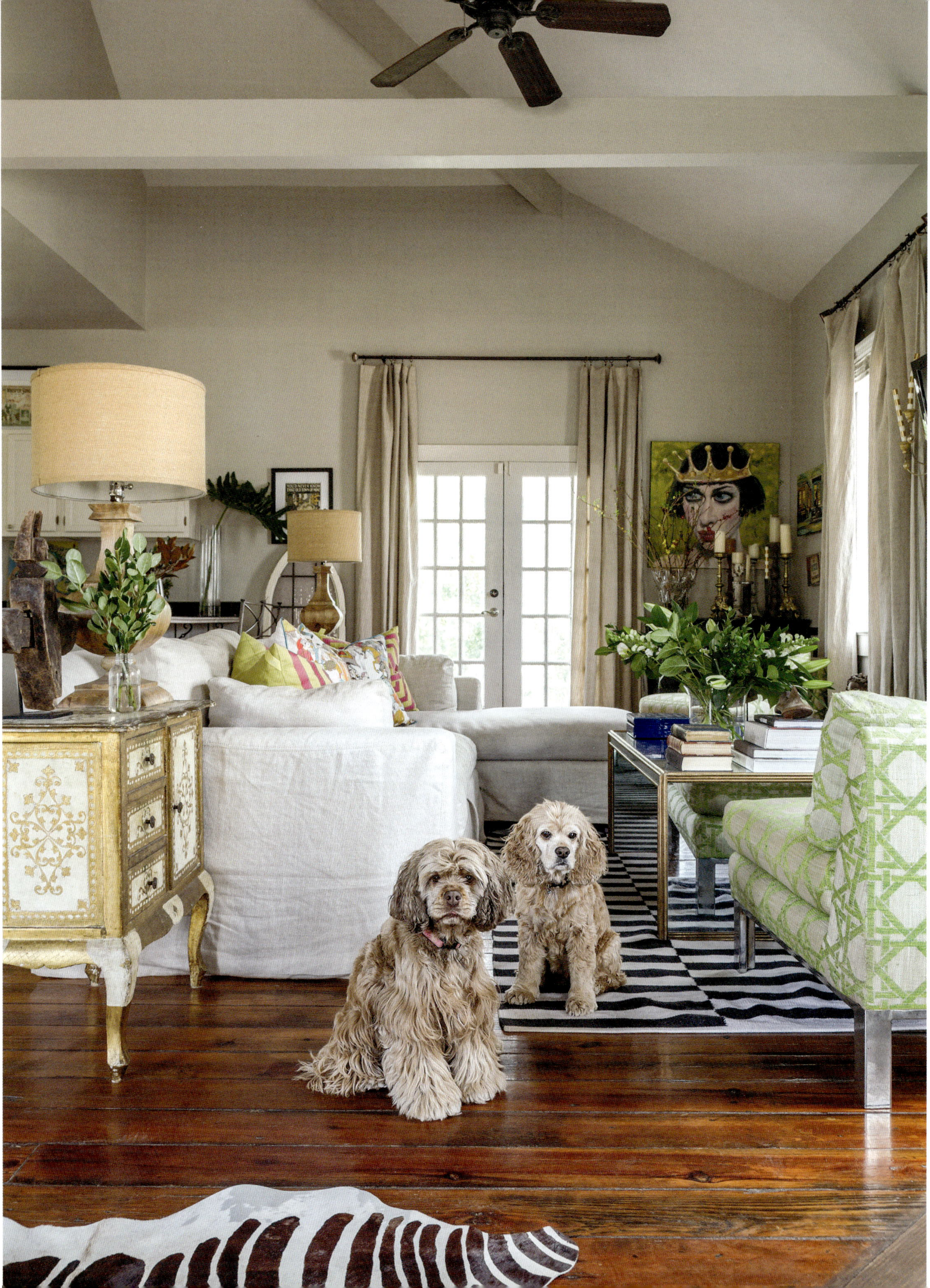

Bella and Lola

"I'm Bella (right), and Lola and I live with Sarah Thorne in the Irish Channel neighborhood of New Orleans. A pharmaceutical salesman by trade, Sarah flips houses on the side. This home is too perfect for her to sell, and she plans to stay forever.

I have been Sarah's companion for twelve years now, staying by her side through many homes, and even the homelessness after Katrina. I am quiet and reserved, unlike the interloper Lola, who came on the scene three years ago.

Lola is blind, and oblivious to my indifference, thinking the whole world is as full of love as she is. Lola navigates her way through the house by memory, so Sarah wanted to assemble a good floor plan and stick to it.

In the living room she combined vintage finds from local antiques stores, with new pieces. The mirrored coffee table is from Neiman Marcus, and the painting in the back is by Nancy Rhodes Harper from AKA Stella Gray gallery.

We're two lucky pups to live in this delicious environment with so much love."

Sasha

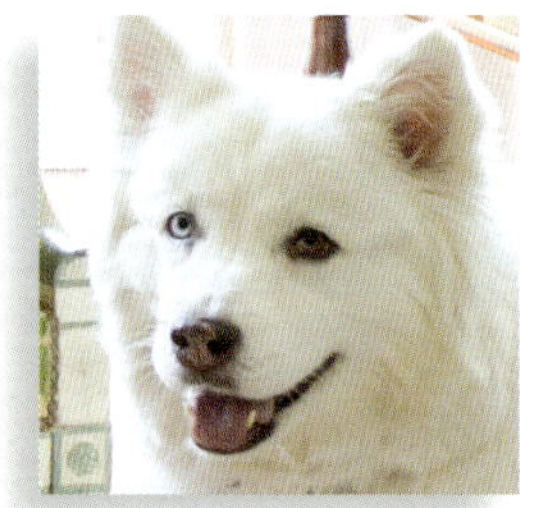

"One of the little-known tragedies related to the BP oil spill actually landed me in the lap of luxury. I was adopted from the Louisiana SPCA after I was abandoned by my previous owners, who could no longer care for me due to financial difficulties following the spill. Since I am such a beautiful, sweet dog, Jennifer Willis was elated to find me.

I can usually be found in my favorite spot, a sunny ladies' sitting room in Jenny and Scott Willis's apartment in the iconic Upper Pontalba Building in the French Quarter. The décor is by Patrick Dunne, with antiques from Lucullus, his culinary antiques shop. The tall windows overlooking a balcony and the treetops of Jackson Square below offer plenty of diversion for an afternoon. The clean lines of the early nineteenth-century period furniture appeal to my sense of calm and order. Though my surroundings are luxuriant, my needs are simple: love, scratches, and the occasional Nilla wafer."

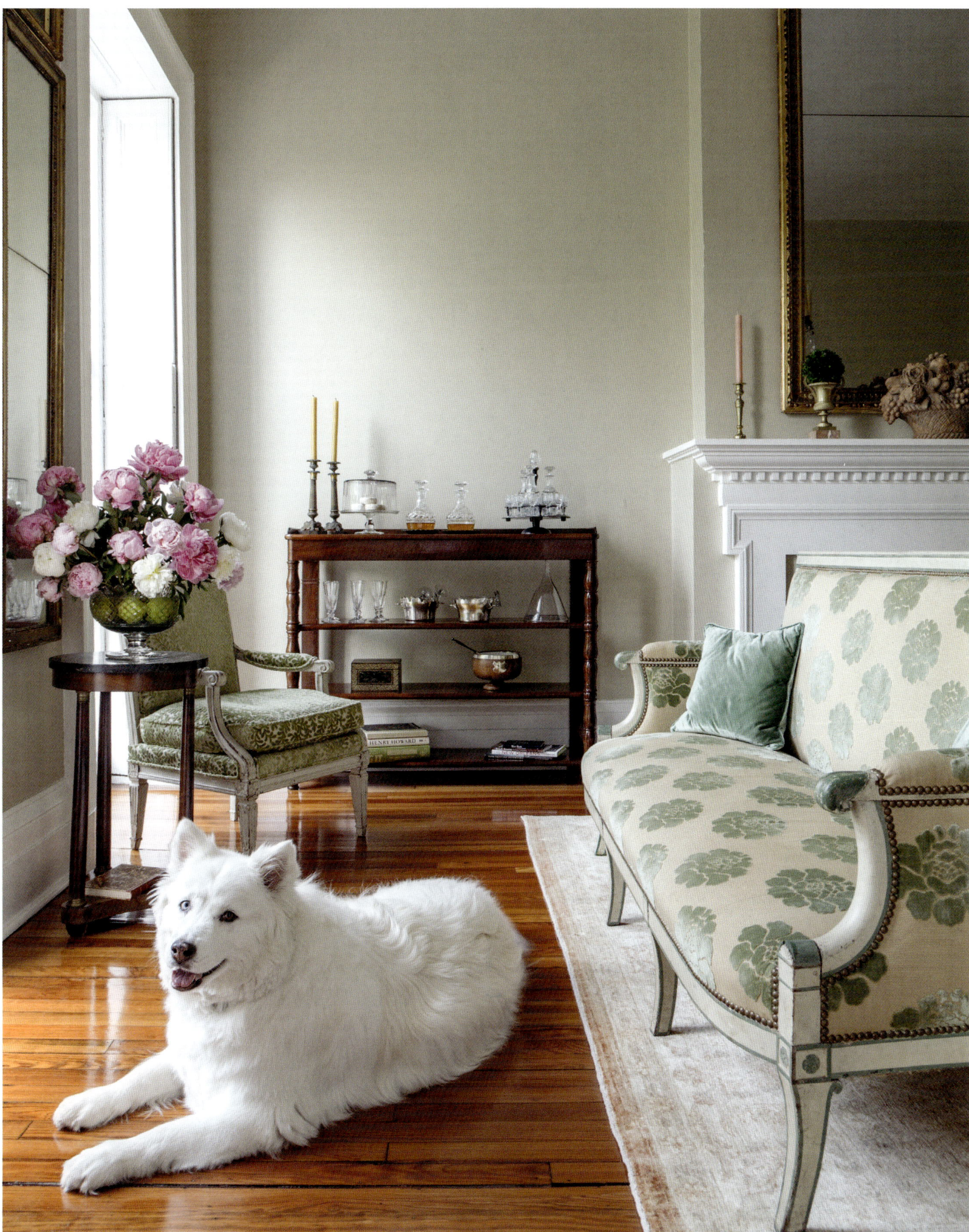
HENRY HOWARD

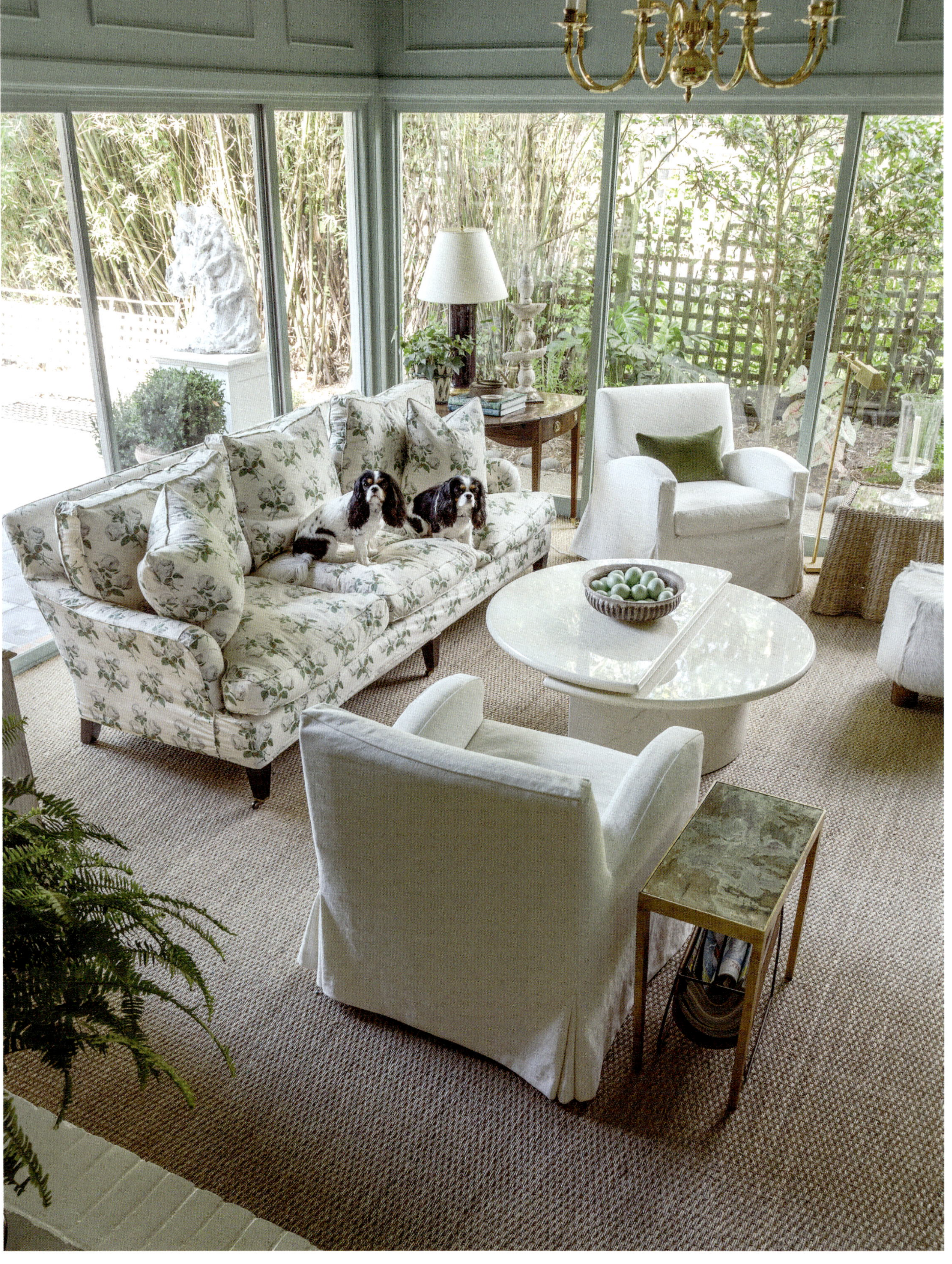

Presley and Harper

"Harper (left) and I are spoiled rotten and we know it. Show-quality Cavalier King Charles Spaniels, we provide calm and peace to in-demand designer Shaun Smith. When Sara Essex Bradley visited us to take our portrait, we were friendly and sweet, and we posed patiently, if somewhat wiggly, for a good fifteen seconds. As she sat and visited over a glass of champagne or two, Harper snuggled up to her and fell asleep with her head in her lap. Harper's a master napper, and actually bed is her favorite word; if you say it, she will run straight to it and go to sleep.

Here the two of us pose in the sunken living room of Shaun's new home in New Orleans, adjacent to the grounds of Long View House. The home had been inhabited by one family for many years, and is a typical seventies-style ranch house in an a typical highly desirable neighborhood. All potential buyers wanted to tear down the house and build a mini mansion, but the owners didn't want their house destroyed. Along came Shaun, who saw the potential of the space.

He has done a loving and elegant light renovation, mostly just paint and finishes with the exception of the kitchen. The den features a comfy couch covered in the Cowtan & Tout fabric 'Boxwood.' On the side table sits a Julie Silvers sculpture. The armchairs are custom by Gerrie Bremmerman. Other furnishings were curated through Shaun's store, Shaun Smith Home, on Magazine Street.

Harper and I fit right in."

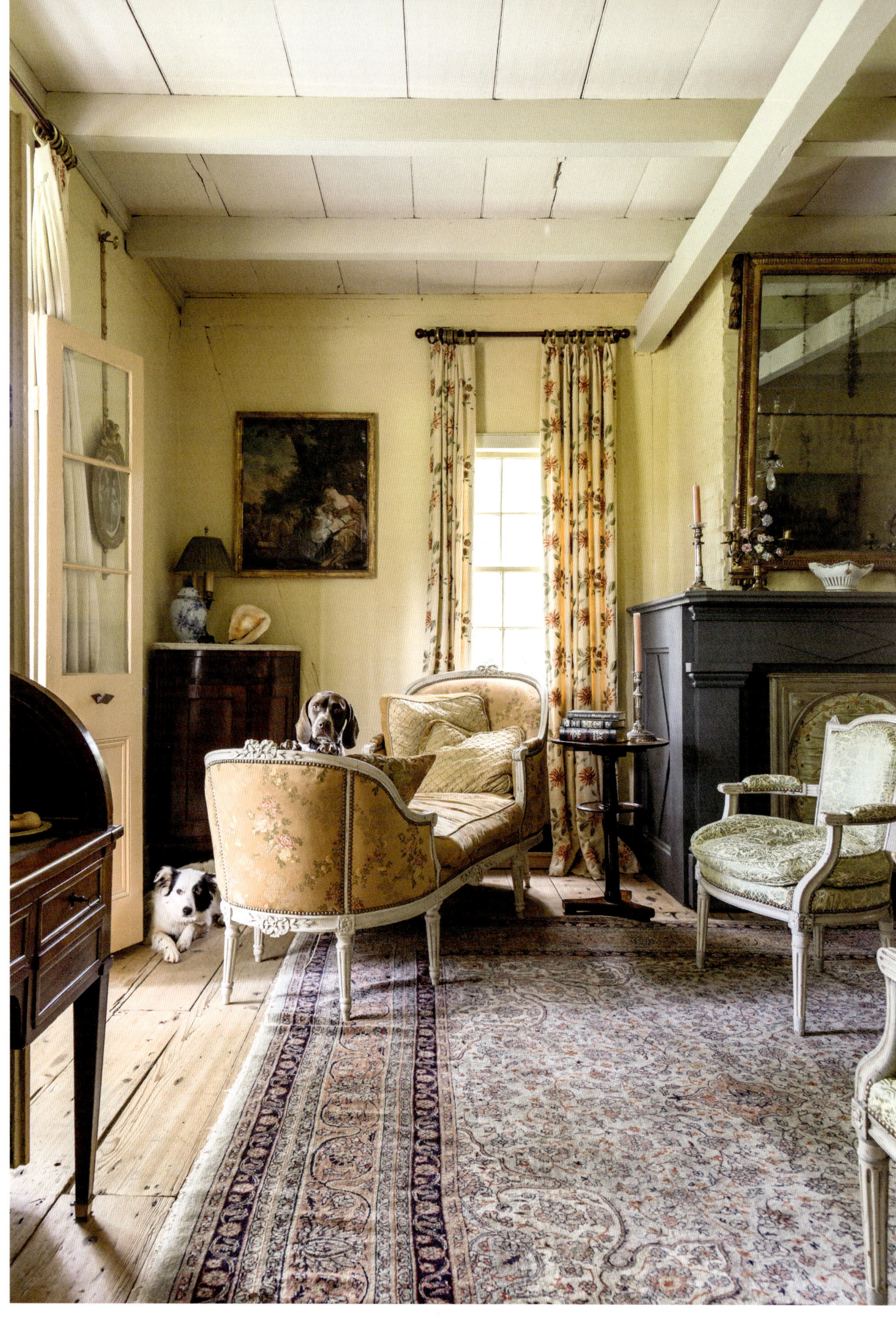

Souci and Chene

"I'm Souci (right), a German Shorthaired Pointer, and I am equally at home lounging on the eighteenth-century painted furniture in the drawing room as racing through the fields surrounding my home in St. Landry parish, Louisiana. The demure Border Collie Chene (French for 'oak') was born in the crook of an ancient live oak tree, thus her name. She prefers the spaces underneath chairs and desks. I like being out in the open!

We're both friendly and affectionate and totally uninterested in having our photographs taken, or posing for the camera. We wiggle to the beat of our own drums, and have no time for 'sit' commands, much less 'stay!'

We live with Patrick Dunne in a gorgeous home that feels like a travel back in time. The early nineteenth-century country Creole manor house was lovingly restored by Patrick, who filled it with family heirlooms (he's a designer). Did I mention he is also the owner of New Orelans' famed culinary antiques shop, Lucullus?"

Lucy

"A red piebald, short-hair miniature Dachshund, I'm a feisty flibbertigibbet, happily following my owners from room to room. I am a willing and happy model for the camera. My tiny size belies my big personality; I am playful, quite smart, and fiercely loyal. I am an adroit hunter, preferring squirrels, lizards, and grasshoppers. When the Harp family returns home at the end of the day, I am there to enthusiastically greet each one, ready for the evening cuddle.

Pam Harp enlisted the help of Cindy St. Romain, proprietor of St. Romain interiors, to help her pull the décor together. The French-style home was designed by architect George Hopkins, and I think he did a superb job."

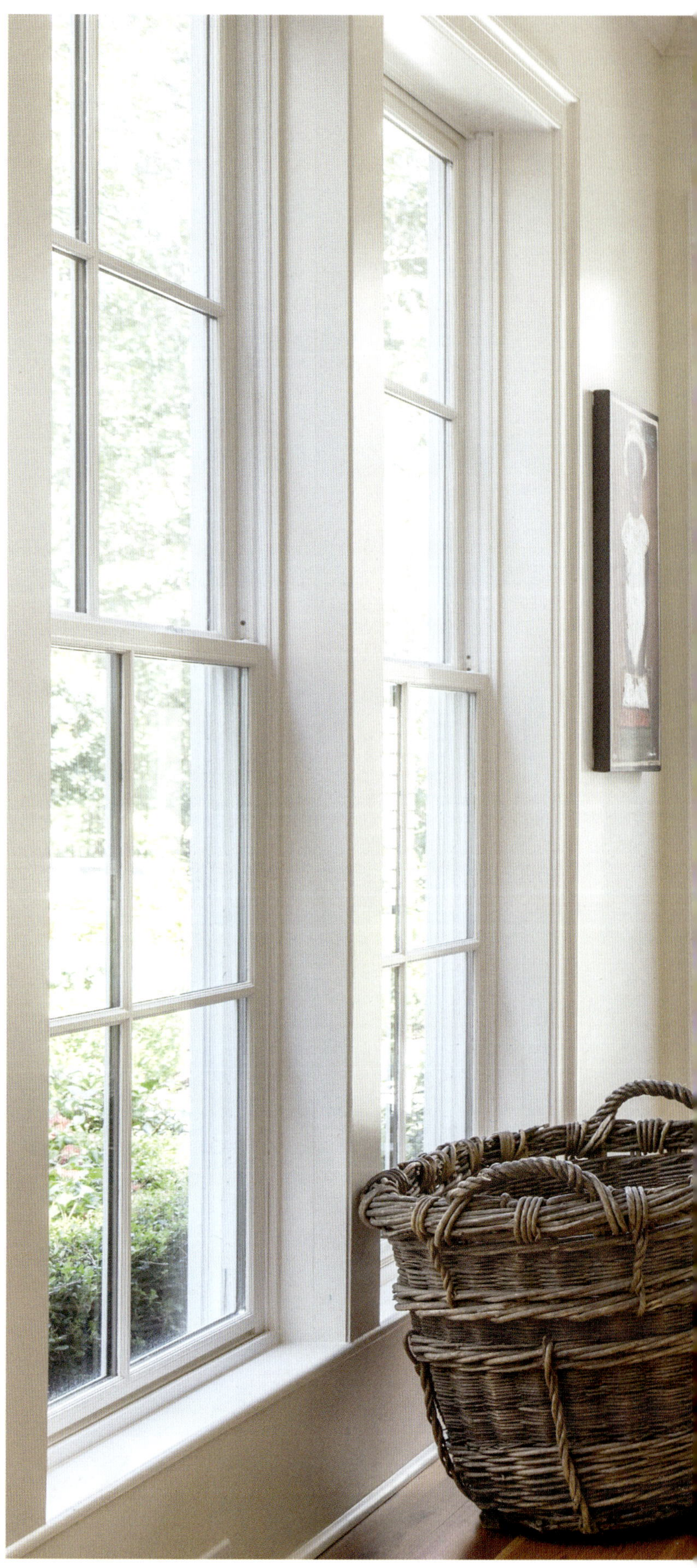

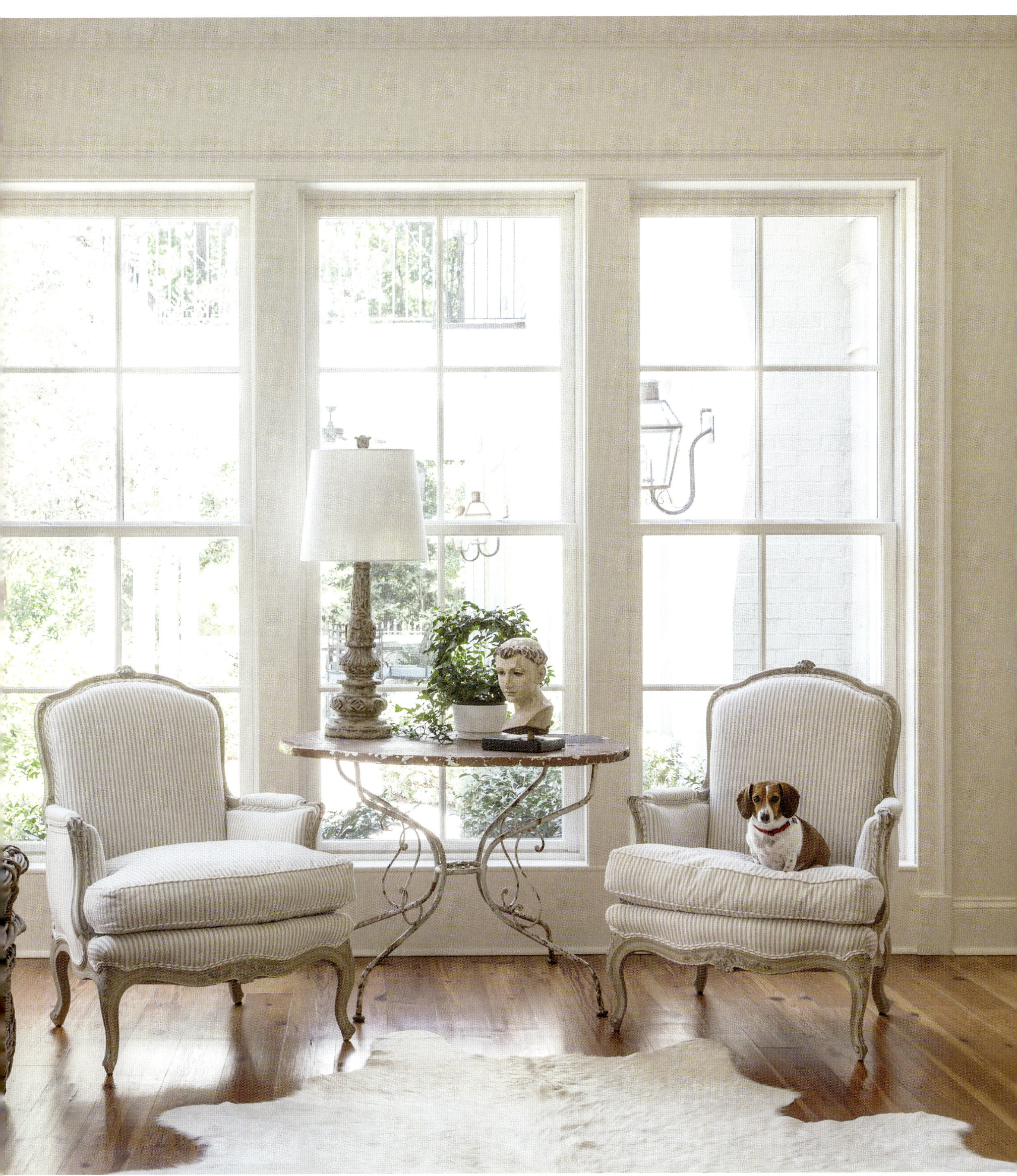

Patches, Pinkerton, and Homer

"I am too busy to pose for photos, as you can see here. My Dachshund pal Pinkerton will do anything for a treat, but my work is never done. My name is Patches, and I'm the family Jack Russell. I'm constantly on patrol, keeping our pack, belonging to Paula and husband Trent, in line. I am Trent's favorite, and I'm extremely intelligent and loyal. Pinkerton, my most troublesome charge, arrived as a gift for Paula and Trent's son, Christian. When he left home for college, Pinkerton remained. He is a loving and playful boy, who has never known hardship.

Towering above Pinkerton and me is loving, lumbering Homer (right), the Golden Retriever. He has been with our family for thirteen years. True to his breed, he is mellow and friendly.

The family worked with designer Cindy St. Romain to create the stylish interiors, blending French antiques from her store with comfortable contemporary pieces. Don't we fit in well?"

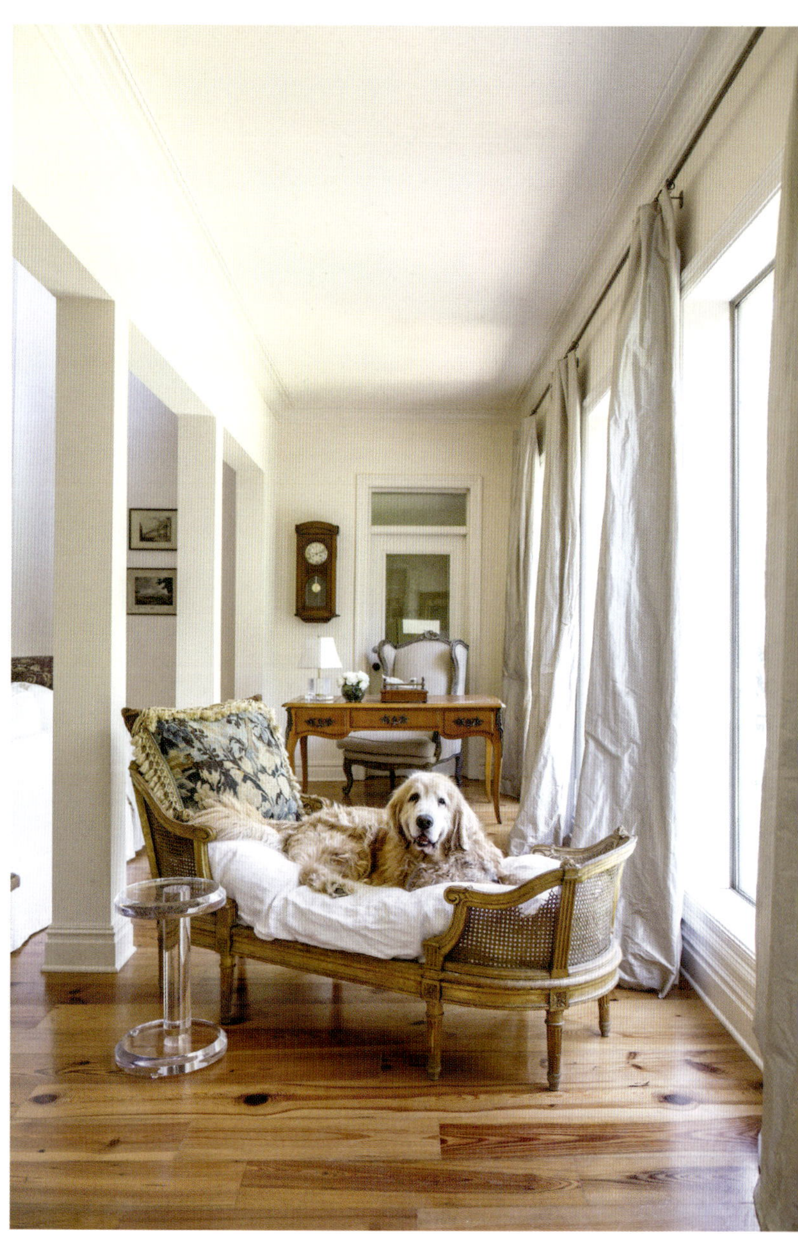

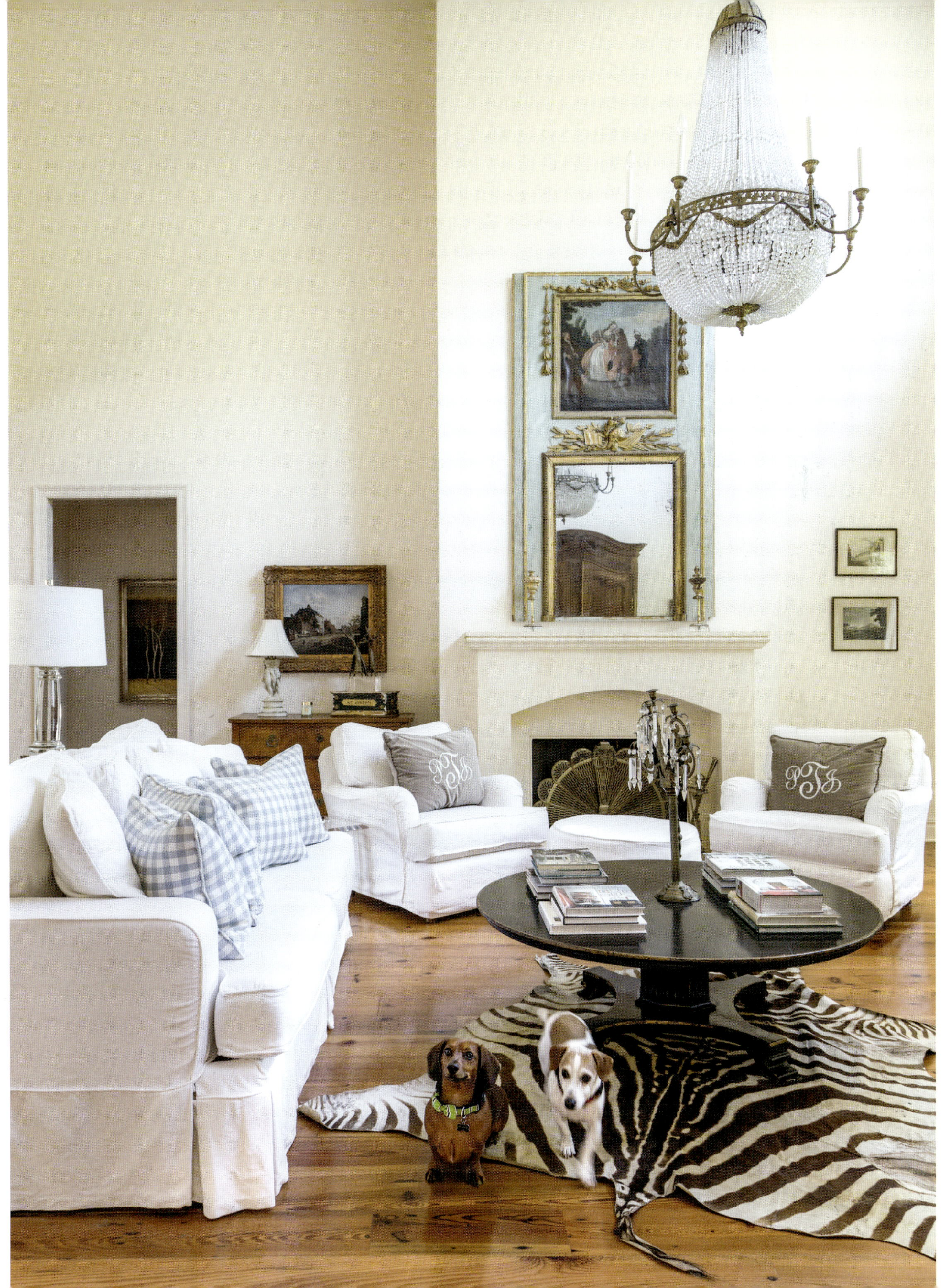

Gus

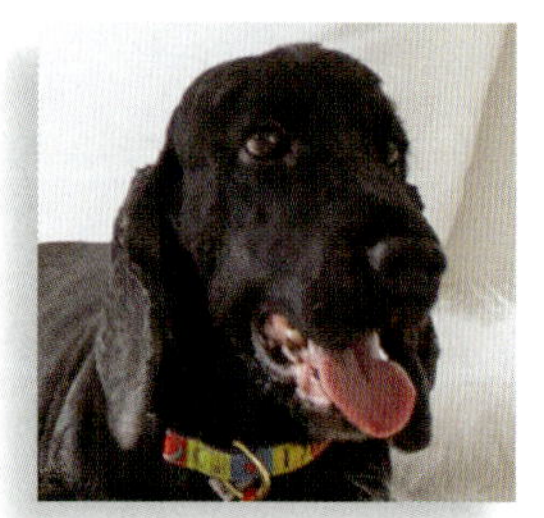

"I must confess that I am somewhat of a furniture snob. When selecting my spot for my beloved nap, I tend to gravitate toward the finer options available in the house, not just any old dog bed. As a nine-year-old English Cocker Spaniel, I have the run of my New Orleans home, and I am not shy about commandeering your seat, if I decide it would suit me better. A bit hesitant with strangers outside of the home, I am sweet and welcoming if you come to visit, dropping a dog toy at your feet for your pleasure and hoping you will play with me a bit.

Paul and Paula Gladden are especially happy to see me at the end of a long work day, as I await them at the top of the stairs, wagging and wiggling my whole body in sheer elation. Sometimes I truly get to sample the high life, when my friend Tanga Winstead brings me with her to work, at the home furnishings store Villa Vici on Magazine Street.

Here, I am luxuriating on a fur throw, atop an Eilersen sectional sofa. The statue is an original artwork by Rod Morehead. The spiky sculpture *Sea Urchin* is by Oly Studio. The painting is by Ed Whiteman. All items are procured through Villa Vici, with the guidance of designer Vicki Leftwich. I think I am the perfect counterpoint to this luscious white environment."

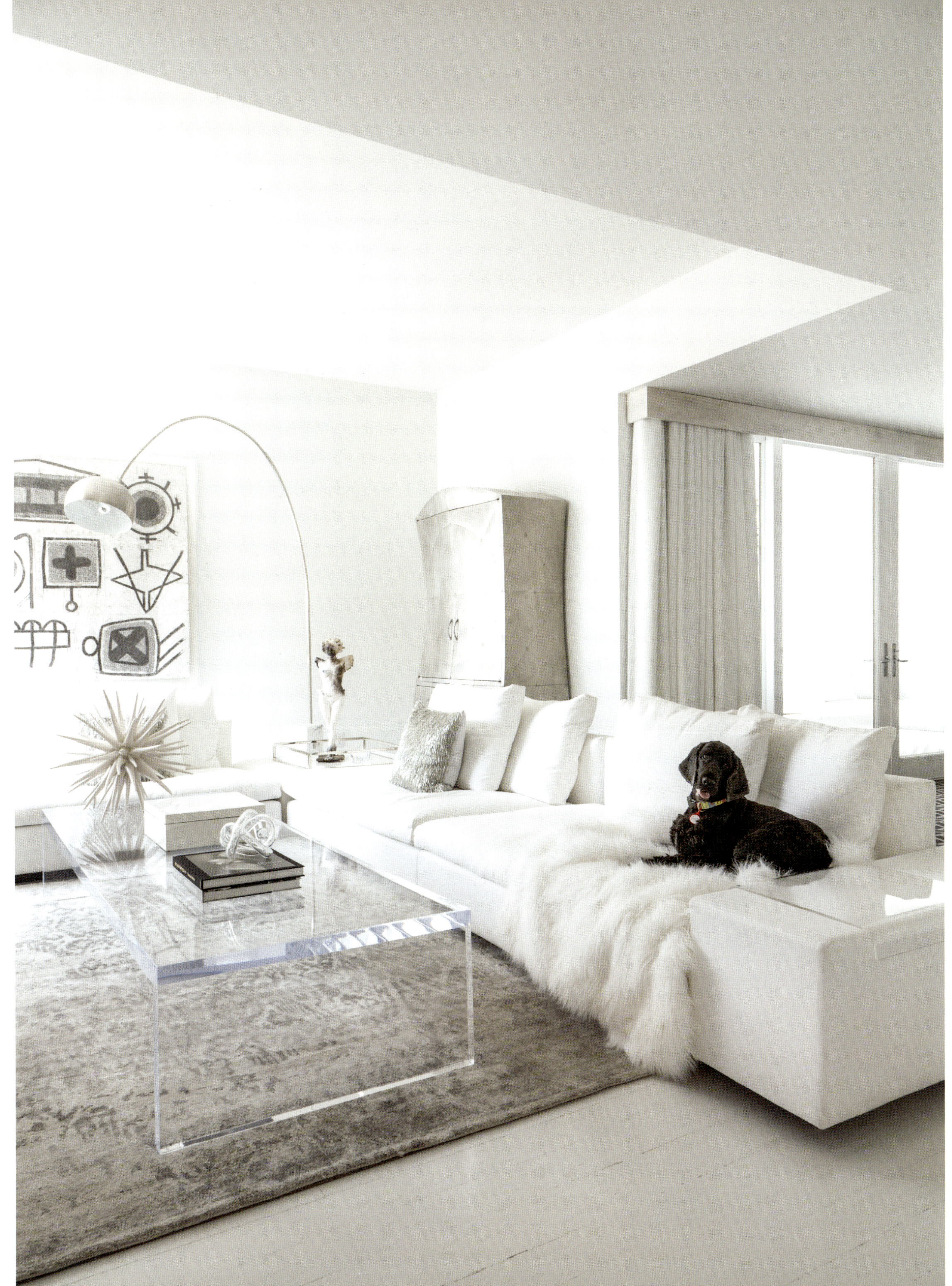

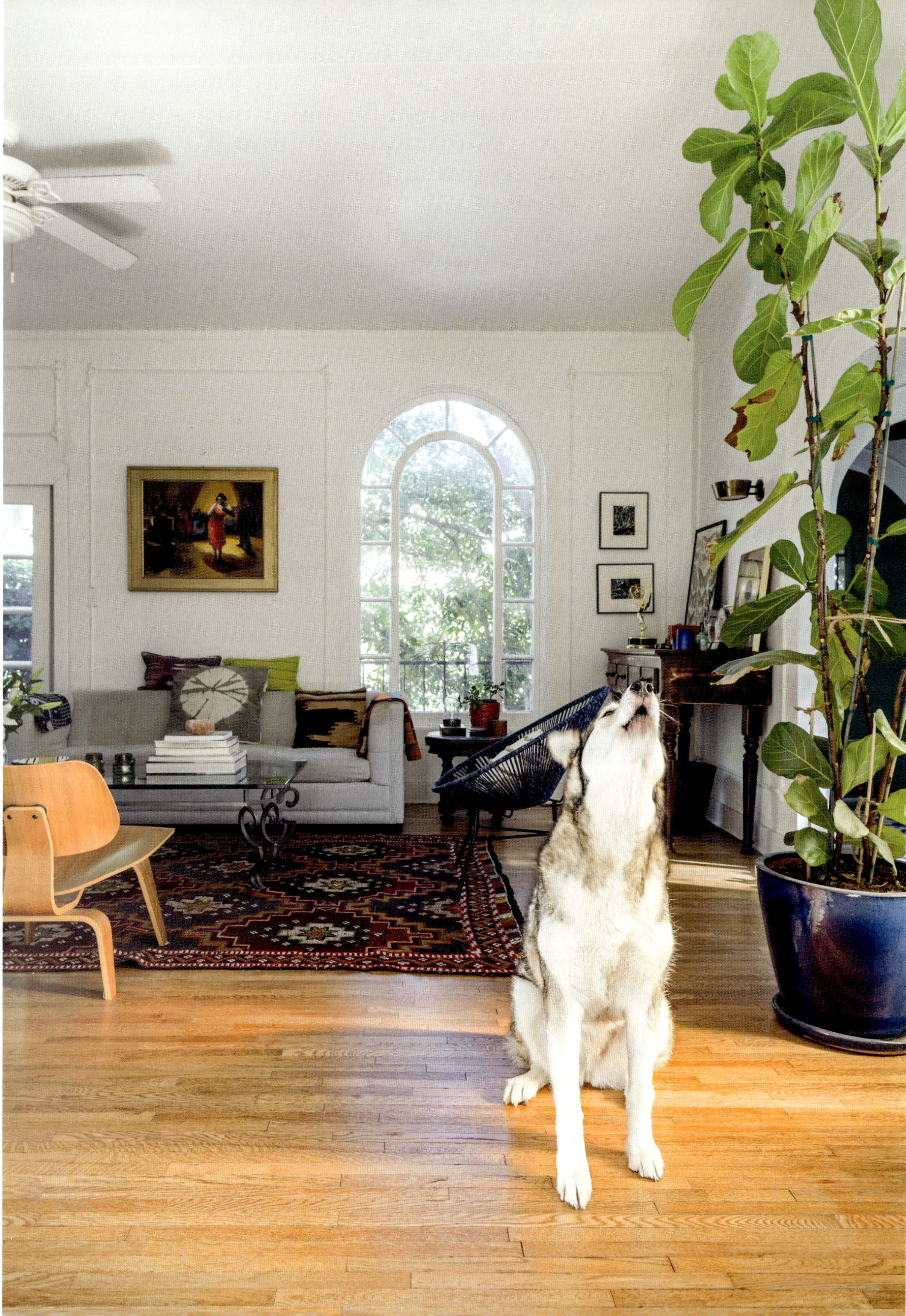

ZEP

"Move over, Robert Plant.

When Los Angeles–based actor Matt Weitl decided he was ready for a furry friend, he set his sights on me, an Alaskan Malamute from Oklahoma. When he collected me at the cargo area of LAX, I was still distressed from the flight, and didn't say a word. Matt put me on the car seat next to him and talked to me for the two-hour ride, but I remained mute. As we neared my new home, Matt turned on the radio to fill the silence. Just then, Led Zeppelin's 'Immigrant Song' came on, with Robert Plant's familiar 'ah ah ahhhhhhh AH!' I love to get the lead out, and know the words to this song well, so I sang along with gusto: 'Ooowwwwwwww! Owwwwwwwwwww!'

Matt and I have been happily howling together ever since. Here, I'm serenading our neighbors, LA-based photographer Amy Dickerson and musician David Ricketts. Amy has quite the creative flair, and appointed their apartment herself, mixing vintage finds, family pieces, art, and David's gold records and Emmy."

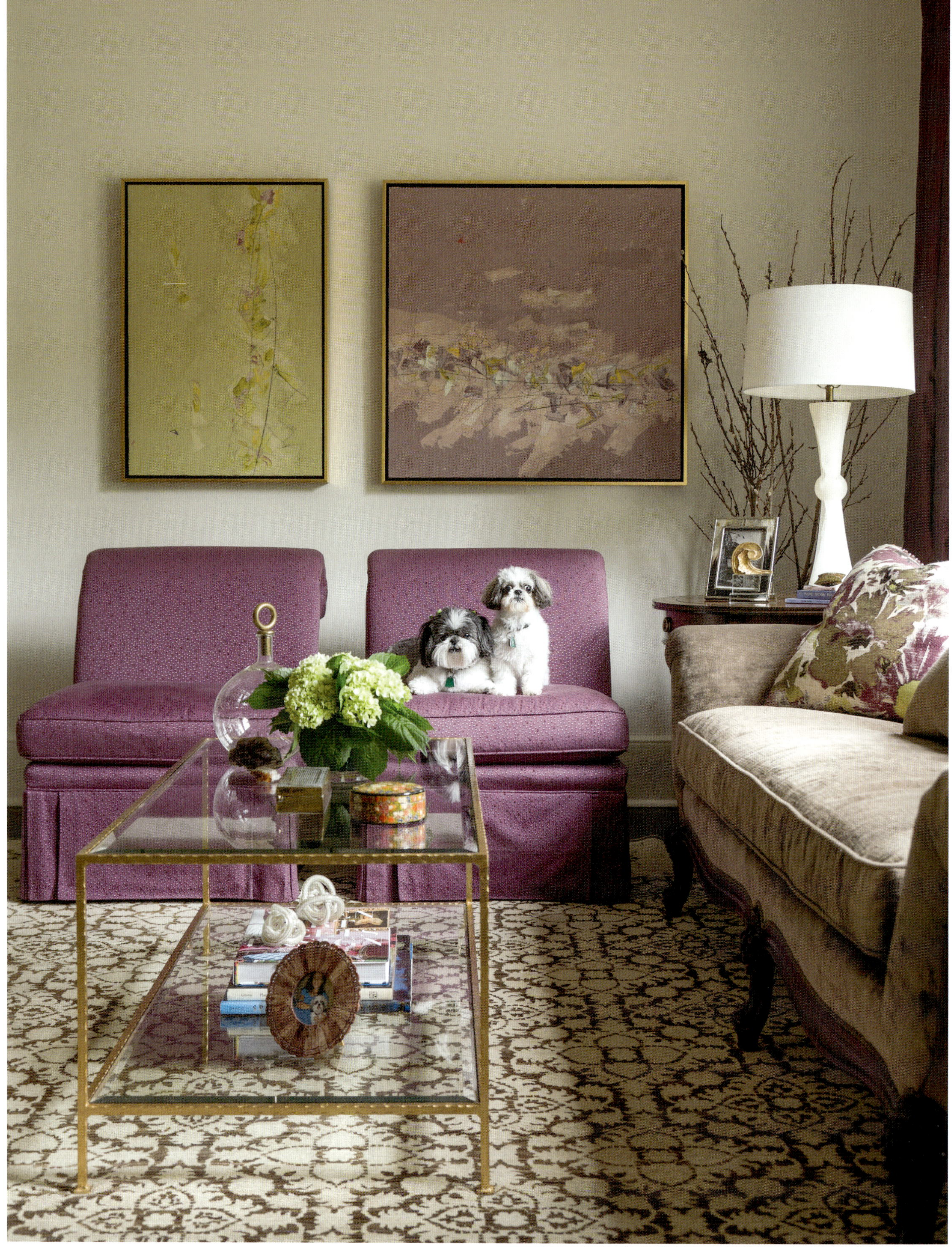

Paisley and Mika

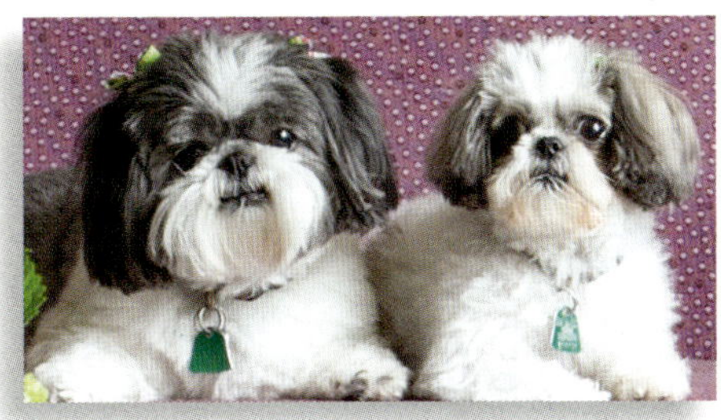

"Designer Susan Currie decided she could use a fluffy companion while living in Atlanta. She soon found me, Paisley (left), a Shih Tzu, at Atlanta Pet Rescue and Adoption. Though smitten with me, Susan sensed that I wanted a friend. After four more visits to the center, Susan and I were adopted by little Mika, who made an immediate connection with me—we are now inseparable.

For this photo, attempts were made to have one of us sit on the sofa and the other on the chair, but that arrangement was unacceptable, as we insisted on being haunch to haunch. And why not? We're besties!

Susan filled her home on Audubon Park in New Orleans with many of her favorite artworks and collectibles. Neutral tones accent her favorite colors of purple and chartreuse, arranged to complement her grandmother's restyled sofa, where we love to sit and gaze out at Audubon Street passersby."

Tater and Spud

"My grandmother, Tater (left), was not altogether thrilled when I joined the household of Janet and Leonard Tallerine. The chocolate Labrador Retriever is well known for its hunting ability, and Grandmother Tater was a champion. She, and two generations of her offspring, trained and excelled at the Black Bayou kennels in South Louisiana. Just as she was settling into the tranquil rhythm of retirement in her lavish Garden District home, Leonard decided to bring home her gangly, awkward, and somewhat shy Cajun granddaughter: me. While I grew into a sleek ninety-five-pound beauty, my hunting career was cut short by Hurricane Gustav. Black Bayou kennels took a direct hit, with the trainers and dogs, including me, barely evacuating in time. Unfortunately, I was never able to take up my training again. I did, however, blossom into a top-notch newspaper fetcher, and have more than three thousand perfect retrieves of *The New York Times* and *The New Orleans Times-Picayune* to my credit.

Grandmother Tater and I pose patiently in our beautifully appointed formal dining room. The scenic wallpaper, Les Monuments de Paris, which was manufactured by Twigs and replicated from the eighteenth and nineteenth centuries, is on permanent exhibition in New York City's Metropolitan Museum's Richmond Room. Janet enlisted the help of design experts Gerrie Bremmerman, John Crestia, Rodney Smith, and Robert Sonnier for furnishings and fixtures to create this sublime environment for us two royal pets."

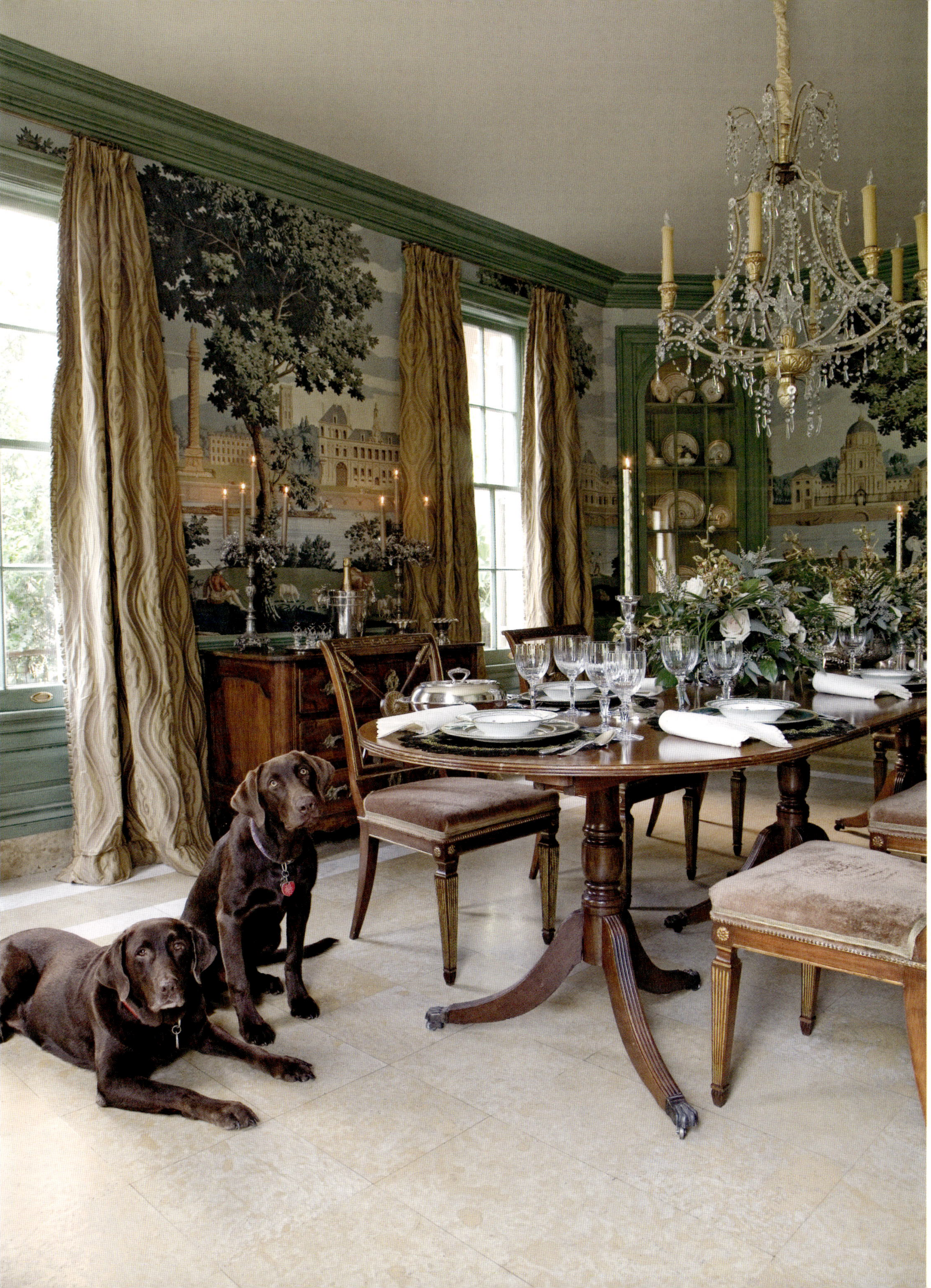

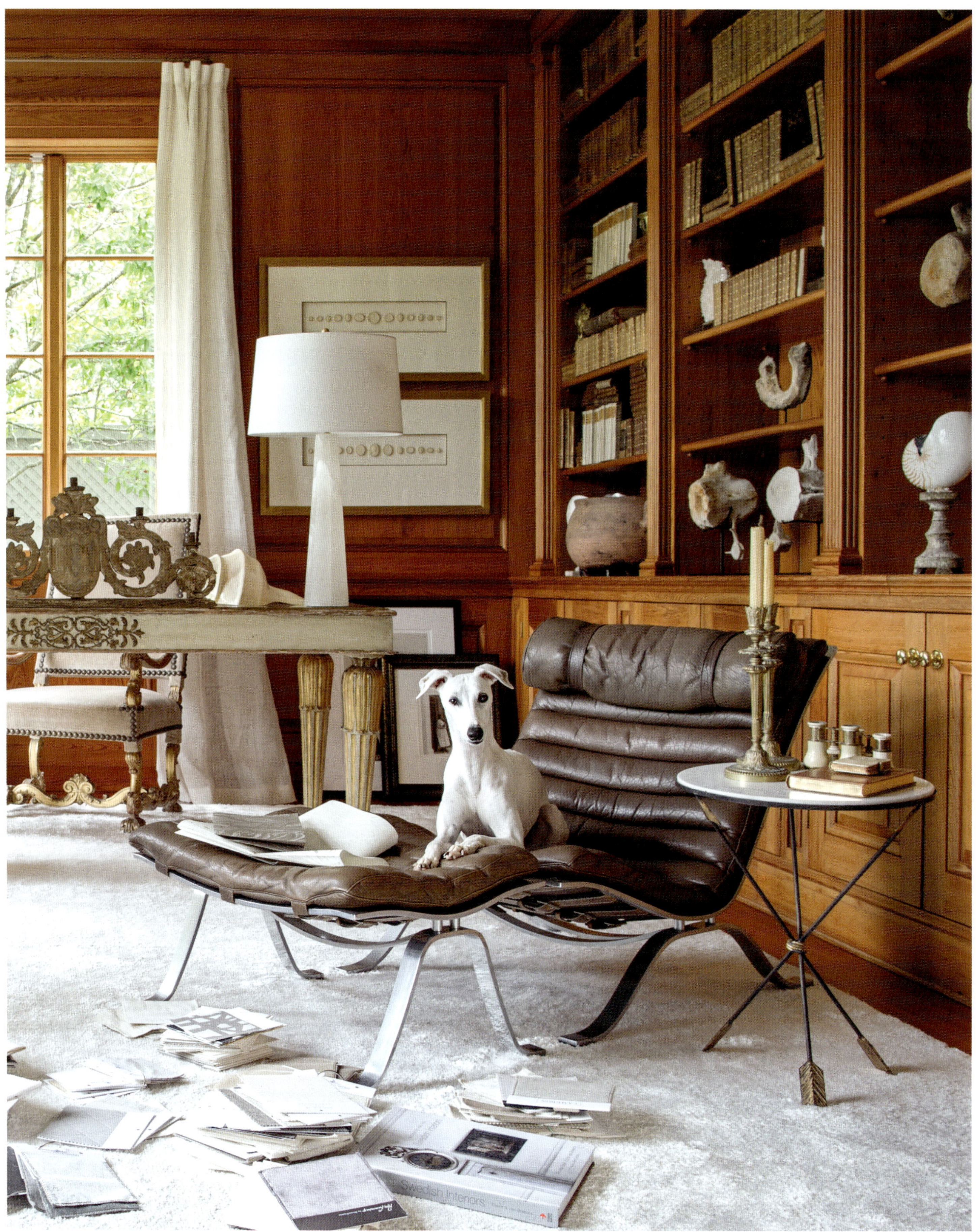
Swedish Interiors

Brother

"I am Brother Lucca Shaw Walsh, a five-year-old Whippet, and I work and play amongst the sumptuous décor of designer Tara Shaw and her husband Jack in Uptown New Orleans.

Tara specializes in European antiques and reproductions, and our home contains a mix of the best of these collections, as seen here in the Italian eighteenth-century Louis XV desk, Louis XIV gilded *fauteuil* (desk chair), and French midcentury arrow table. The horizontal framed cameos are Tara's designs for Restoration Hardware.

I am lounging on the Arne Norell Swedish midcentury chaise. When not sorting through samples with Tara in her office, I patrol nearby Audubon Park, corralling the local squirrel population. I also enjoy visits to Belladoggie daycare in the Garden District, where I am a model student. I am a love bug of the highest order, and I relish my position every night, snuggled in bed with Tara and Jack."

Cholo

"Always ahead of the trends, interior designer Valorie Hart and her now-deceased husband, Alberto Paz, moved into their shotgun double in the Irish Channel neighborhood of New Orleans ahead of the gentrification curve. After living in a large loftlike rental above an Uptown store, they looked forward to owning a piece of the city they had chosen to call home over twenty years ago. Valorie skillfully designed the interiors to reflect her fashion-forward style, and the home has subsequently been featured in many books and magazines. Valorie and Alberto are renowned master tango dancers and instructors, and Valorie was able to reconfigure the new house to accommodate a small studio area where they taught private lessons.

As a balm to soothe Valorie's wounds after Hurricane Katrina, she spotted me, Cholo, a Cavalier King Charles Spaniel, brought me home, and soothe her I have! I am so happy and carefree and a snuggler too and I even like the cat, Kitty Kitty Bang Bang, who lives here too. Alberto, who was at one point reticent, loved me so much and I became his constant companion, following him around and even to tango lessons in the studio.

Sadly, Alberto passed away, but while he was alive the master bedroom was on the main floor and I was a frequent visitor. Valorie designed the headboard with two symmetrical ends of a French antique daybed, mounted on a burlap wall that she hand-upholstered. She's very creative and a master of shopping high and low. The bedding is from DwellStudio, the flower ball chandelier from Perch Home, and the painting over the bed is vintage. Isn't it cozy in here?"

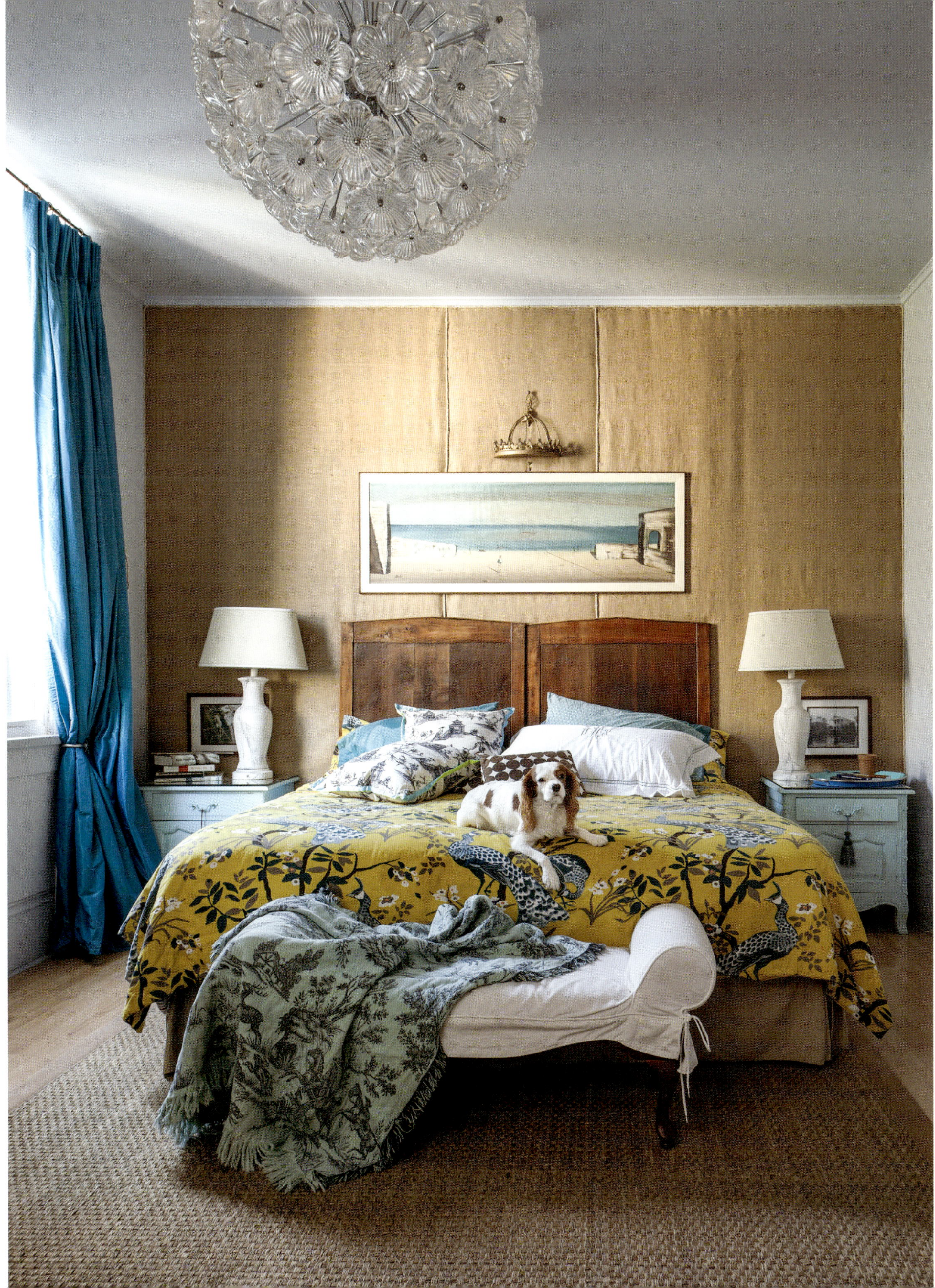

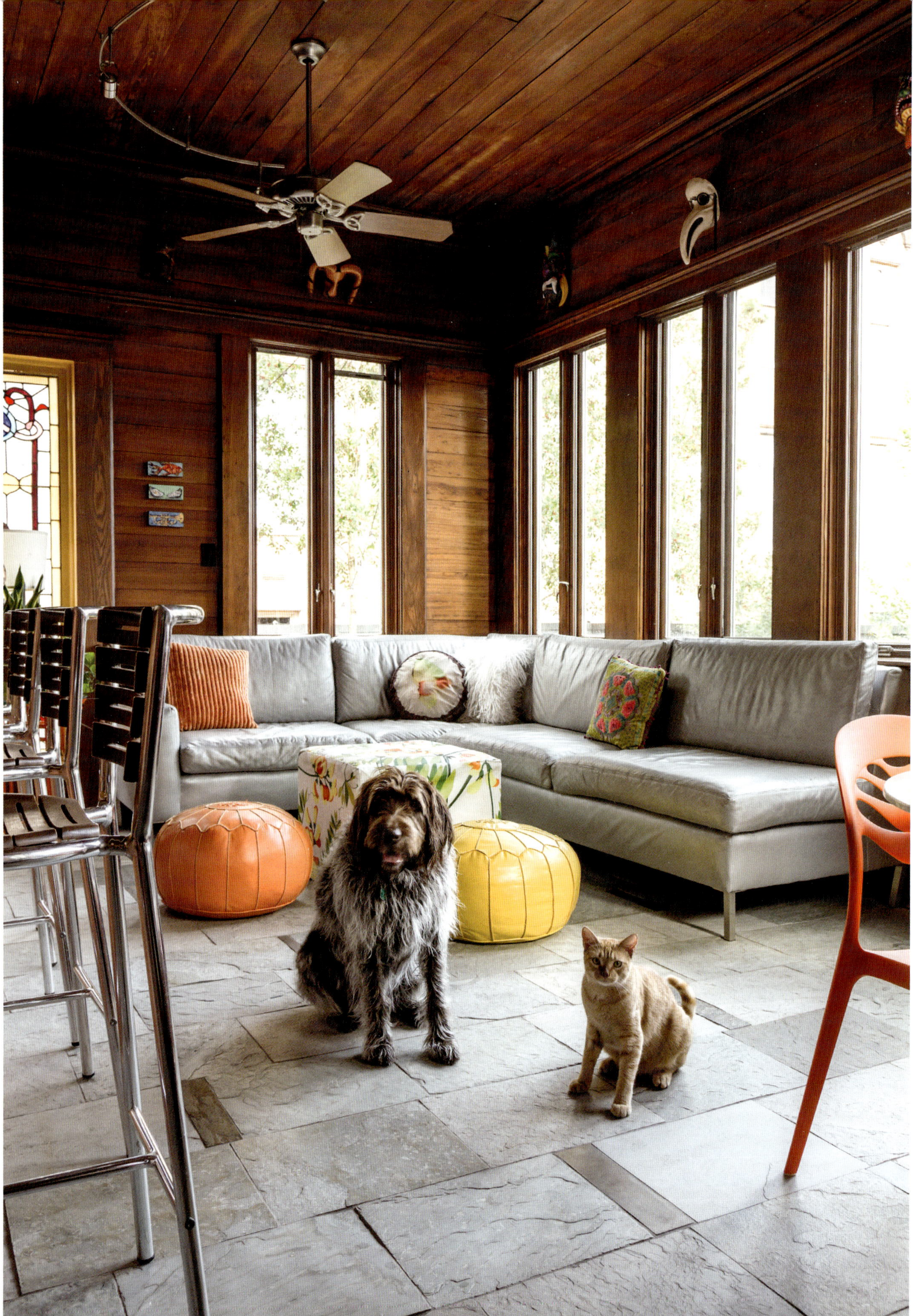

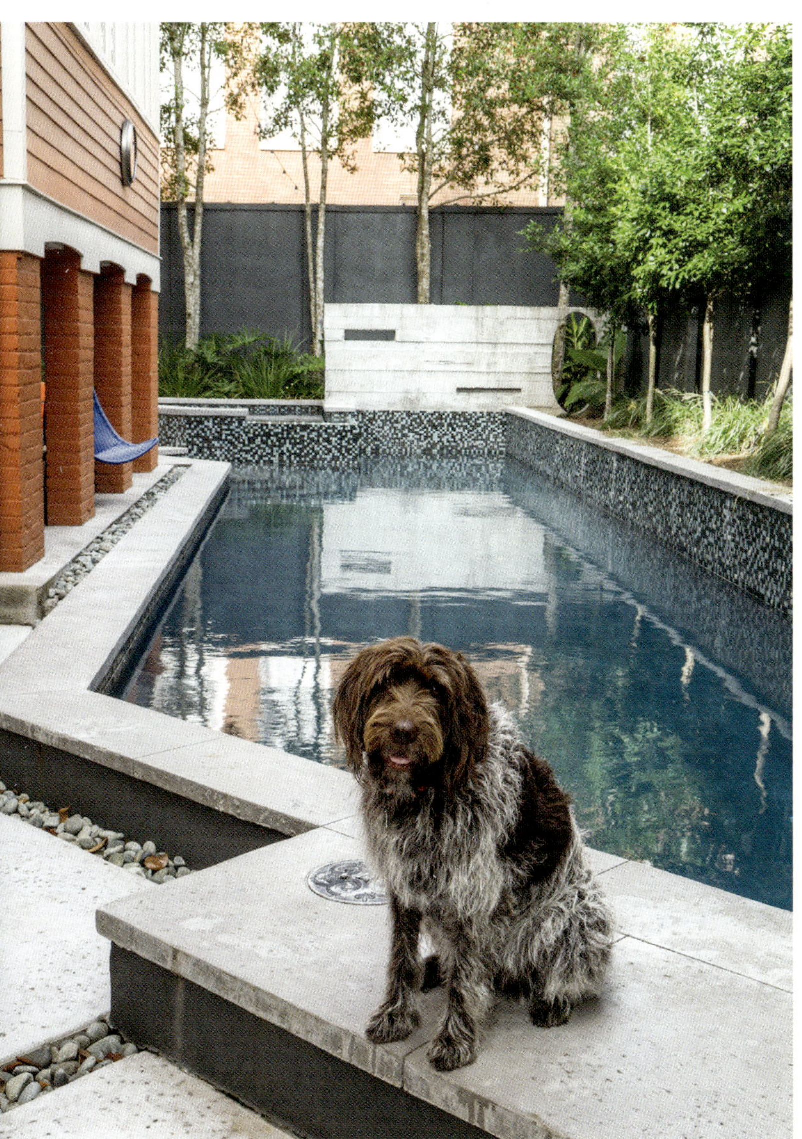

Dusty and Stevie, the Cat

"I'm a natural-born swimmer, so I was delighted when architect Stephanie Adler installed a pool in our side yard; I'm certain that the addition was solely for my pleasure. I'm a Wirehaired Pointing Griffon and I'm a friendly, energetic, and, some may say, silly dog, full of mirth and mischief. I am, however, extremely smart, and know many commands and tricks. Stevie, the cat, takes commands from no one, unfortunately, and rules the entire household. He does seem a bit jealous of the fun I have in the pool, and hints at taking a swim with me any day now, a feat that if captured on video will surely hit your Facebook feed. Stephanie converted this room, which was originally a sleeping porch pre-air conditioning, into a casual den. She had the custom sectional sofa covered in silver-dyed leather. The masks above the windows are from around the world, as Stephanie collects a new mask with every trip she takes, each finding a spot in our home."

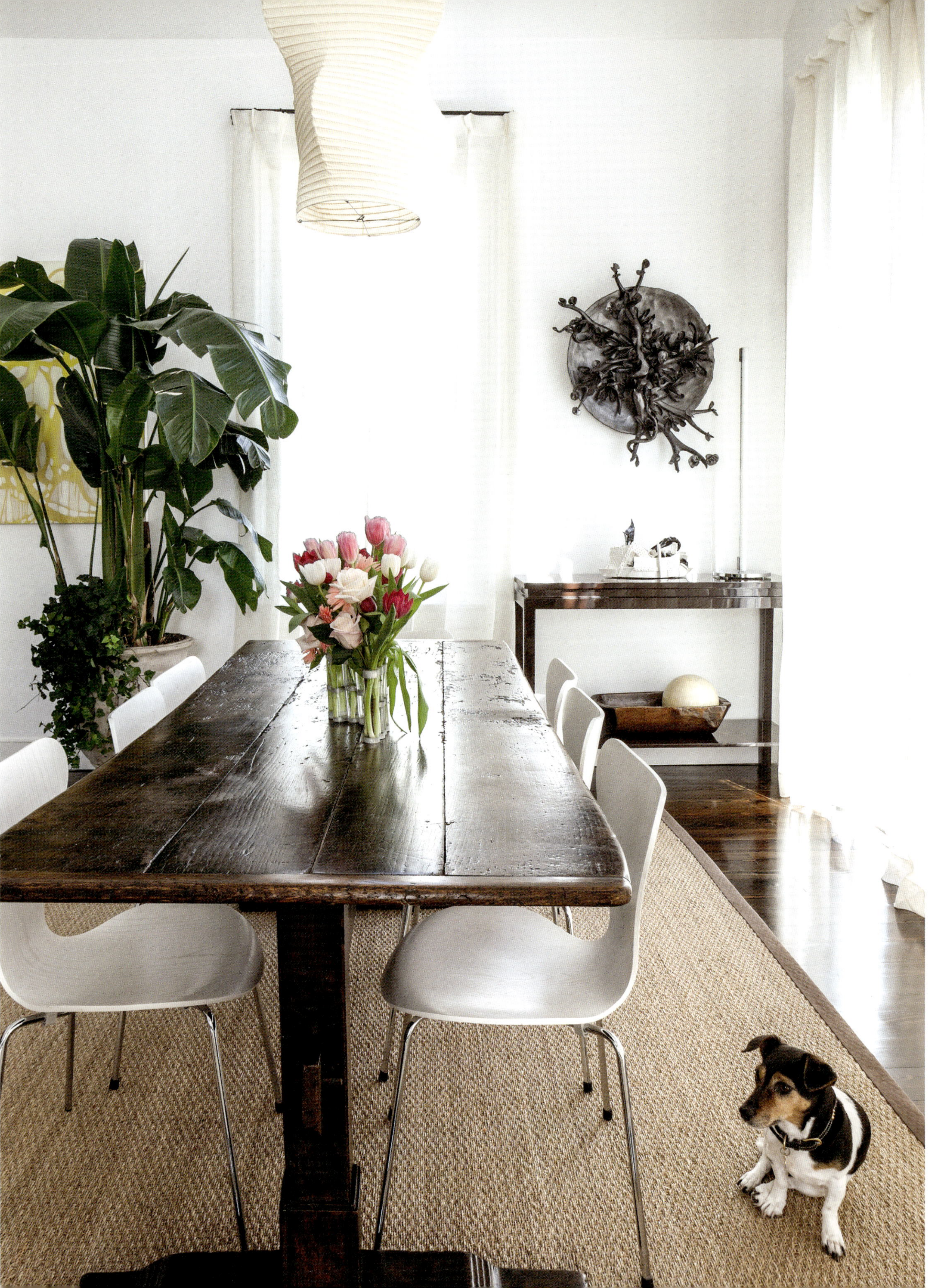

Tipper

Jamie Meeks decided her youngest daughter could use a pal and protector, and selected Tipper, the calmest in her litter. Tipper may not look like a guard dog, but she was mighty in spirit, and took to her role. Named for the dark tip of her tail, Tipper was friendly, and feisty to the end. When her watch came to an end, she was buried in the yard, and a small Japanese Magnolia was planted with her. The tree is now towering to the roofline, indomitable as Tipper's spirit.

Jamie renovated the hundred-year-old house in Uptown New Orleans, with guidance from architect Marion Cage McCollum. The table is from Karla Katz and the chairs are Jacobson. The art peeking through the greenery is by Amanda Talley. The circular ceramic wall installation is by Bradley Sabin, hanging above a custom console designed by Jamie.

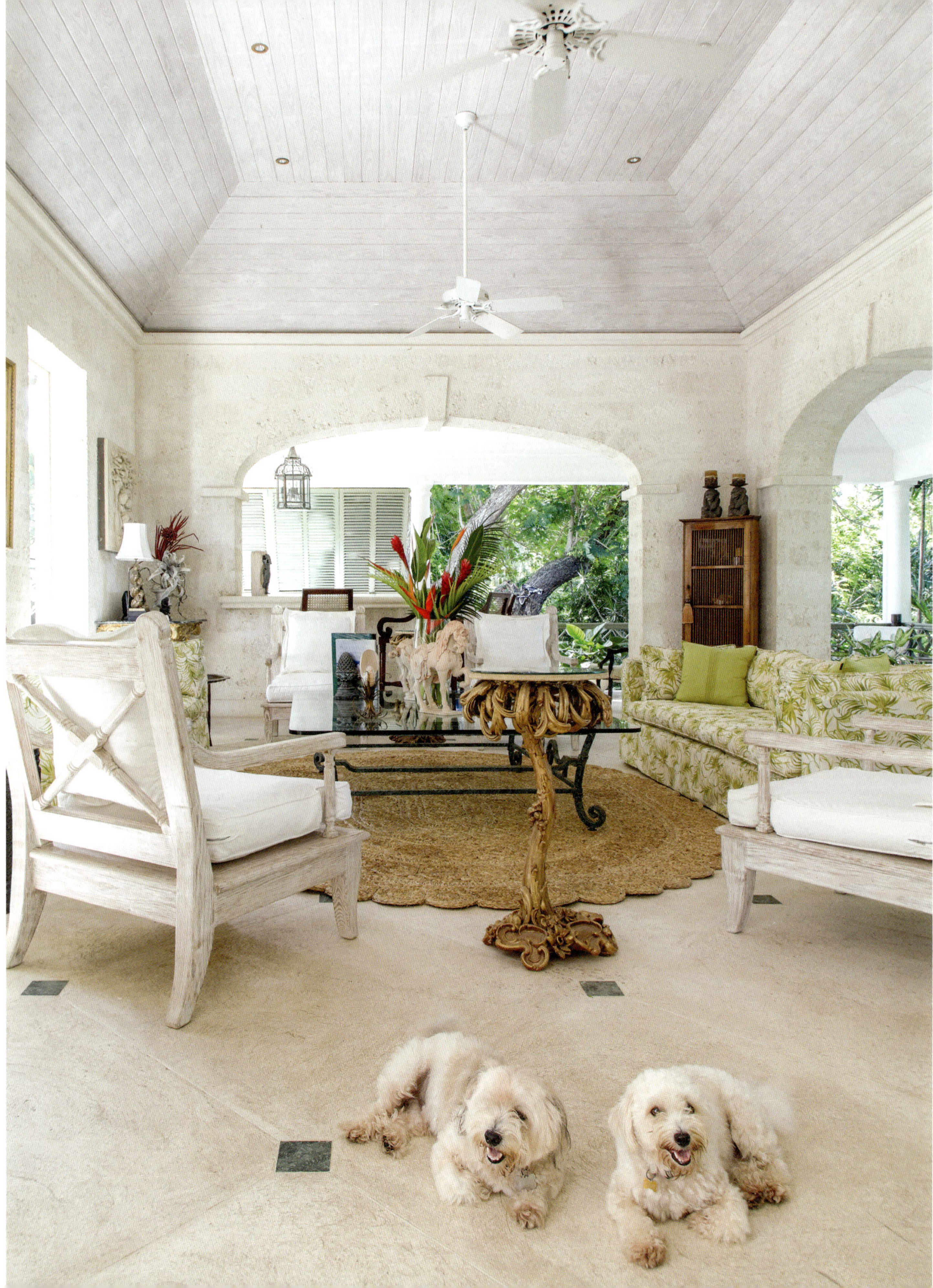

Eli and Ellie

"My daughter, Ellie (right), and I are living the Caribbean dream. We have the run of this sprawling villa in Barbados, built by architect/owner Larry Warren, and decorated by his wife, Anna. The tranquil tropical paradise blurs the lines between outside and in, with multiple living spaces open to the elements. Anna creatively filled the home, combining European antiques, West Indies style furnishings, comfortable seating, and an eclectic mix of art.

Sociable, sweet, and inquisitive, my Ellie and I are inseparable. We were, however, apart from each other when I had to fly to the UK, to undergo cataract surgery. Unfortunately, it was too late to save one of my eyes, but that hasn't affected my self-esteem. Like many small dogs, I am bold and determined. Ellie is more agile and energetic than I, and is always looking to win attention in my shadow. Together, we fill the home with a happy and loving energy."

Thelma

After Hurricane Katrina completely destroyed her home in the Lakeview neighborhood of New Orleans, Karina Gentinetta decided to rebuild in place. As if that wasn't enough of a challenge, the misdeeds of a fraudulent contractor left her with a budget of only $12,000 to furnish the entire house. Astonishingly, the resourceful and creative Karina managed to pull it off, and the outcome is stunning.

Like the city itself, most of the furnishings she found that she could afford were damaged and in disrepair. With love and ingenuity, Karina refurbished and recreated, using items culled and repurposed from junk stores and consignment shops. The rooms are stylish and layered, with an interesting vignette in every sightline. The eighteenth-century French Directoire daybed that wirehaired Dachshund Thelma sits atop seemed beyond redemption when Karina found it, but the piece spoke to her, and like her beloved city, she knew it could be beautiful again.

Thelma was part of a duo, along with her sister Louise, and was the most loyal and devoted girl. On one particularly rainy evening, when Karina returned from work, she found Thelma vigilantly waiting for her outside, shielding herself from the rain under the leaf of a banana tree. She was from then-on known to Karina as her "little banana tree girl."

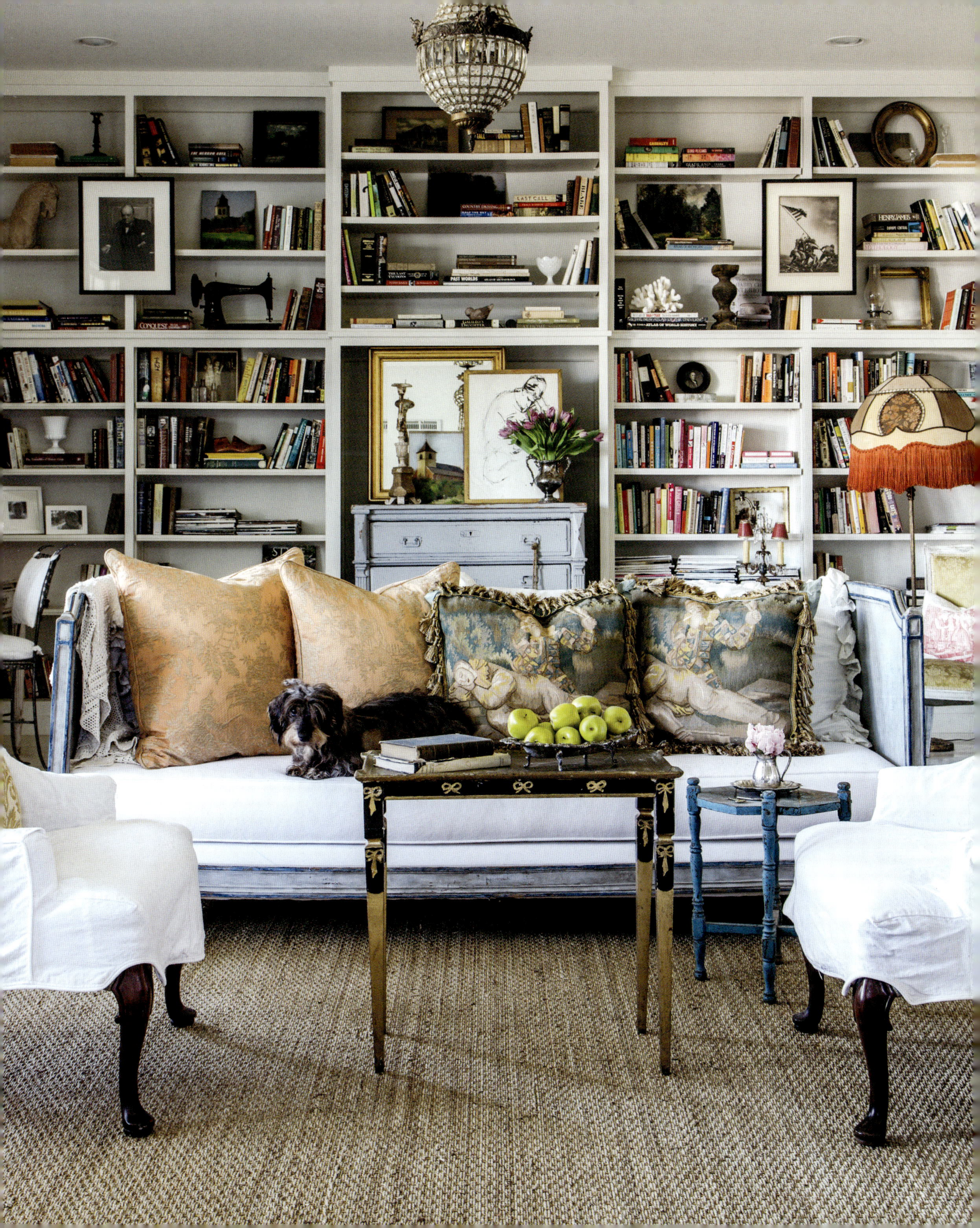

Acknowledgments

First and foremost, I would like to thank all home and business owners, who so graciously allowed me to photograph their beautiful spaces and beloved dogs, and provided me with insight into their dogs' varied personalities. I would also like to thank the talented and generous interior designers, who helped me find great houses with dogs in their décor. Writer and designer Valorie Hart, with whom I collaborated with on my first décor book, *House Proud*, has been instrumental in the production of this book, as well as providing the beautiful foreword. Esteemed designer Patrick Dunn so generously invited me to his own country home to photograph his dogs, as well as helped me gain entrée into some of the most venerable addresses in New Orleans. Chad Graci was extremely helpful in securing access to some photogenic little dogs in grand spaces, as well as his own cheerful pup, Baron. Jennifer DiCerbo's chic interiors provided perfect backdrops for some of the larger breeds. Connie Seitz was vigilant in helping access some of her beautiful projects north of the lake from New Orleans. The French-country stylings of Cindy St. Romain beautifully framed the down-to-earth dogs that inhabit them. Katie Logan and Jensen Killen, of LKI Interiors, helped me round out the homes with their elegant and contemporary décor. Nomita Joshi-Gupta has been a longtime client, supporter, and friend, and shared a few of her beautiful, environmentally-friendly design projects. My final shoot of the book took place in the exquisite home of Shaun Smith. Shaun graciously allowed me to photograph his dogs, as well as connected me with a client in the French Quarter. Shaun also indulged me in an impromptu wrap party, as his shoot was the final one for the book. I thank him for his hospitality.

I would like to thank my old friend, and fellow UGA art school grad, Sean McDevitt, who helped me polish and finalize the images for publication.

The Preservation Resource Center of New Orleans has been an invaluable asset, not just to me in the production of this book, but to our beautiful aging city. I have been photographing grand old homes in the Garden District for their Holiday Homes Tour for almost ten years, many of which, along with their dogs, grace these pages. As a New Orleanian, I am thankful for their mission "to promote the preservation, restoration, and revitalization of New Orleans' historic architecture and neighborhoods."

Tiffany Redding Amedeo has been my editor and art director at *New Orleans Homes and Lifestyles* magazine for many years, and has encouraged and nurtured my work through the bulk of my career. It was in shooting for that magazine that many of these beautiful homes and dogs were discovered.

Taylor Morgan, my editor at *The Scout Guide New Orleans*, has become a great friend and advocate, and her expansive network has been instrumental for this project.

I would like to thank my friends who provided support and encouragement throughout this process: Prisca Weems, Miranda Lake, the Lesters, Jennifer Gardner, Lindsay Ross, and Joe Kight. I would especially like to thank my talented friend Christine Ciarmello, whose expertise helped keep me on track.

Special thanks go to my publisher, Marta Hallett at Glitterati, who had the vision to take a chance on me and this project. Her patience and guidance with this neophyte author were invaluable.

Finally, I would like to thank my husband, Mike, for his support for the duration of this project. Whether helping me with editing (he has a journalism degree—I possess no such training) or keeping the house clean and fridge stocked during the final two weeks that I immersed myself in writing, he has been the best partner imaginable.